T0357431

HOLY MEN OF THE ELECTROMAGNETIC AGE

ALSO BY RAPHAEL CORMACK

Midnight in Cairo:
The Divas of Egypt's Roaring '20s

HOLY MEN OF THE ELECTROMAGNETIC AGE

~

A Forgotten History of the Occult

RAPHAEL CORMACK

W. W. NORTON & COMPANY

Independent Publishers Since 1923

For information about permission to reproduce selections from this book, write
to Permissions, W. W. Norton & Company, Inc., 500 Fifth Avenue,
New York, NY 10110

For information about special discounts for bulk purchases, please contact
W. W. Norton Special Sales at specialsales@wwnorton.com or 800-233-4830

Manufacturing by Lakeside Book Manufacturing
Book design by Brian Mulligan
Production manager: Louise Mattarelliano

ISBN 978-0-393-88110-3

W. W. Norton & Company, Inc., 500 Fifth Avenue, New York, NY 10110
www.wwnorton.com

W. W. Norton & Company Ltd., 15 Carlisle Street, London W1D 3BS

10 9 8 7 6 5 4 3 2 1

Stories about the East and the West are told only by those with a superficial understanding of both.

—Taha Hussein (1889–1973)[1]

~

Much more widespread than the love of truth is the appetite for marvels, the love of the phony *an sich*, in itself and for its own sweet sake.

—Aldous Huxley (1894–1963)[2]

CONTENTS

HOLY MEN OF THE ELECTROMAGNETIC AGE

Prologue

THE WORLD BEYOND

TAKE A WALK ON SIXTH AVENUE IN MANHATTAN AND, as you pass through SoHo, there is an innocuous-looking warehouse on the west side of the street overlooking a small park and a statue of the Uruguayan national hero José Artigas. Set back from the avenue and dwarfed by its more imposing neighbor, the Forhan Building, you might not even notice it, but this building is one of the last remnants of a once-thriving global subculture that tried to change the world. It is the current home of the Dahesh Museum of Art, an institution created to display the art collection of a miracle-working mystic known as Dr. Dahesh, who first appeared in Jerusalem in the late 1920s and could perform amazing feats that contradicted the established laws of nature. Dr. Dahesh, even his enemies agreed, was extremely charismatic and the stories that were told about him defied belief. He could make objects appear out of thin air, heal the sick, and even communicate with the spirits of the dead. In the mid-twentieth century, long before his collection ended up in New York City, he traveled the Middle East, thrilling, baffling, and offending people in equal measure. In Palestine, he was accused of using his paranormal abilities to swindle a wealthy widow out of her fortune. A few years later, in Beirut, he began his own religious movement named Daheshism, which managed to attract a devoted circle of followers among the country's educated elite and terrified some of Lebanon's most powerful men.

Compelling though Dr. Dahesh's story might be, he was just one small part in a much larger transnational movement that flourished in the years after the First World War. Let us call this movement "the occult"—a vague and slippery term but the best one there is. It included a series of philosophies from Theosophy and Spiritualism to Rosicrucianism and parapsychology and was populated by a huge cast of eccentric and charismatic gurus, prophets, and sages. Insofar as a definition is possible, the occult (from the Latin for "hidden") was a belief system that asserted that there is more to our existence than the perceptible, physical world. Other worlds exist, which the tools of conventional science or logic cannot fully understand but which exert a mystical power over everyone. It was a worldview based on wonder, on the possibility that marvelous things were truly possible. Of course, this also sounds uncomfortably like a broad description of religion, and any attempts to define the occult will naturally tread on the toes of several established religions.

If a good abstract definition of the occult is hard to find, perhaps a historical one will make things clearer. Almost every modern occult movement can, directly or indirectly, trace its roots back to a single, seemingly insignificant event in a farmhouse in upstate New York, around twenty miles from the shores of Lake Ontario. In Hydesville in 1848, two young sisters, Kate and Maggie Fox, heard disembodied knockings on the wall of their house. After some investigation, they discovered that these bangs emanated from the ghost of a man who had died in the house many years earlier, and soon they came up with a way to communicate with him. As the girls honed their skills, they found that they had the ability to communicate with a vast range of other departed souls in the spirit world too. What could have been a local ghost story, confined to the pages of obscure histories of upstate New York, quickly expanded much farther. The story of the Fox sisters captured the world's imagination, and by the early 1850s, they were international celebrities. Reports began to emerge that other people had managed to communicate with the spirits just like the Fox sisters, all across the United States and in places as far away as Havana, Paris, Rome, Vienna, Damascus, and London. One writer in America joked that death would no longer have to mean an end to your social life: installing "an electric telegraph across the Styx before they get one across the Atlantic would make death less of a separation from friends than a voyage to Europe."[1]

These astounding phenomena spawned an entire religio-philosophical movement. A significant number of people, disenchanted by the failures of traditional religions and enthused by the possibilities of modernity, were fascinated by the idea that a portal had been opened into the world of the dead. So many barriers were being broken down in the nineteenth century—social, scientific, economic—and, soon, the one between life and death was looking decidedly fragile too. A new creed of Spiritualism was born, and figures from Elizabeth Barrett Browning to Queen Victoria, from Charles Dickens to Abraham Lincoln and Napoleon III, were all said to have experimented with spirit communication. With no central organization or holy texts to speak of, it took only a few years for splinter groups to emerge, taking Spiritualism in strange new directions. There was John Murray Spear, who, in 1853, received a series of instructions from some illustrious spirits (including Socrates and Benjamin Franklin) that gave him a detailed blueprint for the construction of a perfect society. Following their advice, he set up a model community in upstate New York called the Domain (or, sometimes, Harmonia). Surrounded by followers, he set to work on a variety of different projects, including, most notably, an ultimately doomed quest to build a perpetual motion machine.[2] And there was Paschal Beverly Randolph, who immersed himself in the doctrines of occult brotherhoods in the Middle East and returned to America bringing the secrets of hashish and "sex-magic."[3]

The occult expanded and evolved throughout the nineteenth century, and by the beginning of the twentieth, its ranks were filled by a succession of enthusiastic followers. In the front lines came the artists and writers. The great poet W. B. Yeats and the novelist D. H. Lawrence both explored the Spiritualist-inspired, esoteric movement of

Theosophy, which had been created by the eccentric Russian aristocrat Madame Blavatsky in 1870s New York. Arthur Conan Doyle, author of the Sherlock Holmes mysteries, spent his final years as a passionate proselytizer for Spiritualism. Painters found their own inspiration in the new ways of seeing the world that the occult offered, from Wassily Kandinsky and Kazimir Malevich to Hilma af Klint and Piet Mondrian. However, these unusual belief systems did not attract only creative souls, who are typically allowed more license to dream than the rest of us. There were more conventionally minded adherents too—scientists and politicians. The British physicist Sir Oliver Lodge was famous for his early twentieth-century efforts to investigate paranormal phenomena, and he published widely on the subject. Tsar Nicholas II and his wife were devoted to the charismatic and controversial holy man Rasputin. Academics at Harvard, Yale, and the Sorbonne experimented with the paranormal. The University of London and Duke University both had their own dedicated parapsychology labs. Read about almost any major personality of the early twentieth century and you will soon stumble upon some aspect of the occult—if not through them, then perhaps through their aunt, their cousin, or their brother. This spiritual movement reached its last great zenith in the aftermath of the First World War. Palm readers, clairvoyants, hypnotists, mind readers, jinn summoners, and Spiritualists were springing up everywhere. In 1926, one Spiritualist medium testified before Congress that she knew "for a fact that there had been spiritual séances held at the White House with President Coolidge and his family." She also alleged that she knew of several senators who regularly used the services of mediums.[4]

Across the planet, the 1920s were a time of crisis and of rebirth. A new world was forming on top of the wreckage of the past and almost anything felt possible. The occult's belief in the existence of other worlds beyond our own was literal but it also had a metaphorical aspect. The material world was full of drudgery, suffering, and injustice; opening the door to a spiritual world could guide humanity to a brighter future. Occultists promised that they were the midwives of a new modern age, one that would bring untold miracles.

~~~

TELLING THE COMPREHENSIVE STORY of something as vast and obscure as the occult is an impossible task. It is a deep and murky ocean of interconnected ideas, whose adherents plucked philosophies from different sources and stitched them together in their own idiosyncratic ways. Instead, this book will follow the lives of two men who rode this tide of wonders to play their own small but important part in the transnational tale of the early twentieth-century occult. Their stories are now largely forgotten, but they will guide us through the modern world and capture the hopes, anxieties, and neuroses of this troubled age. The miracle men of the 1920s and 1930s talk about hope and progress, but their stories were often tinged with that darkness, which hung heavily over so much of the twentieth century.

The first, Dr. Tahra Bey, born in Istanbul, traveled across Europe out of the ruins of the Eastern Mediterranean until he reached France as a refugee in 1925. In Paris, advertising himself as an "Egyptian fakir" from a long line of mystics, his ability to manipulate his physical body in inexplicable ways using the power of his mind made him a summer sensation. This stranger from the East could control his heart rate, pierce himself with sharp blades without feeling pain, and even shut his body down completely, entering a death-like state that could last hours or even days, then have himself buried alive before a stunned audience. In the years after his awe-inspiring Parisian debut, he became a fixture of the European stages, and crowds lined up to see his strange marvels in the flesh. He had come to a Europe unmoored by the catastrophic events of the First World War and searching for answers in new places. Dressed in exotic Eastern robes and talking about a forgotten Eastern science of the spirit, Tahra Bey gave Europeans exactly what they wanted to hear. In doing so, he became not only famous but also very wealthy. His demonstrations were so popular that innumerable copycat "Egyptian fakirs" appeared across the Western world as fakir fever spread from Warsaw all the way to Los Angeles. Many of these imitation fakirs adopted the Ottoman honorific *Bey* (a title similar to "Sir") in emulation of Tahra Bey. There was a Rahman Bey, a Tatar Bey, and a Thawara Rey, who had obviously slightly misunderstood the significance of the word *Bey*. Some of them lasted only for a few months, but others stuck around for several decades. One of these many copycats, Hamid Bey, toured America in the late 1920s and early 1930s before establishing his own spiritual movement, from a house in the Hollywood Hills, known as the Coptic Fellowship of America, which survives to this day, long after its founder's death.

The second part of this book tells the parallel story of Dr. Dahesh and the Middle Eastern occult. At the same time that Tahra Bey was astounding the European public with his spiritual mastery over his body, Dr. Dahesh was spreading his own form of occult knowledge through the Arab world. From his first appearance in Jerusalem in 1929, Dr. Dahesh embraced the doctrine of Spiritualism and the science of hypnotism to become one of the most well-known proponents of an Arabic-speaking occult. When he finally settled in Beirut to launch his eponymous religious movement, he had managed to shape a persona that was the unmistakable product of the twentieth-century Arab world. There were no appeals to the "mystical secrets of the East," which did not hold the same allure here as they did in Paris or New York. Instead Middle Eastern occultists harnessed the powers of science and progress for their cause, guiding the region toward a new, modern, independent future.

The story of the occult in the 1920s is a truly global tale, and the spiritual movements of East and West interacted in unexpected ways. The action will pass through six continents, touring the cabarets of Montmartre and Cairo, walking the streets of golden-age Beirut, passing through yoga retreats in Los Angeles, seeing riots in Jerusalem and carnivals in Rio, before finally returning to Dr. Dahesh's museum in Manhattan. Along the way, we witness some of the most devas-

tating events of the twentieth century: the fire of Smyrna, the Great
Revolt in Palestine, the Nazi occupation of Paris, and the Lebanese
Civil War. The narrative is based on historical material from across
the world that was written in many different languages—among them
Arabic, Armenian, Turkish, French, Greek, Portuguese, Italian, and
English. The cast of characters includes stateless migrants, a Palestin-
ian nationalist poet, an Anglo-American psychic scientist, a Lebanese
artist, a Midwestern psychologist, and a celebrity Indian yogi.

The interwar period was the setting for a great showdown between
rational and mystical worldviews—the clash that the historian James
Webb called "one of the greatest battles fought in the twentieth century."[5] This book tells the history of this conflict from the perspective
of the losing side. The occult was based on promises about the metaphysical world beyond the veil, where laws of nature and logic did not
necessarily apply. In the fragile and ever-changing world of the early
twentieth century, this made the esoteric a perfect breeding ground
for grifters. Throughout the 1920s and 1930s a battalion of charlatans,
fantasists, and swindlers, armed with little more than their charisma
and some larger-than-life claims, managed to inspire cultlike devotion in their followers. Neither Tahra Bey nor Dr. Dahesh escaped
accusations of fraud or quackery; both had serious run-ins with the
authorities. Were they brave visionaries or unscrupulous con men?
Did they have a noble dream or a dangerous fantasy? Devoted adepts
vigorously defended their prophets, saying that everything new and
unexplained always faced opposition at first. Skeptical members of
the public were less sure and some were actively hostile: just because
something was new did not mean it was good.

These battles between the occult and its doubters were the central
battles of the 1920s and 1930s, decades when many were trying to cast
aside the corrupted relics of the past to reach a brighter future. The
logic of the nineteenth century had been discredited by the events of
the twentieth. Tahra Bey and Dr. Dahesh were offering a new kind of
logic for the new age, which would be built on different foundations.
Like the Surrealists, who were their contemporaries, they revolted

against bourgeois rationalism to create something different. Bizarre and unconventional as these holy men might have been, they were at the cutting edge of modern debates. The central question of the occult was also the central question of the twentieth century: Is another world possible?

Part I

STRANGE AND WONDROUS

We react to facts in the most irrational way.
Without plan or foundations, we build our future
into the circumstances of the time and leave it
exposed to the destructive effects of their chaotic
jostling. "Firm ground, at last!" we cry, and sink
helpless in the stream of events.

—Albert Schweitzer,
The Decay and the Restoration of Civilization[1]

~

In the West, anyway, everyone seemed as lost as
I was: why not try the East?

—Ella Maillart,
The Cruel Way[2]

Chapter 1

THE ANTI-CHRIST
OF ATHENS

ATHENS IN 1923 WAS A CITY IN DESPERATE NEED OF miracles. For several months, a steady stream of refugees had been arriving at the port of Piraeus, driven out of their homes across the Mediterranean Sea. It was a depressing scene. Hundreds of thousands of men, women, and children fleeing war and ethnic violence had boarded cramped and dangerous ships, in search of new shores where they might find safety. One American observer recalled seeing these overloaded ships arriving in Greece, after being buffeted for days in the open seas. Many of the passengers had not had anything to eat or drink for days and were "crowded so densely on board that in many cases they had only room to stand on deck."[1]

Materially, Athens was unprepared for such a large influx of people. Greece had just lost a long and bloody war against the nascent Turkish state. Their ignominious defeat had cost many lives and many millions of drachmas, leaving national morale low, state finances depleted, and the country's politics in turmoil. The Athens of 1920 had been a comparatively small, sleepy city. The population of the entire metropolitan area was less than five hundred thousand. Between September 1922 and the end of 1923, around one million refugees entered Greece, hundreds of thousands of whom ended up in Athens. Between 1920 and 1928, the population of central Athens grew by 54 percent and the population of its port, Piraeus, almost doubled.[2]

At its peak from 1922 to 1923, this crisis put the overwhelmed and under-resourced city under a strain that it could barely handle.

Any available spaces were turned into makeshift dwellings, as the authorities scrambled to find shelter for the new arrivals; factories, warehouses, and schools were all converted into housing. The national theater was taken over and the private boxes, which had once been reserved for the city's wealthy elite, became homes to entire families. A "forced hospitality" law was instituted, compelling the rich to open the doors of their large houses to those in need. Those who refused were fined, and that money was funneled back into aid efforts. Still, this was not enough. Many of the newcomers were unable to find places to stay as the harsh Athenian winter crept in. They slept on the streets, in hastily constructed tents, with barely enough clothing to keep out the cold. Accounts of the terrible situation throughout the country began to emerge. One observer from the League of Nations visited a camp in which five children had died that morning and seven children the day before from either cold or malnutrition.[3]

The Greek refugee crisis became a popular cause for humanitarians across the world. Well-meaning volunteers traveled from Europe and America to lend a hand however they could. They set up soup kitchens and even entire camps in which to house people. Many of them sent further vivid reports back home describing the terrible scenes they had witnessed—people dressed in rags begging for food, disease running rampant through the makeshift dwellings, babies dying in their mothers' arms. Messages and adverts appeared in the press of Western Europe and America imploring people to donate money or their old clothes to charities working on the ground.

In January of 1923, the Greek government announced that it could not accept any more refugees unless it was given foreign aid—the country simply did not have enough money. As diseases spread rapidly through camps, many Greeks became even more suspicious of their new guests. Some doctors refused to treat refugees, worried about the risk of contagion—"Our paying patients do not like us to go among the typhus and smallpox and then come to them," one said. Newspapers reported that in Epirus, a rural region in the north of the country, infected refugees had been herded into a barn, where they were left either to die or to recover.[4]

As these refugees found themselves in a strange land, their old homes and identities taken away from them, many unsure whether their loved ones were safe or not, Athens became a breeding ground for the supernatural. People who had lost family members were desperate enough to try anything. One woman who, like many others, had been separated from her children during the chaos of the past year visited a hypnotist in an attempt to locate her missing son. Miraculously, the hypnotist located the lost boy in a school in the center of Athens and he was reunited with his mother.[5]

Somewhere among this mass of desperate refugees lurked the young, self-styled "fakir," Tahra Bey. In the spring of 1923, pictures of this holy man dressed in the robes and headdress of Bedouins from the deserts of Arabia began to appear in Greek newspapers. He said that he had come from the East to perform inexplicable wonders for the people of Greece, a "land of prophecy . . . land of the spirit." Speaking in the cryptic language of the occult, he told the press that he was in Athens to "prove the existence of mysterious powers in every human being" and promised to "give everyone the key to open the locked door to a world where a powerful humanity slumbers."[6]

Tahra Bey's unusual appearance and his appeals to the supernatural turned heads. Soon after his arrival in Athens he had been embraced by a local magazine called the *Dawn of Humanity*, which had been founded in 1921 and blended modern psychic sciences with stories of the ancient Greek gods and a smattering of Greek nationalism. Its first issue began with a poem in honor of the sun god Apollo, followed by an appeal to reveal the secrets "which have been sealed inside all things and which human ignorance and barbarism have called ancient mythology."[7] The editor was fascinated by the mysterious powers this fakir claimed to possess, which were potential proofs of these hidden secrets that enthralled the magazine's readers. He installed this new visitor to Athens in the small house in the working-class district of Metaxourgeio, just north of the Acropolis, that functioned as the magazine's offices. It was a modest whitewashed bungalow with green shutters and a small wooden door, over which hung a plaque reading "The Spiritual Brotherhood: Virtue."[8]

Almost as soon as Tahra Bey moved in, unexplained phenomena began to occur in the vicinity. One peddler who sold *koulouria*, a ring-shaped Greek bread covered in sesame seeds, saw his stock mysteriously disappear as he walked past this bungalow. Two young women in the city received a series of mysterious letters that, every time the women tried to show their mothers, would vanish from their hands. Rumors spread that a powerful supernatural presence was residing in that small house and old women would cross themselves as they passed by it. One magazine dubbed the city's new visitor "the Anti-Christ of Athens."[9]

Gradually, more details about Tahra Bey's abilities emerged. He could stop his own heartbeat with the power of his mind, pierce his flesh without feeling pain, and even catch a speeding bullet "like it was a bonbon."[10] Using the power of his mind he was able to control his bodily functions and whether he would feel pain or not at any moment. A later observer of his feats remarked that "he inflicted wounds that under ordinary circumstances would have caused serious injury or actual death."[11] But the thing that most caught the public's attention was his ability to bury himself alive for long periods of time, then re-emerge apparently unscathed. He claimed to be able to enter a state of suspended animation—a kind of living death—which allowed him to stay buried under the earth without air for hours or days.

At the end of April 1923, this newly arrived stranger submitted his miraculous abilities to scientific analysis as he put on a special performance for a panel of experts that included medical doctors and specialists in the paranormal. Under controlled conditions, independent witnesses observed his feats and were undeniably impressed; he really did seem able to completely suspend his body's vital functions. First, he miraculously stopped his pulse as the doctors were measuring it. Then, producing twenty-centimeter-long needles, he invited the attendees to insert them into his flesh. When they did, he felt no pain and, inexplicably, no blood came out of the wounds. Finally, he demonstrated his skills of "catalepsy," during which he made his body go lifeless and stiff as iron. The observers could come up with no good scientific explanation for what they had seen. When asked how he could do all of these things Tahra Bey replied, "By will and by faith," and reminded the people of Greece about Jesus's assertion that "the faithful can move even mountains."[12]

When pushed a little further, he told journalists that his feats were part of a long and venerable tradition of "fakirism." Fakirs ("poor men" in Arabic) had been around for centuries and were a part of the cultures of both the Middle East and South Asia. The word itself was first applied to the ascetic mystics of Sufi Islam, who renounced the trappings of the physical world, viewing them as obstacles in the quest for the divine. They cast aside wealth and bodily pleasures, living a simple life of poverty as a form of religious devotion. Some Sufi orders had gradually developed ritual practices that showed their disdain for the physical body and involved subjecting themselves to impressively painful ordeals. Edward Lane, the early nineteenth-century Oriental-ist and traveler, described the things he saw members of one sect do in Egypt (things very similar to Tahra Bey's displays in Athens): "They pretend to thrust iron spikes into their eyes and bodies without sus-taining any injury. . . . They also break large masses of stone on their chests . . . and are said to pass swords completely through their bodies and packing needles through both their cheeks without suffering any pain or leaving any wounds."[13]

By the end of the nineteenth century, the word *fakir* had taken on a wider meaning, particularly in European travel accounts. No longer limited to Sufi Muslims, it was used to refer to any itinerant, ascetic holy man of the "East" (very broadly defined). In the imagi-nation of Europe and America, fakirs were especially associated with India rather than the Middle East. Just as often Hindu as Muslim, these men would perform incredible acts of pain or endurance to demonstrate their piety. They were known for lying on beds of nails or walking across burning coals; but the Indian fakir's most famous skill—one that Tahra Bey assiduously cultivated—was the ability to be buried alive for long stretches of time.

One famous demonstration of this feat occurred in the 1830s at the court of the maharajah Ranjit Singh in Lahore and was witnessed by the British agent in the Punjab, Claude Wade. A fakir who had been put inside a linen bag, sealed inside a box four feet by three feet, and locked inside a sealed room for forty days was released in Wade's presence. A doctor who was present as part of Wade's entourage left behind a stunned account of the moment when the man who had been kept enclosed in a tiny space for over a month was freed. The sack was taken off his body and he emerged, looking like a corpse, cold, with shriveled limbs and no pulse. Quickly, an attendant poured warm water on the fakir and smeared his eyes with ghee, and life returned to his body. The fakir had seemingly entered a deep state of suspended animation, shutting down all bodily signs of life for several weeks and then, in a few moments, had sprung back to life. Wade, after examining him, could find no explanation of what he had seen other than to believe that the man had suspended his bodily functions for the whole time that he was underground.[14]

By the end of the nineteenth century, fakir burials like this had become a minor tourist attraction for foreign travelers in India. Before long, people in Europe started to bring these demonstrations back home too. At the Paris exposition of 1889, a group of North African fakirs entered trance-like states and performed incredible, sometimes gruesome, feats to amazed audiences—putting their hands in burning coals, swallowing cactuses, and piercing their cheeks with knives. In 1892 at the Berlin Panoptikum, "Soliman the Fakir" pierced his tongue, cheeks, and torso with blades. At one point, he popped his right eye out of its socket "so that it hung suspended by the nerve-threads about an inch from his cheek" and then put it back in again.[15]

Tahra Bey had created his own spin on this ancient tradition. Dressed in the clothes of an Arab sheikh rather than an Indian mendicant, he spoke in lofty and evocative tones, promising his audiences both entertainment and enlightenment. He brought together ancient rituals with modern spiritual philosophies with an eye for the theatrical that would soon make him a global celebrity.

However, Tahra Bey was not a member of any Sufi order, nor was he an Indian yogi; he was not even an Arab sheikh, although he dressed like one. He had been brought to Athens by the same tragedies that had brought many thousands of other refugees there. He had arrived alongside masses of people fleeing the destruction that had followed the collapse of the Ottoman Empire, a power that had ruled over a vast expanse of land spanning the continents of Europe, Asia, and Africa for centuries.

For most of its history, the Ottoman Empire had been an extremely diverse polity, where many different religious and ethnic minorities lived in comparative safety; many thrived and some even wielded considerable power within a finely balanced system that had built up over generations. After heavy Ottoman losses, followed by final defeat, in the First World War, this fragile equilibrium started to totter, then collapsed completely. As the once-great empire crumbled, brutal violence descended across its lands. The old logic of a patchwork empire of different ethnicities was gone, replaced by a new ideal of Turkish-Muslim nationalism. Minorities became targets—identified as dangerous and subversive outsiders. Communities turned on one another and the land that was soon to become Turkey was ethnically cleansed of hundreds of thousands of non-Turks who had lived on the shores of the Mediterranean for generations, even millennia.

The majority of the refugees coming to Athens were from the Greek communities that had lived across Asia Minor for millennia and had now been expelled from their homes. Tahra Bey, though, was an Armenian, part of a Christian minority that had been spread widely across Ottoman lands. He was born in Istanbul around 1900 and his real name was Krikor Kalfayan.[16] Beyond that, it is hard to say much about his early life with any certainty. According to one account, his mother died shortly after he was born, and he was raised in the city's Armenian community, moving between Kadiköy, where he was born, and Galata, where his uncle worked in a hotel. He claimed to have attended the illustrious Haydarpaşa medical school—it is unclear whether he completed his studies there, but it was apparently thanks to this training that he claimed the title of Doctor later in his life.

In his teenage years, he began his first, little-documented, experiments with magic and hypnotism. Krikor Kalfayan would have seen many public displays of wondrous feats on the streets of Istanbul as a young boy. When the Armenian writer Zabel Yessayan described her childhood in an Armenian neighborhood of the city in the late nineteenth century, she remembered the impressive street performances by "jugglers, dervishes, and magicians."[17] Krikor Kalfayan may even have spent some time working as a juggler himself as a teenager. Then, after becoming a student, he began to take the occult and supernatural more seriously. Early 1910s Istanbul had a burgeoning occult scene, as a range of scholars and scientists published books and launched journals to debate the merits of psychic and esoteric doctrines. In the early years of the decade, Hasan Merzuk, the Cretan-born son of an Ottoman civil servant and an active writer-translator, wrote one of the most influential occult books of the period, *Talking to the Jinn*, a history and explanation of "Spiritism, Fakirism, and Hypnotism."[18] Krikor Kalfayan had started moonlighting as a bookseller and any number of books like these could easily have passed through his hands.[19]

Alongside these vague, hard-to-verify stories about his early experiments with the paranormal, Krikor Kalfayan's late teenage years were marked by trauma and genocide. When the Ottomans entered the First World War, the Armenians of Eastern Anatolia were instantly suspected of seeking to undermine the Ottoman state from within. Tensions that had been bubbling near the surface of society for several decades turned increasingly violent. The Ottoman authorities took an infamous decision to remove the Armenian presence from Eastern Anatolia, whether by expulsion or by murder. They sent hundreds of thousands of civilians on death marches across the desert and killed others before they could even be deported. In the course of the war, around one million Armenians lost their lives, and an ancient civilization was erased from the land.

Although there were targeted killings and deportations of Armenians in Istanbul, the city was one of the safer places in the Ottoman Empire to be Armenian, and the majority survived the genocide. Still, as they learned what had happened to Armenians in the east of the empire, many of whom were their relatives, they must have been filled with fear, grief, and anxiety. By 1916, gruesome stories of the genocide had traveled as far as the UK, where the British government published a thick dossier collecting eyewitness accounts of the events. This 684-page document gives a sense of the kind of bloody stories that Krikor Kalfayan would have heard in Istanbul as a teenager. There were accounts of Ottoman forces and other irregulars massacring whole towns and burning villages to the ground; troops took able-bodied men into the wilderness, forced them to dig their own graves, and then executed them; thousands of children were made into orphans or were killed themselves; victims were tied up, their heads sticking through the rungs of ladders, and then decapitated; people many miles away saw mutilated bodies floating down the Euphrates River, to be eaten by dogs or vultures. "They engulfed the Christian villages," wrote one Armenian eyewitness. "Plunder, pillage, massacre, and rape were the order of the day. Every village paid its share. First they killed the men, then they took the women—those who had not escaped—and carried them away for themselves."[20]

The Armenians of Istanbul, even if they were not in imminent danger, lived as a people under scrutiny. Police kept a close eye on the entire community, sometimes installing officers outside churches on Sundays to conduct inspections of parishioners' identity papers.[21] Krikor Kalfayan grew up knowing what it was like to be an outsider. In 1920, he left the city of his birth, bound for other shores. Almost all his biographies agree on this, if on little else. The next three years of Krikor Kalfayan's life, until he reached Athens, are hidden behind a haze of rumor and myth.

The most detailed and evocative story, though not necessarily the most reliable, comes from a biography serialized in an Istanbul-based Armenian newspaper in 1926 (and reproduced in the 1930s, with a few changes, in a Turkish-language magazine). It begins in July 1920 on board a Greek ferry bound for the prosperous city of Smyrna on the Aegean Sea.[22]

Smyrna had an illustrious recent history. In the nineteenth century it had become one of the busiest ports in the whole Eastern Mediterranean. Smyrna figs and Smyrna tobacco were famous across the world and many fortunes had been made in those years of plenty. The city boasted all the trappings of modern luxury: cinemas, restaurants, elegant cafés, and its own opera house. Its population was a microcosm of a rapidly fading Ottoman cosmopolitanism—Armenians, Jews, Greeks, and Turks lived alongside "Levantine" families of French and British descent. For those of a nostalgic disposition, pre-war Smyrna is remembered as something close to paradise on earth. "The open market exuded a tantalizing variety of aromas: grapes, fresh figs, apricots, melons, cherries, pomegranates—all so plentiful that the poorest villager could live on fruit and cheese. In season, baskets of rose petals lined the streets; rose-petal conserve and paper-thin pastries heavy with rose-flavoured syrup were favoured delicacies served to guests," wrote one academic in the 1960s, recalling the city's early twentieth-century glory days.[23]

When Krikor Kalfayan arrived in his new home, he quickly found his way into the city's sizable Armenian community—Smyrna, along with Istanbul, was one of the very few places in the Ottoman Empire that still had a significant Armenian population after the genocide. The Armenians of Smyrna had always been bookish and the city had hosted a vibrant intellectual and cultural scene since the nineteenth century. Many famous Armenian writers, translators, journalists, and theater impresarios made their names in Smyrna. The first full translation of a Shakespeare play into Armenian, for instance, was published in the city in 1853—*The Comedy of Errors*, by Aram Teteyan.[24] It was the perfect environment for Kalfayan to set himself up in a career he knew well: bookselling. He acquired a small market stall and began to support himself as one of Smyrna's many bookdealers.

Krikor Kalfayan also brought his childhood interest in the occult with him to his new home. One day, while in conversation with a fellow bookdealer who ran a shop underneath one of the city's Armenian churches, Kalfayan casually mentioned that he had learned the arts of hypnotism in Istanbul. This other bookseller was instantly interested; after this conversation he began to talk to his friends, who were intrigued enough to ask for a private display of this young man's skills. Kalfayan gladly treated them to a demonstration of his hypnotic powers, and they were so impressed that they arranged for him to put on a public show at one of the many clubs near the quay.

Just a few days before the date of his big performance, Kalfayan was strolling through Boudja, a wealthy suburb nestled on the hills overlooking Smyrna that was popular with the English mercantile elite. As he walked past the elegant villas and gardens, admiring the flowers, he peered through one fence and was confronted by the shocking sight of an old Armenian priest engaged in some decidedly non-Christian acts with a beautiful young woman. The priest's face, as he was locked in a loving embrace with an unmarried woman, entered the deep recesses of Kalfayan's memory.

As he took to the stage to demonstrate his hypnotic abilities, Kalfayan looked out into the audience, only to see the very same priest sitting in the first few rows. Even in this early stage of his career, Kalfayan was too savvy to let an opportunity like this evade him. He announced to the crowd that he had the ability to read minds. Immediately, a crowd of audience members rushed forward, clamoring for him to demonstrate his skills on them, but he rebuffed these eager volunteers. Instead, he gestured casually toward the priest and said that he intended to reveal this religious leader's innermost desires.

The priest, nervous about being scrutinized by this unusual performer with supernatural powers, tried to deflect the attention. He insisted that his thoughts were unremarkable; the only love he had in his heart was for Jesus Christ. Why not turn to someone younger with more interesting secrets? he suggested. But Kalfayan was not deterred, excited to reveal the juicy information he had about this upstanding man of the cloth. The priest was in love, he declared, with a young woman in Boudja. He even gave her address, in case people wanted to check the story's veracity. It was the same address where he had seen the couple cavorting in the gardens a few days earlier. The priest tried to deny the claims, but Kalfayan only increased his accusations, until the respected man of God was forced to flee the club.

The confrontation ended up having significant unforeseen consequences for the young Kalfayan, and the second part of this story about his Smyrna years put him at the center of one of the most dramatic and bloody historical moments of the 1920s. As a series of conferences redrew the world map in the aftermath of the war, Greece was granted control of this desirable port on the coast of Asia Minor in 1920. The Greek governor general of Smyrna, Aristeides Stergiades, was given the difficult task of keeping the peace between the sizable Greek population and the other communities—Jewish, Armenian, Turkish—who called the city home.

To add to his problems, Greek forces were engaged in heavy fighting with the armies of the Turkish National Movement, led by Mustafa Kemal, who would later become known as Atatürk—"father of the Turks." Greece had been granted Smyrna and many of the surrounding lands in the treaties that came after the First World War but it was trying to stake a claim to as much of Asia Minor as it could. The Turkish forces were fighting for the creation of a new nation-state on the same lands. Militarily, it was finely balanced, with neither side assured of victory.

In the midst of this geopolitical drama, Stergiades, according to the story, was approached by the wounded clergyman from the mindreading demonstration, who, it transpired, was a personal friend of his, complaining about his merciless tormentor, the troublesome hypnotist turned mind reader Krikor Kalfayan. The Greek governor agreed to help his friend and summoned the Armenian performer to explain himself. Under harsh questioning Krikor Kalfayan stuck to the story that he knew to be true: the priest *was* having a relationship with a woman in Boudja. He calmly told Stergiades to investigate it himself if he had any doubts. In the face of such resolute certainty, Stergiades sent his men to Boudja to verify the tale of sexual dalliances and they managed to confirm everything Kalfayan had said about the priest's affair. Kalfayan was vindicated and Stergiades was supposedly so impressed by this young mystic's powers of clairvoyance that he quickly became one of Kalfayan's most faithful devotees.

In fact, Stergiades was so convinced of the Armenian's ability to predict the future that he installed him in a luxurious villa and put him on a large cash retainer. He even invited him to meet with General Papoulas, commander in chief of the Greek forces that were fighting in the interior, to advise him on military matters. When the hypnotist met the general, he was, at first, reluctant to speak, seemingly nervous of offering his views. It took some convincing but Kalfayan eventually relented and agreed to use his mystical powers to reveal the course of the war. He reached for a glass of water, drew mysterious circles on its surface, then the course of the future battles and skirmishes slowly revealed itself to him. The Greeks would be successful at first, he said, and push deep into the interior of Anatolia. Papoulas was excited but Kalfayan quickly dampened his optimism. The victories would be brief, he said, and the Turkish armies would eventually turn the tide.

"You see a defeat?" Papoulas asked anxiously.

"Yes, a terrible defeat."[25]

Papoulas did not take this news well. Incensed by Kalfayan's prediction of Greek loss, he demanded that Stergiades expel the Armenian clairvoyant from the city of Smyrna. Papoulas was a very powerful man, and the governor general was forced to comply with his request but (in this version of the story) did not completely abandon Krikor Kalfayan. He put him on a ship to Athens, furnished with personal letters of recommendation for when he arrived. As the boat sailed to the Greek capital, a young Krikor Kalfayan retired to his cabin to don his fakir's robes and, like superman putting on his cape, became Tahra Bey.

Of course, his prediction about the war was entirely correct. By 1922, Mustafa Kemal's Turkish National Movement was turning the tide against the Greeks. In a series of military victories, it pushed the Hellenic armies all the way back to the Aegean Sea. At the beginning of September 1922, the ragtag group of soldiers that comprised the remnants of the Greek forces boarded ships and left the continent of Asia entirely. Behind them streamed thousands of refugees from the interior, many of whom entered the now-undefended city of Smyrna and waited for Mustafa Kemal's advancing armies.

Turkish soldiers entered Smyrna on September 9. They reassured the inhabitants that no civilians would be harmed, but both the Greek and Armenian populations were skeptical, having heard many stories of violence inflicted on civilians over the course of this war. It was well known that the Greek armies had killed people and burned villages during their retreat. Would the Turks be hungry for revenge? The Armenian population was especially terrified, afraid that the systematic murder and expulsion of the 1915 genocide might be meted out on them in 1922.

It was not long before their fears were confirmed. Within the first few days of Turkish occupation, troops surrounded the Armenian quarter; the military authorities issued proclamations saying that anyone who was found concealing an Armenian would be court-martialed.[26] Then the atrocities began—looting of property, rape, and murder. Later accounts of the early days of September recall the sight of lifeless bodies lying on the streets of the Armenian district and the smell of death lingering in the air.[27] A few days later, the situation would get even worse. On the evening of September 13, a fire began in the Armenian quarter, almost certainly started by Turkish troops, and within hours the flames had spread across much of the city. As the inferno raged, people sought refuge on the quay. They hoped to board boats and be taken to safety. Many of those who did make it onto boats would end up in Athens as refugees, but many did not make it out at all. Descriptions of the scenes by the water were gruesome—mothers held on to the lifeless corpses of their children, bodies floated in the water. At the time, newspapers estimated that 120,000 people died. Historians today do not significantly differ. According to some reports, no Armenians could be seen on the streets of the city; they were all either in hiding or killed.[28] The *Los Angeles Times* of September 18 described the city as a "vast sepulchre . . . The streets [were] full of the bodies of those who sought to escape."[29] In England, the archbishop of Canterbury called it "one of the most terrible catastrophes which modern civilisation has known."[30]

In this version of Krikor Kalfayan's early life, he is directly connected to one of the most tragic events of the period. Yet it seems extremely unlikely that these colorful anecdotes about the priest or about Kalfayan's meeting with the Greek generals are true. They are certainly not attested in any other accounts of the period, even though they involve several important figures. Perhaps, though, some truth lies behind them. Were these stories of incompetent generals and an untrustworthy priest attempts to sublimate the trauma and religious violence of the early 1920s? Had Krikor Kalfayan escaped Smyrna during the fire, ended up as a refugee in Athens, and created a story to repress his memories? Did Krikor Kalfayan ever set foot in Smyrna at all? The answer to this last question is not clear-cut. Throughout the 1920s, several other versions of his early life appeared, which took him to very different places.

In 1930 Tahra Bey gave an interview to an Armenian newspaper in America. In it, he repeated the story that he left Istanbul in 1920 on board a ship, but he was not bound for Smyrna, he claimed, he was traveling to Egypt. In this land of ancient mysteries and miracles, Tahra Bey said, he had studied the secrets of the fakirs with an ancient order of mystics. He made his way through the country's caravanserais and coffeehouses until he found the wise Sheikh al-Falaki, who taught him the mysteries of the paranormal. In this version of Tahra's early life, he finished three years of training with the mystics of Egypt before he was called to Athens on a mission to spread the fakirs' message among the peoples of Europe.[31]

The final story about Tahra Bey's travels before arriving in Athens happened neither in Smyrna nor in Egypt but in the northern Greek city of Thessaloniki. It comes to us through an unexpected source: the family of the legendary French-Armenian crooner Charles Aznavour, one of the most famous and adored Armenians of the twentieth century. Aznavour was so successful in the twentieth-century entertainment industry that he attained the status of a kind of secular saint; when he died in 2008 his state funeral in Paris was attended by both the president and prime minister of Armenia, as well as three French presidents.

Charles Aznavour's mother, Knar, was also Krikor Kalfayan's cousin, and the family crossed paths with this charismatic mystic a number of times in the early twentieth century, including for a brief period in Istanbul. However, their longest association came in late 1922 or early 1923, when the Aznavour family were in Thessaloniki.[32] Like many other Armenian refugees, they were trying to survive as best they could in this former Ottoman port city not too far from the Greek-Turkish border. Krikor Kalfayan, though, who found himself in the same place at the same time, had more ambitious goals; he wanted to make money convincing people that he had supernatural abilities and access to lucrative secret knowledge. He pursued opportunities at every level, from the mundane (selling good-luck talismans and vials of a liquid of his own creation that he claimed possessed magical powers) to the elaborate (setting up complex ruses to convince greedy and naïve victims that he could reveal the location of hidden treasures).

Aznavour's father, Misha, made some much-needed money working as Kalfayan's secretary while he was deeply invested in a scam involving the local chief of police and a large amount of money that he claimed had been buried in a village not far from Thessaloniki. Kalfayan had convinced the gullible functionary—"the perfect pigeon," as Aznavour called him in his memoirs—to spend six months excavating the village in search of riches. Aznavour recounts a story that happened before he was born but which must have been passed down through family lore. "To lay his hands on [the treasure], it was absolutely necessary for the fakir to fall into a trance; in fact, several trances. Of course, in order to fall into those trances and meditate while they lasted, the fakir needed money, and naturally it was provided by the head of police. . . . Meanwhile a gang of workmen dug up the soil all over the village, making so many holes that the place began to resemble Gruyère cheese."

As time went on and no treasure was found, the pigeon realized that he was never going to find anything, and he was furious. Kalfayan, the proto-fakir, fearful of the potential repercussions of angering an influential local policeman, skipped town in a hurry, leaving Misha Aznavour without a job. As Kalfayan was preparing his belongings to leave, Aznavour sarcastically commented that his much-vaunted vials of magical liquid seemed to have lost their power to protect him. Kalfayan, in no mood for joking, angrily replied, "Go piss in them, that ought to do the trick." Aznavour does not mention what happened after this falling-out, but we can assume that Kalfayan skipped town and made his way south to Athens.[33]

These different versions of Krikor Kalfayan's wanderings through the postwar Eastern Mediterranean before he reached Athens in 1923 are often wildly conflicting or chronologically irreconcilable. At their core, however, they all tell the same story. Kalfayan had lived the life of an Armenian refugee. It is no coincidence that all the places where he was said to have traveled—Smyrna, Egypt, Greece—were well-known destinations for Armenians in the early 1920s. His travels, even if supplemented by fantasies, mirrored the troubled wanderings of thousands in the aftermath of genocide, the First World War, and the fall of the Ottoman Empire.

In 1923, Tahra Bey the charismatic, miracle-working wanderer from the East, who had come to show the people of Greece the secrets of "fakirism," arrived in Athens. Behind this alluring persona lurked his former self, Krikor Kalfayan, a stranger and a member of a recently traumatized people. For his fellow Armenians, there was a grim irony in his ability to withstand mutilation and to raise himself from the dead. One darkly comic article about him in the Armenian press in 1926 observed that "if every Armenian were Tahra Bey and could endure swords and knives and emerge unharmed after being buried underground, the Eastern Question would look entirely different. . . . If the Armenian Fakir had even a smidgen of patriotism, he would share his powers with us."[34]

Chapter 2

"TAHRANITIS"

IN THE WEEKS AFTER TAHRA BEY GAVE HIS INITIAL demonstrations of the wonders of fakirism to doctors and journalists at the small house in Athens, his fame spread through the city. More newspaper articles appeared, enumerating his many skills and trying to explain their origins. One psychiatric clinic in Athens enlisted him to help cure its patients using hypnosis. The police asked him to use his clairvoyant abilities to help them solve crimes, but he refused, saying that the goal of fakirism was to create a world without crime instead of concerning itself with the details of any particular case.

In May, Tahra Bey announced his most ambitious demonstration. He was going to bury himself alive for an entire month under the earth at the center of the city's imposing marble stadium, which had been built for the 1896 Olympic Games and which remains a major landmark in the modern city. Even as his profile rose in Greece, he did not forget the mass of unfortunate people who had arrived in Greece over the past months. All proceeds from his show would go to help alleviate the city's refugee crisis.[1] Unfortunately, despite his big promises, the stunt got caught up in bureaucracy. No permit for the burial was granted and it did not go ahead.

In August, he appeared on a public stage for the first time, stepping out at Athens's Kentriko Theater before throngs of excited fans, who finally had a chance to see his famous miracles up close. The atmosphere was so charged that the police were soon called—not to censor the fakir's performances but to control the raucous crowd—earning

Tahra Bey even more notoriety.[2] Throughout the summer and into the autumn, he put on shows to large audiences in the Greek capital. Over the course of these months, he began to experiment with his act. A few favorite elements emerged: he would pierce his flesh with sharp objects and on request could control whether or not blood came out of the wounds. One of his favorite ways to show that his body was impervious to pain was to lie across two sharp blades, one at his neck and the other at his ankles, and have a large rock broken across his chest. His finale—the feat that was fast becoming his speciality—was always to put his body into a state of living death and have himself buried alive in front of the audience, many of whom would have lived through similarly gruesome traumas in the past years.

In interviews and letters to the press, Tahra Bey was also beginning to form a backstory for himself and was building his fakir persona. He told one newspaper that he had learned his skills from his father, who had been a fakir like him, and from his travels in the lands of Egypt and Anatolia.[3] At this point, he seldom went into more detail, but he did not really need to. The rumors that circulated about his inexplicable abilities quickly made him an object of fascination among the chattering classes of Athens and few were concerned with the vague, confusing stories about his earlier life. According to Giannis Kairophylas, a historian of Athens, his fakir performances had a visceral effect on audiences. "Many of the spectators trembled with fear," he said, and later on in the show "some old ladies turned pale, got up from their seats, and headed for the entrance. . . . One woman fainted."[4] Everyone was soon talking about this fakir; Athens had come down with a disease dubbed "Tahranitis."[5]

As his popularity grew, conservative opinion turned against this mysterious stranger. His extravagant claims were particularly threatening to the Greek Orthodox Church and his supernatural abilities risked shaking the faith of their congregants. To see someone die and come back to life, in particular, undermined a key foundation of the Christian story: resurrection. "A person's death and return to life is not something to joke about," wrote one journalist sternly. As well as the ire of the church, he faced accusations from secular critics who alleged that he was a dangerous and untrustworthy grifter, who had come to swindle the anxious population of Athens out of their money. One newspaper was shocked to see crowds of people "running to the fakir with money in their hands, seeking to know their fortunes."[6]

Tahra Bey responded to the controversy with calm insouciance. Adopting a mildly patronizing tone, he wrote to one newspaper to confess his shock that Greeks were totally ignorant of the doctrines and marvels of fakirism. Elsewhere in Europe the subject was studied academically and even encouraged by the local authorities, but in Greece, Tahra Bey said, he found himself maligned and attacked instead of welcomed. Despite its long history of elucidating the great problems of the mind and the soul, Greece, he lamented, had lost its way.[7]

This appeal to the national pride of his critics did not succeed. Public anger grew and people began to demand that the government expel Tahra Bey from Greece. A few years later he recalled being confronted on the street by an angry mob who believed that he was launching a war against the Christian faith. His activities had touched several nerves and there was a real danger that he could get hurt in this chaos. When he later told the story of this altercation, he described his typically supernatural solution to the threats. He hypnotized the mob and put them into a state of collective hallucination to make them believe that he had fled through the streets in one direction while, in reality, he remained exactly where he was. The bamboozled mob followed the phantom fakir, leaving the real Tahra Bey to blend into the crowd and escape "safe and sound, incognito."[8]

Eventually, an opponent emerged whom Tahra Bey could not deceive. Georgios Maichos, an Athenian dentist and amateur athlete, was not the kind of person you would expect to challenge this holy man. He happily admitted that he was no expert in the occult: "I have not studied books of fakirism or Spiritualism," he told people, "I am just a dentist, devoted to my clinic and my patients."[9] Despite his lack of academic knowledge, Maichos was convinced that he had worked out the secret of Tahra Bey's mystical feats and he intended to use the forces of science and logic to disprove his fantastical claims.

The fakir's supposed supernatural powers, the dentist claimed, were nothing but magic tricks. One by one, he picked apart all the elements of Tahra Bey's act. Sometimes the explanations seemed more outlandish than the tricks themselves. To control his blood flow, for instance, Maichos said that the fakir injected himself with adrenaline in one arm before the show and rubbed the other arm with a balm made from cocaine. If someone asked him to cut himself without bleeding he would stab the adrenaline-injected arm; if the audience member wanted blood he would stab the other one.

When it came to Tahra Bey's most high-profile stunt—the ability to put himself into a cataleptic state and bury himself alive—Maichos went one step further. He made a public offer to the fakir: he would deposit 100,000 drachmas in the National Bank of Greece that would be paid out if Tahra Bey could hold his head underwater for twenty-five minutes. Maichos believed that staying inside a coffin for twenty-five minutes was easy—there was enough air in there for anyone to survive for that long—but that staying underwater was a different story. If he could really enter a self-induced temporary state of death, he would have no problem submerging his airways entirely. If it was just a magic trick, the challenge would be impossible.

At first Tahra Bey agreed, telling Maichos that he would meet him at the offices of a local magazine. But he must have had second thoughts. When the dentist arrived, the fakir was nowhere to be seen. Tahra Bey was starting to feel worn down by the constant attacks from Maichos, who not only offered explanations for Tahra Bey's tricks but had even started a stage show of his own, publicly replicating the fakir's tricks himself. By October 1923, he had decided to leave Athens, in search of new places where he would not be hounded by this hostile and energetic dentist. One Athenian journalist joked, in reference to his famous burial-alive act, that Tahra Bey had discovered that "the soil of Attika might be good for growing tomatoes, but it is no good for burying fakirs."[10]

Once he had left Athens, few people knew his precise location. Tahra Bey himself said that he had passed through Serbia and Romania. However, by early 1924 his name began to appear on the theaters of the Greek provinces. In Patras, in Volos, in Missolonghi, he demonstrated the wonders of fakirism. In reality, Tahra Bey, as an Armenian refugee from Turkey, would have been stateless— eligible for neither a Turkish passport nor a Greek one. In 1924, the League of Nations estimated that there were around 120,000 Armenian refugees in Greece whose situation was similar to Tahra Bey's.[11] Without a passport, traveling outside of Greece was complicated.

A few people managed to acquire passports from the short-lived Armenian Republic, which by 1924 controlled no territory and really existed only in a small network of diplomatic offices in Europe. Most, though, had to survive on one of the League of Nations' newly created Nansen passports, a special international document issued to stateless refugees who had no government to issue them a passport. It was far from a perfect document— there was no automatic right to work nor any guarantees against deportation—but it was the best many people could get. In 1924, Armenians became eligible to acquire a Nansen passport. For much of the decade, questions about passports, citizenship, and residency dominated the minds of many people across Europe. It is no coincidence that several stories about Tahra Bey at the time reported that he had the ability to hypnotize customs officials into believing that all of his papers were in order.

Eventually, Tahra Bey managed to cross an international border, continuing his westward journey from Istanbul, as he reappeared in Rome in December 1924. He was warmly welcomed by Arturo Reghini, a fervent scholar of the occult, who considered the coming of this holy man a great portent for the city. Reghini was a typical example of the kind of person drawn to the occult in the early 1920s. He was well educated and intellectually promiscuous, dabbling in different philosophies—ancient and modern, Eastern and Western—and mixing with Italy's early twentieth-century literary avant-garde. He was also profoundly disillusioned with the state of the modern world, searching for a remedy for the alienation he felt in the 1920s.

After many years of writing on esoteric subjects, Reghini had eventually formulated a complex theory of "pagan imperialism," calling for a return to ancient ways and a system in which people were ruled by an elite group of powerful initiates. Like the editor of the *Dawn of Humanity* in Greece, he had fused modern nationalism with the ancient pantheon of pagan gods. He believed it was Italy's role to spread a new system, based on ancient Roman values and traditions. When Mussolini's government took power in Italy, promising that an era of national rebirth was coming, Reghini was enthused by the fascist revolution and threw his support behind Mussolini. However, his ambitions were grander than Il Duce's. His goal was the total destruction of the Catholic Church and the dawn of a new spiritual era.[12]

Tahra Bey was developing an uncanny ability to embody people's deepest desires, and Reghini saw in him the potential to revive the forgotten ancient beliefs of the East. Reghini, who had recently started a new journal, named *Ignis*, wrote in the inaugural issue that Eastern occult sciences held a key to the progress of the human race and that "humanity's destiny depended on spiritual contact between East and West." He believed that Rome was the city where East and West would meet—"in a land whose history and geography seem to make it predestined to reestablish this contact between East and West, between two traditions and civilisations." The arrival of this Eastern fakir on Italian shores was a sign that the new age was coming and that now was "the right moment to make a concerted effort towards this grand goal."[13] It was as if Reghini had willed Tahra Bey into existence—a man from the East whose miraculous abilities could revivify the spiritual life of the West.

As Tahra Bey traveled farther west his persona slowly became more "Eastern." In Athens, he had been billed as an Armenian who had traveled in Egypt and Anatolia. In Rome, he was now a Coptic Christian Egyptian, Kir Tor Kal Tahra Bey (his full legal name was Krikor Toros Kalfayan). He started telling people that he was the head of a mystical society in Constantinople called the Chavk Institute, founded to investigate and to disseminate "occult Eastern sciences."[14] This mystical traveler cut a striking figure in 1920s Italy. One journalist wrote rhapsodically about his exotic appearance in a way that verged on the erotic: "Dressed in a tunic, a robe, and a turban all'orientale [in an Eastern style] . . . his complexion is brown like his hair and small beard; his face is beautiful, almost breathing sweetness. . . . His form is slight and is a testament to the nobility of his race."[15]

On December 27, he gave the first private demonstration of his abilities in Rome to a panel of doctors and journalists. The display began as he inhaled some incense and went into a cataleptic state, his body going totally rigid. Then, Reghini, who was acting as a kind of manager, invited people from the audience to lay him horizontally across two blades—one at his neck and the other at his ankles—then place a seventy-six-kilogram rock on his chest. Another member of the audience was invited to smash this rock with a hammer, as Tahra Bey remained in a trance, totally unaware of what was happening around him. Once this section of the show was over, he stood up and began to insert sharp objects into his body without feeling pain. Then he prepared for his finale, the burial alive.

He brought the audience outside to a pit that had been dug expressly for the purpose and as they gathered round, he plugged his nose and ears with cotton wool, then put himself in a cataleptic state. He was lowered into a grave and for fifteen minutes, nothing happened—the earth was not disturbed. The audience grew anxious, staring in disbelief, as the rain started to fall. Surely no one could hold their breath that long. People from the neighboring houses stared out of their windows at the fakir's grave. Two minutes before the allotted twenty-five minutes had elapsed, the attendants began to dig Tahra Bey out of his hole, and his body, still covered in soil, was brought back inside. To the amazement of the crowd, exactly on the twenty-five-minute mark an enigmatic smile flashed onto his face as he returned from the dead. None of the scientists who had been invited to attend were able to offer a logical explanation for his abilities. The answer lay in the realm of the supernatural.[16]

Tahra Bey spent the next few months in Italy, traveling through Naples, Sicily, Florence, and Bologna. Many grandiose stories are told about the people that he met on his Italian tour. According to an article in the French press in 1925, "he 'worked' in the most exclusive salons in Rome, in front of the government and diplomatic corps. Mussolini, having seen him at the Duchess of San Faustino's house, begged him to come to the Palazzo Chigi, where he lived."[17] There are also apocryphal tales that the king of England, George V, who was recovering from illness in Sicily, received a personal visit from the fakir. These unconfirmed visits quickly became important parts of the growing canon of lore surrounding Tahra Bey.

During this Italian sojourn, he also added a few new elements to his act: he could transmit his thoughts into other people's brains and hypnotize small animals like rabbits or chickens, putting them into a cataleptic state in front of his audience. He had also developed a complex psycho-scientific explanation for his abilities: "Our body is divided into spirit, astral body, and material body," the fakir told one newspaper in Palermo. His skills as a fakir, Tahra Bey said, were due to the control he had over the spirit, which was itself further split into the "large ego" and "small ego." His mastery of this large ego allowed him to shut down his physical body, to not feel pain, and even to control the flow of blood in his veins.[18]

In the mid-1920s, the scientific frontiers of the study of the human soul were expanding. In 1923, Sigmund Freud had published his pioneering paper on the ego and the id, which argued that the psyche was formed of different parts, not all of which were perceptible to the conscious mind. Tahra Bey, whether or not he was directly referencing Freud, was offering physical proof that human consciousness was much deeper and more complicated than people had previously sup-

Tahra Bey in fakir's robes,
1925.

posed, and his act demonstrated control over the mind that few before him had ever realized was possible.

On June 19, 1925, after six months touring Italy, Tahra Bey got a document that would change his life forever: a French visa. He left Italy behind, along with his great supporter Arturo Reghini. By July 1, Tahra Bey had arrived in Paris, the place where he would attain truly international fame. His two years touring the provincial theaters of Greece and Italy were just the prologue to his grander tale, which would begin that summer.

As soon as he set foot in France, Tahra Bey became the subject of exoticized fascination. As the mysteriously attired fakir strolled in the Place de l'Opéra, he created a huge line of cars whose drivers had stopped to gaze at his long robes and Christlike beard. Within a few weeks, he was giving long interviews to the French newspapers. He told them, as he told the people of Rome, that he was a representative of the Chavk Institute for the study of the psychic sciences of the

East and that he was determined to spread their knowledge to the spiritually backward West. Science was still in its infancy in Europe, he lectured one interviewer, "particularly the science of the spirit," and his goal was to remedy this deficiency.[19] A correspondent for one American newspaper in Paris described Tahra Bey's trip as "the most extraordinary missionary effort imaginable. We have long sent missionaries to the east to tell them they have souls. Now, the east sends missionaries back to us—to prove to us that we have souls."[20]

A short pamphlet about him started to circulate, including a new page-long biography. The stories of his birth in Istanbul and youthful adventures in Smyrna had disappeared. Tahra Bey, the pamphlet claimed, had been born in 1897 in the Nile Delta city of Tanta—a place famous for the shrine of Sufi saint Ahmed al-Badawi. His father was a fakir, the pamphlet claimed, and Tahra Bey had become a fakir in his turn. "The birth of a fakir, like their life, is woven with miracles and legends." According to tradition, a fakir was allowed to have only one child, born from a "virgin that he had selected." During the pregnancy, the parents would then pray over the child in hope that the boy might be given the spirit of a fakir (Tahra Bey insisted that fakirs were always men).[21] Fortunately, he was endowed with the mystical spirit and primed to become a fakir. After spending his early years in Egypt, the family were forced to move to Istanbul in 1905, following an unidentified "Arab revolution." In the Ottoman capital, he trained as a doctor (this element of his story remained consistent throughout his life). In the late 1910s he also became a master of "the mysterious science of the Ancients" and founded his occult society, Chavk, to spread his message to the West. "Tahra Bey is an apostle of science," the pamphlet concluded.[22]

On July 22, he gave his first public performance in the city at the Salle Adyar, the official theater of the French Theosophical Society. By now, Tahra Bey had been perfecting his show for over two years and it was well honed. Incense filled the auditorium in the run-up to his demonstration. At ten o'clock in the evening, he appeared onstage, dressed in his fakir's robes, and, with a dramatic flourish, ripped the material to reveal his bare chest. The audience gasped as his assistants prepared his props and the fakir pressed down on an artery to put himself into a cataleptic state. The act then followed its familiar course, beginning by laying his body across two large blades and breaking a huge rock on his chest, continuing by piercing his flesh with various knives and needles, making some wounds bleed and others heal immediately. As the spectators watched in awe, he lay on a bed of nails without betraying any discomfort. One observer said that "in the hall, there was truly a kind of magnetic current that endowed some of the spectators with a profound faith."[23] He ended by burying himself alive under a large pile of sand for twenty minutes and, once the demonstration was complete, he distributed talismans to the audience, which he said would protect them from evil and bring good luck.

In 1925, Paris was particularly well primed to receive this new visitor. France had endured much in the previous decade, from the mass slaughter of the First World War to the horrors of the Spanish flu, and the potential for total civilizational collapse was very real. The carnage of the past years had ripped a hole in society that felt irreparable. In 1919, the French writer Paul Valéry wrote an open letter that attempted to capture this spirit of hopelessness, "La Crise de l'Esprit": "An extraordinary tremor has run through the spinal marrow of Europe. It has felt, in all its thinking substance, that it recognized itself no longer, that it no longer resembled itself, that it was about to lose consciousness."[24] Intellectual movements in France from across the political spectrum, in the words of a later scholar, "reached the same tragic diagnosis: a failure of the old world, a major crisis in understanding and representation, and the absolute necessity of inventing new forms to give hope back to a society in ruins."[25]

This was a feeling that was shared throughout Europe. The same disenchantment with the modern age that had fueled the occult passions of Arturo Reghini in Italy and the editor of the *Dawn of Humanity* in Greece could be found in almost all Western nations. In Britain, one modern historian observed, "For the generation living after the end of the First World War the prospect of imminent crisis, a new

Dark Age, became a habitual way of looking at the world."[26] Germany more than anywhere in Europe was suffering in the aftermath of its defeat in the First World War, the country was demoralized, and the currency was rapidly losing its value—everywhere was infused by an atmosphere of decay and decadence.

Faced with these ubiquitous feelings of collapse, some retreated into conservatism, trying to reclaim the continent's lost greatness. Others gravitated toward extreme right-wing groups, which promised to rebuild their wounded egos. Still others found solace in universalist and utopian movements, which were emerging to champion values like socialism, world peace, and global cooperation as an antidote to the failures of the past.

The bitter fruits of Enlightenment logic were everywhere to see and those who were disenchanted with the present were ready to consider more outlandish worldviews. This was the cradle of Surrealism, a movement that called for rebellion against the constraints of reason. André Breton, in his 1924 *Surrealist Manifesto*, celebrated the mixed-up logic of a dream and sought to recreate it in his art and literature. Surrealism rejected moral and aesthetic dictates, it rejected the straitjacket of rationality, and above all, it rejected the physical world as it was. "This summer," Breton declared at the end of his manifesto, "the roses are blue, the wood is made of glass. . . . Existence is elsewhere."[27]

Others, similarly dissatisfied with the state of the world as it was, were drawn to the occult and its mysteries. Throughout the continent, as people discarded the past, they found refuge in the miraculous. Spiritualism, hypnotism, and other sundry forms of occult practice were booming. As early as 1920, one American journalist had observed this rising trend in Europe. "Magic is again in vogue. More books on necromancy are being published than on chemistry and have a vastly wider circulation. The worship of Satan reappears and the Black Mass is again celebrated. . . . Witchcraft is becoming popular and is appearing again in the courts. . . . Marvelous incidents which a few years ago would not have been accepted on any amount of evidence are now accepted on no evidence at all."[28] For the world-weary Europeans, there were good reasons to embrace the unexplainable. When life was so corrupt and empty, any kind of change seemed appealing, even if it did not always make logical sense. As one writer said in 1925 of the wonders of the occult sweeping the continent, "If [their] existence could be proven, it would mean turning the world upside down: we would have to change all of our ideas and start from scratch. Right. Is that so bad? . . . Should we not welcome a chance to start fresh again?"[29]

The "East," that ill-defined region that lay somewhere between Morocco and China and was home to abundant miracles and wonders, caught the imagination of many of these occult-minded seekers. In the mid-1920s, a Parisian writer and dancer, Valentine de Saint-Point, who had made her name in the prewar French literary scene as a taboo-smashing futurist, was so inspired by the messages of Theosophy and so convinced by the recently composed obituaries of Western civilization that she moved to Cairo to help launch a global Eastern Renaissance. Soon after arriving, she gave a lecture to a group of Egyptians, laying out her mission. She said that she knew from bitter experience how the West could never offer a suitable model for the future. Colonialism had spread the West's empty hypocrisy through the world and must be stopped. "It is necessary to repair the intellectual, moral, and material ruins that Western civilization has caused by its imperialist excesses," she said. "For it is not possible to found Universal Brotherhood on injustice."[30]

Valentine de Saint-Point believed that the only possible remedy for the violence and inhumanity of the Western system lay in reviving the spiritual wealth of the East. "The health of the world demands that the East again become known everywhere as the light of the world and that the intellectual darkness that has been spread through the world by the West is dispersed by the spirit shining from the East," she declared. As she kept speaking, she became increasingly enthused by her message and called upon her audience in the East to unite, to stand up for themselves and for the future of humanity: "A new dawn is close! It is the East where the spiritual sun is rising! To the task, my friends, my brothers! Lift up your hearts! The universal Powers which preside over the fate of the world are with you: heed their call!"[31]

In the 1920s, Parisians did not have to go all the way to Egypt to find the "East"; it came to them. Many strange travelers and sages appeared during this decade, offering to reveal the hidden secrets of Eastern lands. The enigmatic guru George Gurdjieff was one of the most prominent. He was a refugee from Soviet Russia, born to a Greek father and Armenian mother. When he arrived in Paris in the early 1920s, he was full of stories of travels in various Eastern lands from Tibet to Mount Athos and almost everywhere in between. He claimed to have learned occult secrets from the Sarmoung Brotherhood (a group whose location was unknown and whose existence has not been independently verified). He had come, he said, to spread their message of enlightenment.

In 1922, Gurdjieff bought a former priory in Avon, about fifty miles south of Paris, and set up his Institute for the Harmonious Development of Man, a commune that attracted a mix of faded Russian aristocracy and young bohemian artists. His most famous guest in these early Parisian years was the writer Katherine Mansfield, who was suffering from severe tuberculosis. Her letters back to her husband describe a slightly spartan atmosphere and a heavy emphasis on the improving power of manual labor. She was also struck by the noticeably "Eastern" flavor; the adepts were, at the time, being put to work building a Turkish bath for the old French monastery. Mansfield described the ambience in Gurdjieff's institute as "more like Bokhara than Avon" and she said that "in three weeks here I feel I have spent years in India, Arabia, Afghanistan, Persia."[32]

With Eastern wonders very much in style, Tahra Bey's arrival in the summer of 1925 was guaranteed to attract attention. As he stood onstage at the Salle Adyar in July to give his first public performance, he was surrounded by a mix of people fascinated by the new and unusual trends sweeping Europe: "Writers, journalists, doctors,

THE FEATS OF THE EGYPTIAN FAKIR.

Some Wonderful Performances by a Young Egyptian who has Set all Scientific Paris Agog

TAHRA BEY, THE FAKIR, "LIKE A BIBLE PROPHET IN A COLOURED PRINT," SURROUNDED BY A CROWD OF PARISIANS, EAGER TO TEST HIS WONDERFUL POWERS AT HIS RECENT PUBLIC DEMONSTRATION

Tahra Bey: an early appearance in Paris.

real savants as well as, it was said, a few pseudo-savants, Americans in smoking jackets, some curious onlookers and other maniacs for the occult."[33] The respected neurologist Jean-Athanase Sicard was in attendance alongside the eccentric doctor-philosopher Helan Jaworski, who was putting the finishing touches on a book that explored the possibilities of injecting the blood of the young into the veins of older patients to cure the effects of aging.[34] In addition to these men of science, there were literary figures too. The dandy and aesthete Léon Guillot de Saix was spotted among the crowd; and the poet, writer, and socialite Comtesse Anna de Noailles cut her way through the throngs in an attention-grabbing pink dress and a matching pink hat adorned with roses. She had read exciting reports about Tahra Bey in the Italian press and had vowed to see him in the flesh.

Everyone was asking the same questions. Where had this new visitor come from? How was he able to do these incredible things? The scientists who had come to see this demonstration were a mix of skeptics and sympathizers but none could offer any explanation of how these marvels were accomplished. Tahra Bey's ability to control his body with the power of his mind seemed to defy all notions of Western science. In this fakir, "the mysteries of the East" had come to life.

It is tempting to see symptoms of a troubled imperial psychology in the reactions to this exotic stranger. The year 1925 was a difficult one for France in the Arab world. They were fighting a war in Morocco against the charismatic rebel leader Abdel Krim, who was proving very difficult to defeat. The capable military and political leader had set up the independent Republic of the Rif, which constituted a genuine threat to both French and Spanish colonial possessions in North Africa. In April and May of 1925, Abdel Krim's troops achieved some surprising victories over French forces and the reaction in France was outrage. Le Temps newspaper called for a decisive response, arguing that "the question of prestige is of utmost importance. . . . The complete and utter failure of the Rifians will have a considerable salutary effect in the whole of North Africa." Another writer, in an article so blunt it reads like a parody, advocated for an imperialism based on the French tradition of Enlightenment reason. Drafting René Descartes onto his side, he constructed a long logical syllogism. The first premise was that Moroccans could not govern themselves and that the job could be accomplished only by peoples "more advanced in their technological and economic civilisation." He continued, stating that Morocco was rich in raw materials that France (and many other countries) needed and that the only rational conclusion was therefore for France, which had many other colonies in the area, to rule Morocco. "This logic is harsh, you say? Yes, very harsh. But it is logic and we can do nothing but obey it."[35]

Morocco was not France's only imperial interest in the region. After the First World War, it had also been given the League of Nations' mandate to rule Syria and had been facing resistance from Syrians, who had not consented to be ruled by France. A few months later, sporadic violence turned into a full-scale revolt, which was met by a violent French response, during which the city of Damascus was heavily shelled, prompting international outcry. When a man in

"Arab" robes and a headdress appeared in the Parisian press, it was most often in the role of dangerous enemy of France. But Tahra Bey, a mysterious man from the desert in long white robes and with a dark beard, had not come to take their empire; he had come to save their souls. For some, no doubt, he was a conscious or unconscious salve for their colonial anxieties.

However, ignorance, as much as anything, played its own significant role in the fakir's warm reception. Tahra Bey's public persona was vague (perhaps deliberately so) and his story mixed several disparate traditions—Muslim and Christian, Indian and Egyptian—under the capacious banner of the "East." Most Parisians, who were, in reality, hardly discerning about the world beyond the Mediterranean, did not seem able to place him. Was he a fakir like the one whom Claude Wade had seen in the Punjab? Was he from an Egyptian mystical sect? Was he a divinely inspired Armenian? One newspaper article succinctly captured this widespread confusion about his identity:

The Fakir Tahra Bey is Egyptian by birth, Hindu by culture, and Slavic by his charm. But he does not have the physique of either an Egyptian, a Hindu, or a Slav. What race could he be? . . . Let us just put it simply: he is an Oriental.[36]

Chapter 3

A FAKIR IN MONTMARTRE

AFTER TAHRA BEY'S FIRST PARISIAN SHOW, HIS INEXO-
rable rise to stardom continued through the summer of 1925. Everyone wanted a piece of him, and "not to have seen 'le fakir' and been
stirred by his spiritual emanations . . . was to argue oneself outside
the pale."[1] In August, he put on shows at the elegant Salle Wagrām
and the storied Théâtre des Champs-Élysées. After this, he traveled
to the exclusive seaside resorts of Deauville and Biarritz to give his
demonstrations. It was rumored that the queen of Spain had lured
him across the border to give her a private show—a rumor that he
was happy to indulge. In September, he returned to Paris, where he
took up a residency at the Théâtre des Champs-Élysées. He shared a
bill with more lighthearted acts, including the Champs-Élysées Girls,
the eccentric vaudeville clown "General" Lavine, who had inspired a
short prelude by Claude Debussy, and the novelty dancers Cornelius
and Constance.

Though surrounded by the trappings of the 1920s cabaret, Tahra
Bey maintained that his show was more than simple entertainment;
it was a serious demonstration of the wonders of the East. As his performance began, incense would fill the auditorium and an announcer
would declare, "We are no longer in the music hall."[2] Then the curtain
lifted to reveal Tahra Bey, dressed in his white robes and a white headdress, seated in meditation at the center of the stage. Around him lay
the gruesome tools of his trade. One reporter described the scene at
length: "To the right a coffin made of black wood lies on a huge heap

of sand. To the left, a sombre coloured table filled with long pins and even longer daggers. In the centre an instrument of torture consisting of two large scythes, which shine threateningly in the stage lights."[3]

His performances were known to provoke extreme reactions from the crowd, and nurses from the Red Cross waited in the aisles to tend to audience members who collapsed upon witnessing his onstage mutilations. Fainting spells like these were not uncommon; one journalist counted eight separate incidents during the course of a show— seven men and one woman. Still, Parisian audiences flocked to the Théâtre des Champs-Élysées for the blockbuster late-summer show. The whole city, in the words of New Yorker writer Janet Flanner, was "quivering in excitement" over him.[4] On September 22 the Nobel Prize–winning physicist Marie Curie was spotted among the crowd. Tahra Bey now regularly ended his shows by distributing talismans— small pieces of paper covered in Arabic writing that were said to possess mystical powers—which quickly became coveted collector's items and provoked a "wild scramble" among the audience at the end of his shows.[5] "All of Paris wants their own," said one journalist, who had witnessed audience members wrestle with each other to get their hands on one of these souvenirs.[6]

Tahra Bey's die-hard fans were known for their passion, which could sometimes veer into violence. In early 1926, there were ugly scenes at a courthouse where one disgruntled spectator was suing the fakir for the price of his entry ticket, claiming that Tahra Bey had failed to read his mind accurately and demanding his money back. Supporters of the fakir gathered on the street outside the trial to lend their support, and when his opponent came out of the court, they set upon him. A violent altercation quickly ensued as one man grabbed Tahra Bey's opponent and a woman walked up and attempted to hit him with her handbag. A large crowd of the fakir's supporters descended on the courthouse to confront supporters of the man who was suing him and the whole scene quickly developed into a mass brawl.[7]

Tahra Bey's name was rarely out of the newspapers. He took advantage of the frequent publicity, turning his gruesome but impressive stage show into something bigger that he hoped would be the basis for an entirely new spiritual movement in modern Europe. By September, he had acquired a local manager: Professeur M. H. Bardez, who described himself as an "independent professor of psychology."[8] Bardez was himself a writer on occult subjects under the pseudonym Francis de Mirclair and had long had an interest in the outer reaches of human experience. He had written books on Spiritualism and a scholarly article on his own experiments with the psychedelic peyote cactus. During Tahra Bey's run at the Champs-Élysées, Bardez appeared onstage as his interpreter, explaining the significance of the fakir's abilities to the excited crowd. The next year, Bardez helped Tahra Bey release a book, *Mes Secrets*, on the small imprint Editions Fulgor, whose only other author was Francis de Mirclair—some cynics even suggested that Bardez himself wrote Tahra Bey's text.[9]

Mes Secrets was a 160-page manifesto-biography in which Tahra Bey laid out his spiritual mission. He lamented that, for five years, he had been so busy doing "demonstrations before kings, princes, scientists, and crowds" that he had not explained his philosophy in depth. His fellow fakirs had always been afraid to engage with people outside their circles—"they fear your scepticism and I see now that they were not wrong."[10] But because of his medical and scientific education, as well as his ability to learn different languages, he saw it as his duty to be the ambassador of fakirism. Addressing his words to "those who search, those who suffer, those who toil," Tahra Bey compared himself to a Christian missionary, spreading the good word among heathens.[11] His demonstrations, like piercing his flesh with sharp objects and burying himself alive, might have seemed extreme but they were necessary to prove the existence of hidden forces buried in the soul that could control the physical body. Onstage, he declared, "I give my blood for the truth."[12] Withstanding pain like this was only the beginning. The skills he showed could be put to many other uses, including the control of physical desires. One could be trained to "adjust the movements and appetites of one's own body, as a horologist adjusts a clock."

Tahra Bey's book was a mix of mysticism and self-help for a disenchanted generation. It offered the chance to escape the Western world
with its rampant individual greed and its endless pursuit of unattain-
able desires. "Modern life, thunderous and chaotic, is an externalisa-
tion. The interior life of the spirit is dying a little bit more every day."[13]
Tahra Bey made no claims to being unique—modern fakirism, he
said, was a doctrine that anyone could embrace. However, it was an
extremely powerful weapon. Doctors and surgeons might be able to
save individual patients, but his message could save the whole human
race. The fakir was offering a remedy to the poor souls ground down
by Western modernity and promised to "excise the monstrous cancer
gnawing away at humanity."[14]

Amid these grand statements about pain and psychic development
the book offered relatively little detail. Tahra Bey gave few specific
instructions about how someone might embrace modern fakirism,
beyond saying that they had to submit their body to the power of
their soul. Nevertheless, he remained unequivocal about one thing. If
his readers did embrace the message, it would give them the answers
to all their problems: "What a relief it will be the day that this science
becomes universal! The golden age will not be far away; every man
will have happiness at his door."[15]

Tahra Bey had come to change the West, but the West soon began
to change him. Paris in the 1920s was a famously intoxicating city
and a magnet for ambitious people from across the world. There were
the artists: young Americans, Canadians, and Brits came in droves,
exploiting the exchange rate, to live as bohemians on the Left Bank
as part of the famous "lost generation." There were many others who
were not so fortunate: victims of displacement, migrant workers, and
political exiles rather than privileged young tourists on journeys of
self-discovery. Paris was the major refugee capital of Europe in the
1920s and 1930s. The most recognizable community were the White
Russians, who had left their homes after the revolution of 1917 and
subsequent civil war. There were members of the former Russian
nobility—the heirs to grand titles who had never worked a day in

their lives—forced to take on jobs, well below their accustomed status, as taxi drivers or washerwomen. Those who had managed to bring their family heirlooms with them survived by selling them for vastly deflated prices.

Alongside these Russian exiles, Paris hosted a significant Armenian diaspora—sixty-five thousand came in the years after the First World War and the genocide.[16] Tahra Bey was among this sixty-five thousand, as were his parents and siblings. His cousins, the Aznavours, also wound up in Paris's Armenian community, and Charles Aznavour himself was born in the French capital in 1924, though there is no evidence that the family ever saw Tahra Bey in Paris. Life was often difficult for these new immigrants, packed into cramped living spaces with few possessions. According to one French newspaper article from the 1920s, up to sixteen Armenian refugees would squeeze into one three-room apartment.[17] In his later memoirs, Charles Aznavour described the conditions of his first apartment in the Latin Quarter, a place well known at the time for its insalubrious lodgings. Their family of five lived together in one twenty-square-meter room, with a sink in one corner and a small stove that served for both the cooking and the heating. At night Charles Aznavour's parents would pull a curtain across the alcove that contained their bed to give them some privacy, his grandmother was on a broken sofa, and he slept on a fold-out iron bed alongside his sister. When they needed water, they brought it in from a tap in the staircase, and when they needed the toilet they went to the communal bathroom on the floor above. "What luxury and comfort!" Aznavour joked.[18] Armenians like Tahra Bey and the Aznavour family were the subject of considerable confusion, sometimes hostility, from local Parisians, unsure of how to categorize this new group of refugees. They were not quite like the Russians, though there were some similarities. They were not like the Moroccans or Algerians, though there were some similarities there too. Members of the extreme right, steeped in the anti-Semitism of the early twentieth century, had an answer of their own. Armenians, they claimed, were "the Jews of the East"—a deracinated minority who lived across the

Ottoman Empire, often thriving as a kind of merchant class—"just as rapacious, vulturous, and vampiric as the true Israelites," in the words of one.[19] The connection between Armenians and Jews was a common one in the fevered minds of European race scientists in the early twentieth century. The Armenians were among the closest relatives of the Jews, it was claimed; some people even argued that both Jews and Armenians got their distinctive characteristics from something that was dubbed "the Armenoid race."[20]

The Armenians, driven from their old homes in the Eastern Mediterranean, found themselves the subject of renewed suspicion in their new country. By the 1940s, the xenophobic furore had dissipated, and Armenians avoided the genocidal racism that Europe inflicted upon the Jews—the Nazis eventually concluded that the Armenians were an Aryan race. But any Armenian living in Paris in the 1920s would have been aware of the level of prejudice that existed against them. They were seen as insular, dishonest, and selfish. When George Orwell was working menial jobs in Montparnasse at around the same time that Tahra Bey came to the city, studying for his book *Down and Out in Paris and London*, he had part of his paycheck stolen by an Armenian man. The incident brought to his mind a popular proverb of the era: "Trust a snake before a Jew and a Jew before a Greek, but don't trust an Armenian."[21]

Tahra Bey's Armenian identity was a complicated part of his life in France. Publicly, he did not advertise that he was Armenian, preferring to hide behind the guise of the "Egyptian Fakir." In his book, *Mes Secrets*, he makes only one oblique reference to his true identity: "I belong to that race which has suffered so much over the course of the centuries and which is now scattered through the Balkans, Greece, Romania, Serbia, and Turkey."[22] But, in practice, he maintained significant ties to the Armenian community. He supported his family—his parents, siblings, and uncle—through much of the 1920s and maintained both ties to Armenian organizations and friendships with Armenians in Paris.

At the height of his career the fakir demanded substantial appearance fees and performances earned him enough money to avoid the difficult life of a new immigrant, sharing a tiny, cramped apartment with several others and the penury of the Left Bank. Sixteen shows at the Champs-Élysées earned Tahra Bey 160,000 francs, and at Deauville, he made 75,000 francs from just three nights of work (for comparison, an average working-class annual salary at the time was around 6,000 francs, and the average monthly rent was 360 francs).[23]

With this money, Tahra Bey could afford to live in some style. He soon became a devotee of the city's famous fleshpots. "He has rapidly acquired most of the habits of the music hall artiste," wrote the Paris correspondent for *The Observer*, "and is not above joining a supper party after the show and taking his champagne like a gentleman."[24] His admirers came from the highest echelons of the aristocracy. *The New Yorker*'s letter from Paris reported that "his dressing room was filled with flowers sent with little warm notes from Princesses, Countesses, and others not less elevated; and he has been entertained in royal ways that would leave the finite American mind utterly flabbergasted."[25] He was renowned for spending long nights in cabarets and music halls, befriending some of the era's most recognizable stars. He was once spotted with the actress Georgette Leblanc, and another night with Mistinguett, the artiste who famously insured her legs for half a million francs, then again with Cécile Sorel, known at the time as "France's greatest living actress."[26] Tahra Bey did not escape the lure of the casinos either. The English theatrical impresario and writer Albert de Courville recalled spotting the fakir one day in Deauville pouring franc after franc into low-stakes games, "his face white with excitement, his eyes gleaming, and his losses mounting up and up."[27]

The fakir reached the pinnacle of his 1920s glamour in September 1925, when he played a part in launching the career of the twentieth-century Parisian icon Josephine Baker. The *Revue Nègre*, which claimed to bring the glamour of the Harlem revue to Paris, was set to start at the Théâtre des Champs-Élysées immediately after Tahra Bey had ended his run. The Champs-Élysées Theatre would go from one form of exoticism to another as "the Divine Josephine" danced, almost nude, in front of a crowd of baying Parisians. On September 26, the Saturday before the *Revue Nègre*'s official opening night, the troupe of Black musicians and dancers gave an early performance to a select crowd, late at night after the curtain had gone down on Tahra Bey's show. Some illustrious names were present: the music hall stars Mistinguett and Cécile Sorel, and the influential art dealer Paul Guillaume, who helped popularize African Art among the Parisian modernists. Tahra Bey led the proceedings at the afterparty; "minus his flowing robes and turban, he had donned smart Western attire to act as master of ceremonies. . . . And it was well into the new week before the Egyptian fakir released his cataleptic control over the merry company and permitted them to find their ways home."[28]

On the night of February 11, 1926, as Tahra Bey was on a tour of Paris cabarets, accompanied by two women, an ordinary night on the town descended into violence, the precise details of which would later be fought over in court. There had been nothing unusual about their evening, but as the revels dragged on into the early hours of the morning, Tahra Bey and his companions ended up in the Canari, a small cabaret in the heart of Montmartre's theaterland, where events took a strange turn. The Canari's proprietor, Georges Varounis, was one of the many unusual characters that populated the Parisian nightlife scene. A Greek, born in Sparta in the 1880s, he had spent the first decades of the twentieth century traveling between Europe and North America, going from one money-making scheme to the next. Different sources claim that he was at various points a lawyer, a journalist, a newspaper salesman, and a graduate of the universities of Athens and Berlin.[29] He occasionally dabbled in inventing—in 1913, a patent for a collapsible steamer was registered in France under the name Georges Varounis—and in the lucrative American import-export business. In 1919, he had made some unsuccessful attempts to convince several American companies to finance the construction of an international shipbuilding yard on the Mediterranean island of Crete.[30]

In the early 1920s, Varounis had given up his international business ventures and settled in Paris, where he noticed a significant gap in the nightlife market. The city was now full of White Russian refugees who had nowhere to go at night. Always keen to pursue a new opportunity, Varounis opened a string of Russian-themed cabarets in the city, most famous of which was the legendary Caveau Caucasien on the rue Pigalle. By the mid-twenties, this nightclub, which served shashlik kebabs with vodka to the accompaniment of loud Russian folk songs, was a well-known meeting spot for the White Russian elite. Varounis knew how to advertise. He played heavily on the myths of destitute Russian aristocracy, banking on the fact that tourists would come to see these new curiosities. At one point, he claimed to have five titled Russian princes among his performers, including a sword juggler, a folk dancer, and the conductor of his orchestra.[31]

On that February night in 1926, Varounis was sitting in the Caveau Caucasien when someone informed him that Tahra Bey, the man who was the talk of Paris, had been spotted in the Canari. Never one to miss a chance to promote his businesses, the Greek nightclub baron went to seek out the fakir, made his way toward his table, and invited Tahra Bey for dinner and drinks at one of his venues, the Gabriella on rue Gabrielle. Varounis had recently opened this club, aiming to create a more intimate and exclusive alternative to its more ostentatious cousin, the Caveau Caucasien. He must have hoped that the famous fakir's presence at his cabaret would get people talking about this new addition to the Montmartre scene. Tahra Bey, for his part, graciously accepted the offer of free food and drink.

Over a mile separated the Canari from the Gabriella, but when the group finally arrived at their destination, Varounis made sure it was worth their while. They were treated to Russian-Caucasian delicacies from the kitchen and a bottle of Monopole champagne as the band played songs of the Caucasian steppes. By all accounts, the night was going well. Tahra Bey, who had learned some Greek in the early 1920s, talked to Varounis about the old country. According to one report, he was also sporting enough to give a few demonstrations of fakirism to the other guests in the cabaret.[32] After a while, his mission accomplished, Varounis left his guests to enjoy his hospitality and retired for the night.

It was about seven or eight in the morning when the group finally got up to leave. Unexpectedly, the waiters came over brandishing a very large bill, totaling almost 500 francs. Tahra Bey protested that he could not possibly owe any money; they had come as invited guests of the owner. Since Varounis had departed long before, the waiters, who had no way to confirm this story, insisted that he pay the full amount. Tahra Bey, who had been drinking for some time at this point, did not back down. The argument quickly turned heated; "the fakir, svelte but strong, grabbed some chairs and threw them across the room. Several glasses were broken," alleged one account.[33] The fight ended, as the sun was coming up over Paris, with Tahra Bey sprawled out on the floor of the nightclub with a black eye, laid low by a blow across the head from an ivory-topped cane.

The police were called and an investigation followed. The precise details of what had transpired would be vigorously disputed in front of a judge. Tahra Bey hired the flamboyant young lawyer René Idzkowski, whose client list read like a checklist of Paris's cosmopolitan underworld: Algerian hitmen, drug-dealing nightclub singers, a female Estonian international thief, and a con man known as the "pseudo-baron" Richard Reith. The thirty-year-old Idzkowski, not afraid of the rough-and-tumble of the courtroom, came out swinging. He told the judge that Tahra Bey had been forced to cancel his performance the following evening, and argued on this basis that he ought to be compensated for the fee, 50,000 francs. He also demanded a further 200,000 francs for the fakir's injuries. Varounis, for his part, asked for the more modest sum of 10,000 francs to cover damage done to his cabaret.

The proceedings themselves quickly took on the quality of a performance—or a farce. The newspapers had fun trying to ascertain the precise details of Tahra Bey's nocturnal carousing—how much did he spend? Who was with him? And so on. One paper dubbed the case "the after effects of a light supper or the misfortunes of the unlucky fakir."[34] The press were particularly amused to see that the fakir, who claimed that he was insensible to pain, was suing for the injuries he had received. Varounis's lawyers also pointed out this irony, contending that since fakirs did not feel pain, a bang on the head shouldn't amount to 200,000 francs' worth of damages. Naturally, Tahra Bey did not think much of this line of argument. He explained to the court that fakirs were insensible to pain only once they had entered a cataleptic state; otherwise, they were just like ordinary people. He even called his manager, the "independent professor of psychology" M. H. Bardez, as an expert witness to back up his claim.

After several months of back-and-forth, the police tribunal eventually returned its verdict on July 1. Neither party's demand for money was accepted. Tahra Bey and the head waiter at the Gabriella each received fines of five francs for the violence. Tahra Bey, on top of this, came out looking a little silly. The man who had come to Paris proclaiming to be the prophet of a new psychic revolution that would free the world from pain and misery was now exposed as a late-night cabaret crawler and a violent brawler. "Fakir though he might be," a writer for *Le Figaro* concluded, "in Montmartre he is just a man, a man who can suffer, and drink champagne, smash plates, break his cane, and exchange blows. In other words, a very ordinary man."[35]

Georges Varounis came away with some hard-won publicity, as the name of the Gabriella cabaret had been in all of Paris's newspapers. He continued his successful nightlife ventures for the rest of the 1920s. In 1926 he opened a venue called Harem, which ran on an "Oriental" theme. After the success of Josephine Baker's *Revue Nègre*, Varounis changed its name to Harlem and turned it into an American jazz club. But after the financial crash of 1929 and the subsequent global depression, the bottom fell out of the Parisian cabaret scene, and Varounis moved on to other things. In early 1930s Los Angeles, as Prohibition was coming to an end, he reinvented himself as a wine dealer, playing on his experience running various French cabarets and the knowledge of French vintages that came with it. Still, he never recaptured the glory of his days as a king of Paris's cabarets.

Chapter 4

RAHMAN BEY (ALMOST) CONQUERS AMERICA

THE STORY OF TAHRA BEY MIGHT HAVE ENDED THERE—A tale of an extraordinary Armenian refugee who beguiled Paris in the 1920s, reaching heights of fame and glory that he could never have imagined. He might simply have faded away, as many other celebrities did, to become a curious footnote in the history of interwar Europe. But fate had something else in store for the fakir; his influence was destined to spread across the world, shaping the 1920s and 1930s in unforeseen ways.

From his earliest performances in Athens, Tahra Bey had spawned imitators. The first articles about him had appeared in the spring of 1923. By the end of the year, Greece was filled with fakirs. In October, Doctor Kara Iki, a man from the Greek port town of Volos, demonstrated mystical powers to rival Tahra Bey's. In the same year, another challenger, Taarhan Effendi, emerged.[1] As late as 1925, when the original Tahra Bey was in Paris, the Greek right-wing politician and later anti-communist strongman, Ioannis Metaxas, saw a hypnotist on the island of Kefalonia who was also claiming to be Tahra Bey.[2]

Likewise in Italy, almost as soon as Tahra Bey started performing his fakir act, people were imitating it. In May of 1925, a "false fakir" by the name of Agostino Sioli was arrested by the police in Milan when trying to put on an imitation of Tahra Bey's show.[3] Adolfo Manetti, a man from a small village outside Florence, took the act in a different direction, starting a career in 1925 as an "authentic national fakir." He did not dress in robes, had no exotic backstory, and made no claims to the secrets of the East. He was just a simple Italian man fascinated by the teachings of the fakirs. He proved that, with enough will and determination, people of any background could be part of this new craze. Manetti's crowning achievement came in the autumn of 1925 when he had himself sealed in a coffin, loaded onto a train from Alessandria to Milan, and taken to the Palazzo dello Sport for his resurrection. Crowds gathered to send him off from Alessandria station and another large crowd gathered to greet him one hundred kilometers away in Milan. The casket was then rushed to the Palazzo dello Sport, where people nervously watched as the lid was removed to reveal Manetti in a cataleptic state, rigid and apparently lifeless. After a short but agonizing wait, Manetti sprang to life, opening his eyes wide and taking a sip of cognac, much to the relief of the audience.[4]

After the summer of 1925, France entered its own "fakir period," during which, in the words of a contemporary writer, "the fakirs came to Paris in their swarms."[5] However, after Tahra Bey's exploits had appeared in the world's newspapers, thanks to his Parisian fame, fakirs started to appear in cities where he had never even set foot. In the second half of the 1920s, fakir fever spread through Europe and farther afield. You could have seen the fakir Witry in Algeria, the fakir Ben Kuro in Krakow, the fakir Thawara Rey in Budapest, Blacaman in Berlin, or the unusual female fakir Laila Hanoum in Vienna. In Stuttgart, the fakir To Kha was allegedly buried alive for 120 hours. In Warsaw, one Moyshe Shtern stuck pins through his body under the borrowed name Takhra Bey.[6]

In April 1926, the city of London got its first taste of this global craze. A previously unknown fakir calling himself Rahman Bey announced that he would put on a private demonstration of fakirism on April 27 at the Savoy Hotel. Rahman Bey claimed to have been born in Eritrea and to belong to an Egyptian psychic union called Chams ("sun" in Arabic)—a rival to Tahra Bey's own union, Chavk. Rahman's performance was, in most elements, almost identical to Tahra Bey's—Rahman Bey "pushed hatpins through his cheeks until they protruded from his mouth," lay on a bed of nails, hypnotized rabbits, and read the contents of sealed envelopes.[7]

Before this, Tahra Bey seems to have been happy enough to let the other European fakirs perform without a challenge, but Rahman Bey's attempts to take England provoked a response. In public he was dismissive of this new rival to his crown: "I have never heard of him. I can only suppose that he attempts a poor imitation of my own achievements."[8] In private, he was nervous and decided that he should make a trip across the channel to assert his dominance. On April 28, the day after Rahman Bey's performance, Tahra Bey took to the stage of London's Scala Theatre, offering free tickets and an open bar. Perhaps thanks to the latter promise, the original pioneer of fakir performances drew a bigger crowd than his challenger, and he also attracted some important establishment figures. Mingling among the audience was the internationally known travel writer and adventurer Lady Dorothy Mills, and the novelist and yoga enthusiast Francis Yeats-Brown. Tahra stood on the stage and, surrounded by a large group of doctors, including one of the founders of the London School of Tropical Medicine, Sir William Simpson, and the renowned neurologist Sir James Purves-Stewart, he ran through his well-rehearsed act. Alongside his usual demonstrations, including his showstopping burial alive, Tahra Bey also included several examples of his mind-reading and clairvoyance skills. His most impressive feat was to pick the horse that would win June's Epsom Derby, Coronach, a prediction that turned out to be correct.

The fakir show had proved a reliable hit in France, but London in the 1920s was more conservative. The arbiters of public taste were not impressed by these gruesome and unusual acts. After Rahman Bey had given his private performance at the Savoy Hotel, the "Londoner's Diary" in the *Evening Standard* published a disparaging report:

Repellent feats by fakirs became enormously popular in Paris a few months ago. A fakir, one Rahman Bey, an

Egyptian, gave an exhibition in London last night, and it is to be hoped that this is not the beginning of a similar craze for the horrible in this country. Fortunately shows which capture the fancy of the French often meet with a luke-warm reception here. Negro revues are the rage of Paris still, but in London they failed utterly and immediately.[9]

The two consecutive nights of fakir demonstrations in England were called "morbid," "revolting," and "disgusting" by people who had seen them.[10] Members of the audience fainted after viewing the stomach-turning feats of physical endurance. There was little time to hear the larger philosophical messages of fakirism, but they were unlikely to have been received well anyway, especially in the atmosphere of casual racism of England in the 1920s. One journalist who attended Tahra Bey's night at the Scala Theatre said that he could not understand why "religious societies should send a couple of negroes to Europe to stick hatpins through their cheeks."[11]

The day after Tahra Bey's first performance, complaints had already reached the Home Office. The graphic displays were thought to be too much for the London audience. The Royal Society for the Prevention of Cruelty to Animals, for its part, added its own animal welfare objections to the live rabbit-hypnosis. The day after Tahra Bey's private performance, the lord chamberlain's office, which had the power to censor any theatrical performances in England, banned all public shows by "Egyptian Fakirs" in London.[12] For many, this was a relief. Potentially vulnerable audiences would not be subjected to the grisly displays that had held Paris rapt. London was spared the excesses of the fakir craze. Neither fakir saw any reason to hang around—the British were beyond hope, deaf to their messages. Tahra Bey returned to France. Rahman Bey, on the other hand, decided to travel to America, where, as his manager told the press, "you can cut your head off on stage . . . and nobody minds."[13]

With that, Rahman Bey boarded the SS *Leviathan*, bound for New York City. The ship was "without question the most luxurious" vessel on the Atlantic, complete with Turkish baths, an onboard library, and its own Ritz-Carlton restaurant.[14] Rahman Bey was traveling first-class. His fellow passengers included the managing director of a large American department store, a wealthy Canadian diamond merchant, and a Soviet filmmaker. But as the vessel pulled into the Forty-Second Street docks in New York on May 17, Rahman Bey was the most striking figure on board, dressed from head to toe in his white robes and a white headdress, the uniform of the fakir.

New York, unlike London, was ready to receive him. America may not have experienced the catastrophic decade that Europe did in the 1910s, but there were still many who were seeking a remedy to the rising tide of materialism sweeping the globe. Even the president, Calvin Coolidge, was worried. In his Independence Day address in 1925 he warned Americans that they "must not sink into a pagan materialism," advising them, "we must cultivate the reverence which they had for the things that are holy."[15] Americans looked around them and saw that postwar culture had become obsessed with money and material gain and had forgotten the spiritual foundations that had thrived in previous centuries.

New York City, home to the financial center of Wall Steet and a growing number of towering skyscrapers, built high into the clouds, was the beating heart of American materialism. However, it was also home to many people who rebelled against this conception of progress. In their quest to remedy this empty acquisitiveness, many New Yorkers, like Europeans, opened themselves up to the so-called spiritual wisdom of the East. In 1923, Hari G. Govil, a recent immigrant to New York from India, intent on showing New Yorkers the cultural glories of the East, decided to set up something he called the Orient Society, which quickly started publishing the *Orient* magazine, which became *New Orient* the following year. This journal, which featured work by some of the era's best writers and essayists, was aimed at a generation that was turning its attention to the lands out East—or, as Govil called them, "dissatisfied sons of the West, who find ourselves cramped in the old house, and who . . . confess its insufficiencies and its narrow pride."[16] In the same year, the Lebanese-American writer Kahlil Gibran published what is now his most famous work, *The Prophet*: a long collection of aphorisms, meditations, and observations about the nature of existence, dripping with the spirituality of the "East." Other Eastern religions, like Baha'ism, which started in nineteenth-century Persia and preached a message of radical equality, were starting to attract adherents across class and race lines in the city. The vogue for the East had not bypassed New York.

In America, just as in Europe, this vague curiosity about the East often led people into the outer reaches of the occult. People flocked to mediums, spiritual guides, and anyone who claimed access to secret knowledge. "In every American city of any size there lies a Hidden Empire. It is ruled over by sovereign 'high hokum peddlers,'" said one article in the *Christian Herald*. The author decried the overwhelming presence of "prestidigitateurs, charlatans, fakers, jugglers, mountebanks and thieves," as well as the "fortune tellers, mediums, seers, crystal gazers, and others of the same ilk."[17] Another observer in the 1920s said that "it should be obvious to any man who is not one himself that the land is overrun with messiahs. . . . I refer not to those political quacks who promise in one election to rid the land of evil," he continued, "but rather to those inspired fakirs who promise to reduce the diaphragm or orient the soul through the machinery of occult religion."[18] New York in particular, according to one Baptist minister, had "the most variegated menagerie of cults anywhere to be found." Quoting a friend who was a little blunter, he said that the city was full of "fads, freaks, fakes, supported by women of a certain age suffering from suppressed religion."[19]

When Rahman Bey arrived, he spoke the language of these new gurus, claiming to be "a living weapon sent to fight the supreme curse of our alleged civilization—the curse of materialism."[20] He hoped, it was reported, to make converts to a new creed that he called fakirism.[21] Rahman Bey was also a performer. At the end of May 1926, he took to the stage at the Selwyn Theatre on Forty-Second Street, steps away from Times Square. Arch Selwyn, the theater's owner, had sponsored

A. H. WOODS and ARCH SELWYN Announce
THE FIRST APPEARANCE IN AMERICA OF
THE ORIENTAL FAKIR

RAHMAN BEY
The Wonder of Europe in An Amazing Demonstration of
The Miracles of Fakirism
SELWYN THEATRE, West 42nd St.
BEGINNING TUESDAY EVENING, MAY 25
Matinees Wednesday and Saturday   PRICE 50c to $2.50

Playbill for Rahman Bey's first New York performances.

Rahman Bey's performances in London and now he was opening up his New York venue for the fakir show. As the audience took their places, atmospheric music filled the almost one-thousand-seater auditorium. Slowly, the curtain rose to reveal a dimly lit stage and Rahman Bey sitting on the floor in his flowing robes. In this city that wanted to see the mysteries of the East, he gave the spectators the show that had been unceremoniously banned in England—rabbit hypnotism, cheek piercing, burial alive, and all.

The critics' responses were suitably incredulous. The *Brooklyn Eagle* called it "weird and uncanny," while another newspaper said his "astonishing feats . . . completely mystified an audience that filled that Manhattan playhouse."[22] *The Billboard* magazine said that his performance "would defy the most astute to establish evidence of trickery or the use of the magician's subterfuges and artifices."[23] The show was strange, but it was also popular. The theater critic Burns Mantle called Rahman Bey's show "the most dramatic of the current events" and its first week grossed a respectable $8,000.[24]

Rahman Bey cut an unusual figure on the Broadway of the 1920s as he walked onstage dressed in exaggerated "Oriental" garb, with a thick beard and piercing dark eyes. He was accompanied by his manager, Victor Bartelloni, who claimed to be the secretary of something he called the Psychic Association of Alexandria.[25] Since Rahman Bey spoke no English, he answered all questions through an interpreter. However, his nationality, his history, and his reasons for being in America remained something of a mystery, mired in conflicted information. Sometimes he was billed as an Indian, sometimes as Egyptian, and sometimes simply as an "Oriental Fakir." The *New York Sunday News* explained that he was "a scientist, an adept, a representative of the oldest sect of mystery worshipers in the world."[26] Other publications claimed that he was from Eritrea, born to an Italian father and an Arab mother.[27]

But Rahman Bey was not from Egypt, India, or Eritrea. He was a young Italian called Antinesco Gemmi, who had lived in Florence before adopting this new Eastern persona. There is no evidence he had ever been east of Naples, let alone to Egypt. Like most fakirs, Rahman Bey was a character and details of his life before taking the stage remained a mystery. At some point in 1925 he was probably discovered by Victor Bartelloni and given his stage persona to mimic Tahra Bey. Soon after, he managed to attract the attention of the important American impresario Arch Selwyn, who owned several theaters in the United States, and was taken across the Atlantic for his Broadway debut. In the mid-1920s, the ambiguity about his identity did not seem to matter; the secrets of the East sold well, and few people had enough knowledge to prove that he was lying.

The most important thing that Rahman Bey did in the early days of his American sojourn was enlist the help of the local psychic celebrity Dr. Hereward Carrington, to act as his interpreter and inform the audience about the doctrine of fakirism. In the 1920s, Carrington was well known as a prolific scholar of strange and supernatural occurrences. He was also a minor eccentric—a vegetarian, in a time when it was uncommon, and a teetotaller who held "exotic" parties where "white-clad turbaned servants offered Oriental delicacies."[28] Carrington had been born on the island of Jersey off the coast of England in the late nineteenth century, but moved to America in 1899. In his early years in New York, he worked in a variety of jobs to make ends meet: bookstore clerk, editor of dime novels, and small-time magician.[29] Before long, he found his way into the world of psychic investigation, studying the paranormal and the supernatural under the tutelage of Professor James Hyslop, a leading light in the Society for Psychical Research. Carrington's work first made headlines in 1907 when he made an unusual public proposal to weigh the bodies of murderers before and after their execution to establish the precise weight of a human soul. For the next years he worked as a ghost hunter, applying scientific methods to allegedly psychic phenomena across North America. Although he did expose several fraudulent mediums, Carrington remained a believer in the existence of a spirit world and the truth of many paranormal phenomena. In 1909 he was so convinced by the genuine mediumship of superstar Italian Spiritualist Eusapia Palladino that he arranged her American tour.

Through the 1910s and 1920s, Carrington dedicated himself to the study of Spiritualists, mediums, conjurors, mystics, and occultists. He published work at an astounding rate, often releasing several books and articles in one year, on magic, Spiritualism, and the psychic sciences. Some of his more popular titles included *Your Psychic Powers and How to Develop Them*, *Death: Its Causes and Phenomena*, and the more lighthearted *Magic Is Fun: Magic for Everyone*. He also worked as a scriptwriter for the Hollywood serial inspired by occult activity, *The Mysteries of Myra*. Struck by Carrington's ubiquitous presence and prodigious output, one reviewer joked that he seemed "to have taken over all syndicate rights on the 'other world.' . . . He must work three shifts in the spiritist factory, catching cat-naps in some divinely intercalated hour."[30]

As part of his study of occult phenomena, Carrington had been interested in fakirs for some time. In 1909 he published the book *Hindu Magic*, which investigated, among other things, the apparent miracles of Indian fakirs. In it he mentioned the phenomenon of "voluntary internment" (burial alive), saying that he found it theoretically impressive but needed a "considerable amount of first-hand evidence" before he could pass judgment.[31] Seventeen years after these words were published, Rahman Bey appeared to give him that firsthand evidence. For Rahman Bey, Carrington gave publicity and a veneer of scientific research, but Carrington also came with some very powerful opponents, not least the world-famous magician Harry Houdini.

Since at least the early 1900s, Houdini had committed himself to the methodical study of supernatural phenomena, exposing the occult to skeptical, rational investigation. His particular focus was on the Spiritualist mediums who claimed to communicate with the spirits of the dead. He believed that they were exploiting vulnerable, grieving people for their own personal gain. Houdini had some experience in this field. In the late nineteenth century he had started his career putting on fake Spiritualist séances for entertainment. In 1924, he had published *A Magician among the Spirits*, the detailed history of his crusade against Spiritualism. At the time of writing, he said, he had not found a single case of communication with the dead that he believed to be genuine or indeed anything more than "the result of deluded brains."[32]

By the mid-1920s, Houdini was totally consumed by his battle against charlatanry. His motivations were complex. He justified his crusade on humanitarian grounds. He was a seeker after the truth, attempting to demystify the fraudulent "miracles" that were used by the unscrupulous to mislead the credulous. The strange knockings and spirit communications that Houdini had observed in countless séances were all untrue—simple magic tricks, as he knew all too well—and this was enough for him to want to expose them. However, according to some critics, there was a more egotistical reason for Houdini's campaign against Spiritualists. Arthur Conan Doyle, an ardent believer in the world of the spirits and a longtime friend, concluded after Houdini's death that his vanity, combined with his desire for publicity, was a large motivating factor in "his furious campaign against Spiritualism." He was hoping to ride the coattails of Spiritualism's popularity to boost his own fame, Doyle believed. Houdini was, at heart, a performer and he craved an audience.[33]

A few years before Rahman Bey arrived in New York, Houdini entered into an acrimonious feud with Carrington, centered around the claims of a Spiritualist medium from Boston called Margery Crandon. The whole affair began in 1923, when the magazine *Scientific American* decided to offer a prize of $2,500 to any medium who was conclusively proved to be genuinely communicating with the dead. The magazine assembled a panel of five scholars, including both Carrington and Houdini, as well as other scientists and psychic investigators, to oversee the prize. Carrington, the well-established paranormal expert, was an obvious choice. Houdini was selected because of his knowledge of magic tricks as well as his reputation as a skeptic of Spiritualist phenomena who was believed to be reasonably fair-minded.

Over a long series of visits and tests, Carrington and Houdini found themselves coming to opposite conclusions: Carrington was convinced that Crandon was genuine and Houdini thought that she was simply "a very cheap fraud."[34] The scientific disagreement quickly became personal. Carrington called Houdini a "pure publicist," who wanted to be on the committee only for his own personal fame and whose implacable anti-Spiritualist agenda meant he could never be a fair judge.[35] Houdini hinted that Carrington was part of a scam to help Crandon fraudulently win the prize money and unsuccessfully tried to get him kicked off the jury.[36] Rumors even circulated, some perhaps spread by Houdini himself, that Carrington was having an affair with Margery or that he was heavily financially indebted to the Crandon family. Eventually, Houdini's argument won; Crandon was not awarded any money by *Scientific American*.[37]

Even after the verdict was given, the enmity between the two men continued to boil. In 1926, Houdini appeared before the House of Representatives to demand harsher legal punishments for fake Spiritualists. He took the opportunity to air his opinions about Hereward Carrington, even attacking his academic integrity by claiming that he had purchased a mail-order PhD from a scam artist. (Carrington proudly and assiduously referred to himself as Dr. Hereward Carrington.) Carrington, by this point, although he maintained his objectivity, often seemed to be acting as a propagandist for Spiritualism. Houdini tried to undermine his famously prolific research output and said that his books were of questionable worth. "Carrington is a hacker," he declared. When asked to explain this clearly derogatory term, which many present had not heard before, Houdini told Congress that it was a British phrase: "A hacker takes other people's books and writes a book with a pair of scissors."[38]

Before the arrival of Rahman Bey in New York, Houdini had taken little interest in the miracles of fakirs. However, when Hereward Carrington's name appeared on the bill, Houdini must have seen another opportunity to triumph. He attended a performance on May 30, sending his magician friend Joseph Rinn onto the stage to observe the act. Rinn was unimpressed; Rahman Bey did not seem to be doing anything he hadn't seen in a magic act before. While he was up on the stage, Rinn took the chance to whisper his disapproval to Carrington: "This is the rawest deal you've ever put over."[39] After leaving the theater, Houdini began to hatch a plan that would both disgrace the fakir and land a blow on his old rival Carrington.

At first, Rahman Bey, unaware of the moves being made against him, continued his attempts to crack America. At the beginning of July 1926, his management planned an attention-grabbing stunt that would keep him in the headlines. The fakir would be sealed inside a metal coffin and thrown into the Hudson River in front of a crowd of onlookers. News of this potentially death-defying feat quickly spread; this was no stage show in the easily controllable surroundings of a Broadway theater. Just after midday on July 7, a group of curious spectators—"half of New York City," according to one newspaper—made their way to the docks at the bottom of Seventy-Ninth Street to witness Rahman Bey's biggest performance.[40] The crowd boarded a small tugboat and set out onto the choppy waters of the Hudson, to an anchor point near the New Jersey coast.

Rahman Bey on a boat on the Hudson River,
preparing to enter his coffin.

On the boat, which was weighed down with the excited audience, Rahman Bey ate a light vegetarian meal and, at around three o'clock, entered into the cataleptic state that would allow him to survive underwater without breathing. The atmosphere was tense, with the people gazing on in worry as he was placed in the coffin, which was then soldered shut and lifted into the air with a crane. The casket was swung round and slowly lowered into the water. If this exploit had gone according to plan, Rahman Bey might have been catapulted into fame and his name might still live on in the annals of New York history, but a technical malfunction turned potential glory into unfortunate embarrassment.

Rahman Bey's team had installed several safety features into the equipment before the demonstration, among these an emergency bell that the fakir could ring if he encountered any problems while underwater. Almost as soon as the coffin containing Rahman Bey had gone below the surface, the bell started ringing. This was not supposed to happen. People started to realize that something had gone wrong and a commotion was quickly raised. Some scrambled across the deck to help guide the casket back on board. As the crane swung the fakir out of the river and they guided it back down onto the boat, Rahman Bey's manager, Bartelloni, stood by in a panic, shouting "Allez, allez" as several men grabbed hammers, chisels, and shears to unseal the coffin. As the metal was torn away, Rahman Bey's calm face was revealed beneath it, very much alive and blissfully unaware of all the panic. He insisted that he had never left his trance state and told the crowd that the bell must have gone off by mistake. Still, it was hard to think that this had been anything but a failure. He had been in the coffin for a total of only twenty minutes when his grand publicity stunt came to an anticlimactic end.[41]

About a month later, Harry Houdini's preparations were done and he announced that he was ready to publicly replicate Rahman Bey's most difficult stunt—the burial alive. For Houdini this was a matter of professional integrity. If Rahman Bey had admitted that he was doing a trick, Houdini would have left him alone, but he was claiming to have some kind of miraculous powers that others did not. Houdini could not let him deceive anyone into believing there was *real* magic at work.

Houdini had acquired his own bronze coffin for the challenge, which he brought to the swimming pool at the upmarket Shelton Hotel on Lexington Avenue. There, surrounded by newspapermen, he endeavored to prove that you did not need to enter a "cataleptic state" or know the secrets of the fakirs to accomplish this feat. Houdini took some steady breaths, then lay down in the casket, where he was sealed in and lowered into the swimming pool. With a group of sturdy men standing on top of the coffin to ensure it did not resurface, Houdini lasted for one hour and thirty-one minutes, comfortably exceeding Rahman Bey's record. When he emerged, the magician was visibly out of breath but triumphant.

The trick was simple, he told the assembled journalists. All you had to do was breathe very deeply for a few minutes before entering the coffin, then, once inside, take light and shallow breaths for as long

*Harry Houdini in casket shortly before it was sealed
for submersion.*

as you could manage. Physically, it was tough, but there was nothing
to it beyond endurance. The metal box could be airtight, he said, but
there was still enough oxygen inside to survive for a surprisingly long
time. "There is nothing supernatural about it at all," he was happy
to announce.[42]

When the news broke the next morning in the New York press,
Rahman Bey and Hereward Carrington were over one hundred miles
away preparing for a show at the Capitol Theatre in Wilkes-Barre,
Pennsylvania. Refusing to grant his old rival the victory, Carrington
continued to insist that Rahman Bey's powers were supernatural;
Houdini might be able to replicate the stunt with magic but the fakir
could *genuinely* enter a breathless trance. He told the local newspaper
that he was willing to add another layer to the challenge that would
prove it: "The Egyptian was willing to undertake to stay underwater at
least thirty minutes in a coffin filled with poison gas."[43] Houdini never
answered the challenge.

A few days later, yet more embarrassment appeared for Rahman
Bey. On August 10, the *Brooklyn Eagle* published an interview that
the Arabic-speaking journalist Habib Katibah had conducted a few

days previously. Katibah had been born in Syria, graduated from the American University in Beirut, and then moved to America, where he studied at Harvard University. In the 1920s, he was working for the *Eagle* as their expert on Arabic affairs—later in the decade he went to Egypt as the paper's special correspondent in Cairo. In the 1930s and 1940s, Katibah became a prominent mouthpiece for Arab causes, including the Palestinian national movement. In 1926, he was still a jobbing journalist, sent to interview this mysterious "Egyptian fakir." Katibah immediately addressed Rahman Bey in Arabic and was a little shocked to discover that his interviewee did not speak a word of the language. Rahman tried to justify himself, saying that he spoke a very specific dialect of Alexandrian Arabic that Katibah did not know. Neither the interviewer nor the newspaper bought this desperate excuse. "Rahman Bey, the Egyptian who spoke only Italian, had proved himself a supernatural phenomenon, which only the press agents can explain."[44]

For a while Rahman Bey managed to continue his show; his association with Houdini—even if it had ended in defeat—made him a hot ticket. He left New York behind to spend the next year touring his show across America, from Pittsburgh to Detroit, from Allentown (PA) to Toledo (OH). But after an early run of successes, his "buried alive" act started to lose steam. By the end of 1927 the audiences were no longer turning up at his shows—he was old news. Once Houdini had taken the magic out of his act it could not survive much longer. In 1928, Rahman Bey left America and traveled across the world to Australia. At first, he tried to repeat his act in the major cities of the antipodes, playing at the Sydney Stadium, as well as some lesser venues, including the Masonic Hall in the small town of Bathurst, New South Wales, and announcing that he would be buried alive in the sands of Bondi Beach.[45] But his Australian career did not flourish in the way he might have hoped. He continued to perform in the subsequent decades and even started a romantic relationship with the Australian filmmaker Isabel McDonagh. But as years went by, he disappeared from the public eye—rumors said that he had given up performing, made a failed attempt to become a farmer, and eventually entered the silk-stocking business.[46] By 1937 he and his father were living in "the most squalid poverty."[47]

Houdini, Rahman Bey's great opponent, had a tragic story arc of his own. A few months after his stunt in the Shelton Hotel pool, his appendix burst, probably as a result of being punched in the stomach as part of an offstage stunt, and he died of peritonitis. In a strange coincidence (or perhaps due to the supernatural vengeance of a fakir), the coffin in which he had beat Rahman Bey's record was used to transport his body to his final resting place in Queens, New York. Some even say he was buried in it.[48] Hereward Carrington later wrote, with a hint of triumph, that the magician's dramatic attempt to challenge Rahman Bey may have been the ultimate cause of his demise: "It is my opinion that Houdini appreciably shortened his life by this endurance burial."[49]

Chapter 5

THE MAN FROM
JUAN-LES-PINS

BACK IN PARIS, WHERE TAHRA BEY HAD BEEN PERFORM-
ing since his showdown with Rahman Bey in London, the tide of
opposition to fakirism was growing. Tahra Bey's sudden appearance
in 1925 had exposed some of the anxieties buried in 1920s French
society. For some the "East" was the exotic home of ancient spirituality; for others it was a source of mysterious dangers. Tahra Bey was
the embodiment of that threat. He was powerful, charismatic, and
inscrutable. He also had an undeniable sexual allure, with his dark
eyes, neatly trimmed beard, and habit of exposing his bare chest at
any occasion. Wherever he went, newspapers reported that scores of
female fans were seduced by his magnetic gaze.

There was genuine paranoia that this strange Eastern man might
be coming to take French women. At the end of the 1920s the ninety-
five-page thriller *L'Amoureuse du Fakir* (The fakir's lover) dramatized
the French neuroses about this fakir craze. The book tells the story
of Ourahm, a charismatic fakir, who has taken Paris by storm with
a sensational act in which he is buried alive. All of the city is talking
about him and the Kabbalistic talismans that he distributes after his
show. A fragile, bored, and rich French widow, Lise, attends one of
his shows and is drawn into the fakir's thrall. Ourahm manages to
bring Lise into his total control, taking her to his villa in the South of
France and slowly sucking out her life force. Eventually, her devoted
friends manage to save her from the clutches of this "magnificent

brute," and the pulp novel ends with Ourahm's murder at the hands of his former lover.[1]

The unscrupulous protagonist, the fakir Ourahm, was not, like Tahra Bey, an Armenian in disguise. He was someone even more terrifying and suspicious to an early twentieth-century European audience—his real name was Yosef ben Youssouf and the author said he was an "Arab-Jew" from Algeria.[2] Both Tahra Bey and Ourahm represented fears of mysterious, potentially deceitful men coming from the East to seduce the women of France. Concerned critics, who said that they were not taken in by the claims of the fakirs themselves, maintained that they were worried for their weak-minded and gullible victims. Someone needed to protect the vulnerable maidens from the foreign miracle workers of the East. The French needed their own Houdini, and soon they found him.

Paul Heuzé was everything that Tahra Bey was not. He was a well-connected, respectable, rational skeptic. A journalist, minor historical novelist, and amateur artist from Le Havre, he had served with some distinction in the First World War. After the armistice, he published well-regarded (if not exactly best-selling) works about the finer details of the French war effort. Around this time, Heuzé also developed an interest in Spiritualism and psychic phenomena. Like Houdini, he was anxious about the rising tide of mediums who were exploiting the "spirit world" for their own gain. He knew many people who had been taken in by these fakes; he even knew one couple that had divorced following arguments on the subject.

In the early 1920s, Heuzé published a series of articles in *L'Opinion* magazine about the results of his investigations into Spiritualist occurrences and the claims of mediums who purported to contact the dead. They were popular enough for him to turn them into the book *Do the Dead Live?* and to cement his name as a leading authority on psychic matters. His stance was undeniably sceptical, but at this point, he remained respectful about the central theories of Spiritualism. "We are on the threshold of an entirely new science which will doubtless tell us nothing definite for years," he said of these strange phenomena. "Therefore I am not *opposed* to the Spiritistic hypothesis," he assured people.[3] He was just worried about the large number of charlatans out there deceiving innocent people with their false Spiritualist phenomena.

Soon after the arrival of Tahra Bey in Paris, the fakir's opponents started to mention Heuzé's name as a potential ally. As early as the winter of 1925, an article appeared in *La Victoire* begging Paul Heuzé, now that he had defeated the spirit mediums, not to recoil before the fakirs.[4] Heuzé, for his part, did not demur. By March 1926, he had started his own investigations into the claims of Tahra Bey. In the summer of that year, he published the 211-page study, *Fakirs, Fumistes & Cie* (Fakirs, fakes, & company), a comprehensive effort to debunk every single one of Tahra Bey's miracles. The balanced tone of his early articles on Spiritualism had disappeared and Heuzé was on the attack—a dogged crusader for the truth, who was committed to exposing this charlatan.

Western civilization and the rational methods of the Enlightenment had been kind to Paul Heuzé. He had no desire to see them overthrown, nor did he welcome this new mystical Eastern revolution. In his introduction, written from his home in the stylish resort town of Juan-les-Pins on the French Riviera, he informed readers that Tahra Bey's abilities were simple "jongleries" (tricks), which anyone could accomplish and which had been common in the entertainment industry for decades. Heuzé was methodical in his attack. He set out to prove that nothing supernatural or unexplainable was happening during Tahra Bey's shows, by dissecting the workings of each trick to remove its mystique or, failing that, by giving examples of other people who had done exactly the same thing before him. "Decidedly, Tahra Bey has invented nothing," he told his readers.[5]

First, he addressed Tahra Bey's ability to remain insensible as a huge rock was smashed on his chest. This, Heuzé claimed, was nothing special. He recalled a strongman in Paris in 1902 or 1903 who could break an enormous stone on his head, which was even more

The cover of Paul Heuzé's 1926 book, Fakirs, Fakes, & Co.

impressive. The rock itself took most of the impact, Heuzé said, so all that was required was enough stomach strength to balance the stone. Then he offered other explanations for the supposedly incredible feats. Some, like piercing himself with needles, were not fraudulent, strictly speaking, they just required tolerating a tiny amount of pain (the needles were thin and they didn't go that deep into his flesh). Tahra Bey's ability to stop his blood flow on demand was accomplished by pinching his skin to either push blood out of the spot where the needle would pierce or gather blood into it. His trick of putting animals into a cataleptic state could quite easily be replicated by applying a little pressure to their carotid arteries. Heuzé dropped the name of a famous friend, the writer Maurice Maeterlinck, who had reported seeing the same thing done in Algeria.

Even the big climax to Tahra Bey's show, his burial alive, was an easy trick. Following the same tack that Houdini was taking with Rahman Bey in New York at around the same time, he asserted that there was enough air in a coffin to survive in it for a decent period.

"Anyone could stay alive in one for an hour and a quarter or an hour and a half. With a little training one could last two hours without too much inconvenience. So 'miracles' are accomplished," he concluded sarcastically.[6]

To prove his point, Heuzé performed a few of Tahra Bey's tricks himself, supervised by experts, at his villa on the Riviera. He published accounts written by respected medical doctors attesting that they had witnessed him successfully accomplish many of the feats mentioned in the book—putting himself into a cataleptic state, lying on a bed of nails, and piercing his cheeks with sterilized needles. As part of the publicity for the book he also released a film in which he replicated Tahra Bey's stunts, including the famous burial alive.

Faced with these meticulous public criticisms, Tahra Bey decided not to repeat Rahman Bey's errors. He did not face his opponent directly; instead, he disappeared. Posters went up around Paris announcing that Tahra Bey was going back to Egypt to bury himself alive for three years. The fakir claimed to be tired of the relentless campaigns against him and was giving up on his mission to save the souls of the West. Despite his feelings of persecution, Tahra Bey was not ready to give up on Paris. But it would be nearly two years until he announced, in the autumn of 1928, that he was ready to come back to France and stand up to his accuser. To help him, he enlisted the help of the impresario Edmond Roze to plan a performance that would vindicate him. Roze was a successful actor, director, and producer with a particular speciality in musical comedy. He knew a good show when he saw one—in the early 1920s he had been the director of Théâtre des Bouffes-Parisiens, which had been putting on operettas for decades. So he approached Paul Heuzé about a showdown. "It is very simple," he said. "Tahra Bey is coming back to Paris; he wants to make a sensational comeback and he challenges you to face him publicly."[7]

Heuzé, confident that he could defeat the mystical forces of fakirism with logical argument, quickly agreed to the face-off. He had spent the past year confronting the minor fakirs who were still working in Paris, but he longed for a chance to confront the original, Tahra Bey. The date and a location were decided—November 21 at the Salle du Trocadéro—and a jury consisting of "eminent doctors, officials, and literary men" was assembled to determine the winner.[8] On Paul Heuzé's insistence, proceeds from the event would go to a charity that supported the wounded of the First World War.

Few events involving Tahra Bey ever ran entirely according to plan. The day before the performance, after the running order had been decided and all the preparations had been made, Heuzé received an urgent message that Tahra Bey was very ill and could not come. Heuzé was convinced that this was an obvious case of cold feet; the fakir knew he was going to be shown up so he feigned some ailment that would keep him from having to appear. In a last-ditch effort to salvage the event, Roze and Heuzé sent three doctors from the theater to inspect the patient. But when they knocked on Tahra Bey's door, he refused to let them in. Spectators who turned up to the Trocadéro were greeted with a poster informing them that the show had been canceled and their tickets would be reimbursed.

Afterward, the newspapers came to their own conclusions. One journalist claimed to have gone to Tahra Bey's house on Friday night (two days after the canceled show) and seen him not confined to his sick bed as he had doggedly maintained but "dining happily in the company of friends."[9] The whole fiasco turned into showbiz joke and popular songs started doing the rounds mocking Tahra Bey's weak excuses for his absence.[10] Edmond Roze, who had taken on considerable expenses to hire the venue and make preparations, was left 35,000 francs out of pocket. He decided to take matters into his own hands, sending people round to seize some of Tahra Bey's personal belongings, including his embroidered robes and dinner jackets, as recompense. Despite the wealth of evidence against him, Tahra Bey stuck resolutely to his story. He instructed his lawyer to launch legal proceedings against Roze. Eventually, he managed to secure the release of his belongings but only on the condition that he commit to a definitive showdown with Heuzé on December 11, this time at the Cirque de Paris.

This initial false start only added to the suspense. Paris was avidly watching to find out what would happen when these two men finally clashed in person. Tickets sold out within hours and, on the newly arranged date, the Cirque de Paris was packed. Heuzé later claimed that almost twenty thousand people had turned up, desperate to be let in. Unfortunately, the venue could not hold everyone who wanted to see the show and scuffles broke out in the street outside; "a lamp post was knocked over, a café window broken, chairs and tables destroyed."[11] The doors were scheduled to open at 8:30 but it took until 9:30 to get the mob under control and everyone seated. Estimates of the final size of the audience admitted to the venue range from five thousand to eight thousand.

The Cirque de Paris was more accustomed to hosting boxing matches than fakir shows, and the atmosphere inside was closer to a heavyweight bout than an impartial scientific experiment. The audience were split into pro-fakir and anti-fakir camps, each cheering for their man and each committed to their view of the world—one that proclaimed the mysterious powers of the soul to control the physical body and the other that doubted the arcane claims of the occult. "The 'believers' and 'non-believers' showed themselves equally committed to die for their respective mystics," one journalist observed.[12] Tahra Bey, it was said, had the support of the majority of the women in the audience; one particularly devoted group of his female fans had reserved several boxes in a row from which they loudly cheered and applauded the fakir.

On the sands of the circus lay the many instruments of torture that would be used through the evening—the nails, the blades, and the pins. The panel of judges was in one corner, including the writer Clément Vautel, the lawyer César Campinchi, and the eminent neurosurgeon Dr. Thierry de Martel. Paul Heuzé, dressed conservatively in a dinner jacket, stood beside them, chatting. Finally, Tahra Bey emerged to greet the waiting audience, clad in his long white robes, introduced by the former Comédie-Française actor André Polak, whom he had invited along specially. The fakir's fans erupted into raucous whoops as he took to the sands.

In the charged atmosphere of this long-anticipated performance, it was hard to follow the action in detail. Tahra Bey and Heuzé quickly abandoned the pre-agreed timetable. Accounts of that night's events differ significantly, but most reports agree that the fakir, undeniably a seasoned showman, had the better of the fight's early rounds. He began, as his show usually did, by making his body totally rigid, lying on top of two sharp blades, and having a stone broken across his chest. As he accomplished this first feat, the crowd cheered. Tahra Bey beckoned Paul Heuzé to replicate the feat, but the journalist demurred. So the fakir laid down another challenge. He calmly pierced himself with needles and inserted a dagger into his flesh, demonstrating no signs of pain. Then he turned again to Paul Heuzé and instructed him to do the same: if these feats were as easy as his book had claimed, copying them would be no problem.

Once more, Heuzé refused. This was not a good start for the Frenchman, whose entire argument hinged on the assertion that anyone could accomplish Tahra Bey's tricks. The audience grew impatient. Heuzé had turned down the fakir's offers twice and was starting to look like a coward, happy to attack his opponent in print but unable to face him in the flesh. André Polak, who was now filling the role of commentator, declaimed in a loud voice, "He is asking him to do it, he is not doing it."[13] The audience were incensed; "Actions, actions," Tahra Bey's partisans chanted, calling for physical proof, not academic explanation. Four women leaned out of their box and "cried out for Paul Heuzé's blood." Some others theatrically blew kisses to the fakir. Heuzé had no desire to submit to the will of the crowd. Stubbornly, he wanted to wait as long as possible before replicating any of these gruesome tricks. But he knew that Tahra Bey was making him look like a fool. "I understood all the treachery of that Armenian, and the trap that I had fallen into," he later said.[14] Eventually, as the crowd increased the pressure, Heuzé gingerly inserted two needles into his neck. This small gesture was not enough to please Tahra's supporters. At that moment, "the East crushed the West under the weight of its mysteries."[15]

Despite this fevered opposition, Paul Heuzé claimed never to have been nervous. "Awaiting my time, I am proud to say with no false modesty, that I never lost my cool." In the next test—lying on a bed of nails—Paul Heuzé seized his chance. He had studied the fakir's act and, as Tahra Bey lay down on the painful-looking array of spikes, Heuzé immediately asked him to take off the robe that was wrapped around his torso. When he did, the fakir uncovered a large piece of leather underneath, designed to cushion the sharp points of the nails. Tahra Bey, it seemed, had been caught cheating. But the veteran showman took control of the moment. Removing the leather corset, he pulled down his robe to expose his bare chest and got back onto the bed of nails, betraying no signs of pain. One newspaper report mentioned that, as Tahra Bey lay on his back, a group of excited women rushed to the higher levels of the circus to get a better view of his naked torso. He had managed to save some face.

At the burial-alive portion, Heuzé did not attempt to imitate Tahra Bey; instead, he projected the film he had made showing himself doing the burial alive for an hour and a half. But the audience, those who could crane their necks to see the film, were again unimpressed.

Had Paul Heuzé challenged Tahra Bey alone, the result would have been hard to predict. But he had a secret weapon: he had brought the "false-fakir" Karmah to help him. This drama now had another character. This magician, born in the city of Carcassonne, in the South of France, did not claim to be a real fakir nor to have any unexplainable powers. Yet he could do everything that Tahra Bey could. He could put himself in a cataleptic state and he could lie on the bed of nails without displaying discomfort, making no claim to the secrets of the East nor arguing that his skills were the result of his manipulation of the spirit or his training with a secret society of fakirs. It was all a

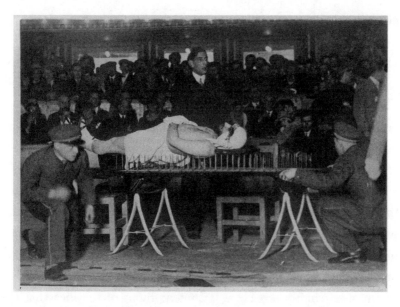

*Tahra Bey at the Cirque de Paris during his showdown
with Paul Heuzé.*

simple trick, he said. Heuzé summoned his assistant onto the sands of
the circus and invited him to repeat Tahra Bey's feats.

Tahra Bey was not happy with the inclusion of this professional
magician in this head-to-head. He cited Heuzé's own book back to
him, quoting a passage in which Heuzé had insisted that, if called
before a court, he could repeat Tahra Bey's act himself—not that he
would get someone else to do it. But Heuzé was unmoved by this criticism. He retorted, somewhat weakly: "I could do it in front of a court
but doing it in front of a circus crowd is not the same thing."[16] Instead,
he had brought Karmah to do his work for him, and Tahra Bey could
only watch as this French magician repeated his entire act.

Shortly after midnight, it finally came time for the jury to cast their
votes. After seeing everything on display, especially the feats easily
accomplished by Karmah, they came to the obvious conclusion that
Tahra Bey had not done anything an illusionist could not, and found
in favor of Paul Heuzé. Tahra Bey's supporters in the audience could

not help him anymore. The next day, the headlines were damning: "Tahra Bey: A Fakir? No, an Illusionist";[17] "The Illusionist Karmah Has Defeated the Fakir Tahra Bey."[18] News of his loss reached the foreign press around the world. *The Observer* in the UK proclaimed, "Tahra Bey Meets His Waterloo."[19] The duel was covered in newspapers from India to San Antonio, Texas; all declared the fakir's defeat.

A few years later Paul Heuzé published a final book on the subject of fakirism, *Dernières Histoires de Fakirs* (The latest fakir stories), in which he recounted his victory not only over Tahra Bey but against the whole institution of fakirism and even the East itself; Western science and logic had prevailed. In his conclusion Heuzé warned his readers against the dangers of following Eastern philosophy and mocked anyone who thought that the West lagged behind the East in any way whatsoever. He was contemptuous of the idea that the people that had produced great minds like Plato, Dante, Shakespeare, Molière, and Beethoven could learn anything from "the savages of the Himalayas—who have produced what, exactly? Except perhaps the crudest, most licentious, and cruelest religions!"[20]

Chapter 6

HAMID BEY:
SELF-HELP GURU

FAKIRISM WAS AT A LOW EBB AT THE END OF THE 1920S. Rahman Bey was defeated; Tahra Bey was defeated. But alongside this parade of failure, a new fakir was being born in America, one who would take a very different path and return fakirism to its mystical foundations. His name was Hamid Bey and he announced himself with great fanfare at the beginning of 1927 when, in the front garden of a suburban house in Englewood, New Jersey, he buried himself alive for almost three hours, smashing Houdini's record.

The event itself was a master class in vaudeville publicity. On the morning of January 20, a crowd of nearly five hundred people gathered around a nondescript New Jersey home as Hamid Bey, dressed in the robes of a fakir, prepared himself for the stunt. He was accompanied by a striking entourage, including Rahman Bey's old manager, Victor Bartelloni (who was now claiming to be the leader of a Coptic cult in Egypt), a mysterious "Turkish medium" called Zulficar Effendi, who wore a pink tunic and carried a purple umbrella, and, perhaps unsurprisingly, the famed psychic researcher Hereward Carrington. He claimed to have eaten only one egg in the past three days to prepare himself to enter his cataleptic state. According to his later memoirs, the first time Hamid Bey had tried this trick in Italy he had eaten a whole plate of spaghetti beforehand and been so full that he nearly died in the coffin. Since then, he was always careful not to overindulge before a show.

Just after one o'clock in the afternoon, as a heavy rain fell, Hamid

Bey was ready to be interred. He stuffed his mouth and nose with cotton wool to prove that he was not breathing while underground and, with a kiss on each cheek from Bartelloni, entered the coffin. Workers shoveled earth on top of him, and the assembled crowd then went into the house to wait out the rain, eating sandwiches and drinking coffee. Hamid Bey, while underground, stayed in psychic contact with his medium, Zulficar Effendi, for the duration of his stunt. Although few braved the weather for the whole event, a dancer called Señorita Martinez went out into the rain to perform a fandango on top of the grave while holding a rose between her teeth, giving the newsmen some color for their articles.

At four o'clock, Hamid Bey finally emerged, having spent around two and a half hours underground and smashing all previous records. Such a long interment could not have been accomplished by anything but supernatural methods, he claimed. When doctors examined him, they found his vital signs were all fine; his pulse and breathing were slightly reduced but returned to normal as he slowly came out of his cataleptic state. Some people heard him mumble the words "Houdini, Houdini" as he came to. When questioned, Hamid Bey said that, while he was in the grave, he had been talking to the magician's soul in the spirit world.[1]

Like Tahra Bey and Rahman Bey before him, Hamid Bey was not exactly who he claimed to be. He was not an Egyptian; he was Italian, born Naldino Bombacci into a large Catholic family in a small town near Ravenna. He had first come to America to work as Rahman Bey's assistant, riding with him on the SS *Leviathan* in the spring of 1926.[2] The fact that both of these American fakirs were from Italy might say something about the way that, in the early twentieth century, people from the north and south of the Mediterranean were regarded as much alike by the country's Anglo-Saxon mainstream. It also showed how interchangeable the people under the fakir's robes were. The fakir was a character to step into, and Hamid Bey effortlessly followed a path laid out for him.

After his stunt in New Jersey, Hamid Bey successfully toured the

*Hamid Bey emerges
from his burial alive
in New Jersey.*

American vaudeville circuit. Traveling across the country accompanied by Victor Bartelloni and Hereward Carrington, he topped bills in Brooklyn and he was buried alive in front of a crowd of thousands in Piedmont Park in Atlanta. According to later reports, he even planned to stage a crucifixion in Times Square but was warned that it might anger the city's Christians, so he backed out.[3]

In the late 1920s, Hamid Bey had lost all traces of the philosophical and mystical backstory of the fakir acts before him. Audiences simply wanted to see miraculous tricks and he was happy to oblige. But wondrous feats without any story behind them did not hold the crowds for long. By 1929, the fakir's popularity had waned significantly. In April of that year, he was giving demonstrations to high school students in the small town of Adams, Massachusetts, and performing in the window of a hardware store.[4] In June 1929, he sailed to Europe, in the hope of finding some work there, but by January 1930, he was back in America. For most of that year he traveled the carnival Midway circuit with a group called the Hamid Bey Revue. It was far from the glamour of Broadway. In September of that year, for instance, he performed in Toronto alongside acts including Silver King, the "wonder dog of the screen"; the Submarine Girl, with a team of trained sea lions; a pair of Siamese twins; and a monkey circus.[5]

Tahra Bey had arrived in Paris with a spiritual message, but as the fakirs moved to America it was lost, and Hamid Bey became more of a freak-show performer than a prophet. Fakirism, shorn of any philosophy, was simply a magic act and one that was beginning to look old. If he wanted to keep going, Hamid Bey would have to return to his show the psychic depth that it had lost. In November 1930 he took the first steps in this new journey. At the auditorium of the Hotel Missouri in Saint Louis, he took to the stage alongside the Indian guru Paramahansa Yogananda. Hamid Bey was buried in an airtight glass coffin as Yogananda delivered a lecture on "the mystery of death and after."[6]

"Swami" ("teacher") Yogananda would set Hamid Bey on a path that would end with his founding his own religious movement in Los Angeles a few years later. Yogananda was not a circus performer; he was a spiritual leader, who had first come to America in 1920 as an enthusiastic young man, intent on educating the country about Hinduism. Initially, he had moved to Boston, setting up an ashram ten miles outside the city and attracting a small following. He spent much of the 1920s touring America and giving self-improvement lectures inspired by yoga and Hinduism—his talks had titles like "Power of Will," "Mastering the Subconscious by Superconsciousness," and "Using Cosmic Consciousness in Daily Life."

This young Indian lecturer had managed to find a sizable following. He traveled the country dressed in a turban and long robes and immediately caught the attention of the American public wherever he went. In 1923 he came to New York, "wrapped in a salmon-pink robe, well brushed black locks cascading over his broad shoulders." The newspapers were stunned, or perhaps amused, by his entourage of disciples made up of Boston elite: "Robert Raymond Eliot, described as a nephew of President Emeritus Eliot of Harvard, wore a yellow turban with a topknot rising erect from its rear. Mrs. Jessie Eldrige Southwick, of the Emerson School of Oratory in Boston, had on a henna-colored robe, and two unidentified middle-aged women wore robes of gold with flowing cowls of the same color."[7]

Yogananda offered his followers a mélange of ancient Eastern philosophies and twentieth-century American self-help. He took the affirmations and positive thinking that had been central to the American New Thought movement and put it in an Eastern garb. As many of the popular self-help writers at the time did, he said that positive thoughts would bring positive outcomes. People who did not imagine themselves to be rich could not become rich. His 1924 book, *Scientific Healing Affirmations*, gave a set of affirmations that he advised readers to recite to bring them health, wealth, and success, interspersed with references to meditation, yoga, "God-realization," and Hindu sacred texts like the Bhagavad Gita.

In 1925, he moved his base of operations to Los Angeles, buying a large former hotel in Mount Washington, a quiet neighborhood less than ten miles from Hollywood, and turning it into the Mount Washington Education Center for the spread of his doctrine of yogoda. The *Los Angeles Times* gave a typically exotic description of the swami's philosophy: "Yogoda, as Swami Yogananda describes his scientific system of applied life vibration, seeks through concentrated absorption from cosmic energy a recharge of life-giving elements into the physical and spiritual system."[8] In the late 1920s, using California as his base, Yogananda traveled the country, lecturing to sold-out halls and proclaiming that the spiritual wisdom of the East was a way to attain success. Many were receptive to his message. He was invited to a luncheon by the women's rights activist Grace Gallatin and was joined by the Egyptian chargé d'affaires Ismail Kamel Bey and the American major general James Harbord.[9] In Miami in 1928, the authorities received complaints from two hundred men that their wives had fallen under the swami's thrall; one man even threatened to kill Yogananda if he caught his wife attending one of the lectures, and another claimed to have found his mother trying to walk on the

Miami River because "Yogananda told her he could do it."[10] The police chief, H. Leslie Quigg, ordered the swami to leave Miami. When he did not comply, Quigg sent his men to surround the hall where Yogananda was set to speak and not let anyone enter.

During his travels across America, Swami Yogananda had crossed paths with Hamid Bey at least once. In 1927, both men were performing in Buffalo, New York; Hamid Bey was performing his fakir act at Loew's Theatre and Yogananda was giving a series of five lectures at the capacious Elmwood Music Hall on subjects such as the "magnetic law of attracting friends" and the "magnetic law of prosperity."[11] While in Buffalo, the two men met and Yogananda was impressed by the fakir's ability to pierce his flesh without feeling pain, to put himself in a cataleptic state for up to twenty-four hours, and to read other people's thoughts. He was disappointed, though, that Hamid Bey was not interested in the spiritual aspects of his abilities. Unimpressed that Hamid Bey went into a cataleptic state simply by pressing down on his temples, he "told Mr. Bey to produce trance by love of God, rather than merely by glandular pressure, as the results produced by devotion are safer and greater."[12]

Eventually, Hamid Bey would heed this advice, and in 1930, the two men started working together. Hamid Bey had just finished his contract with the Rubin & Cherry carnival company and Yogananda was looking for new acts to jazz up his lectures. At their first joint show in Saint Louis, Hamid Bey was brought onstage to amaze the audience by being buried alive in an airtight glass coffin while Swami Yogananda gave a spiritual explanation for this feat in his lecture. As he moved further into Yogananda's world, Hamid Bey left behind the character of "Egyptian fakir" in favor of "Indian yogi." He lived in Yogananda's Los Angeles compound and became an active member of the movement. "Yogi Hamid Bey," the "miracle man and magnetic healer from Egypt," appeared onstage accompanied by Yogananda a number of times in 1931, mostly in Los Angeles.[13] When he was not performing with Yogananda, he appeared with another important member of the swami's entourage, Bramachari Nerode. In 1932,

Hamid Bey's shows began to spread the word across California. In February, Nerode and Hamid Bey went to Oakland for a series of eight lectures—Nerode gave philosophical lessons and Hamid Bey demonstrated his skills, most notably burial alive.[14] In August, the two men traveled to Santa Cruz to give a series of lectures entitled "Higher Science of Living: Rhythmic Breathing, Rhythmic Living, Rhythmic Thinking."[15]

Yogananda and his fellow travelers tailored their messages for American audiences. They were influenced by the growing trend for self-help and motivational speakers, which had particular resonance during the economic depression of the 1930s. Beyond giving general spiritual advice, Yogananda, Nerode, and Hamid Bey insinuated that these lectures might help make you rich; ease physical, mental, and spiritual sufferings; or guide you toward success. It was a simple but effective tactic. As one observer wrote, "We modern Americans will have none of religion if it does not offer us something practical for the wear and tear of the life we live. Swami Yogananda knows that; even the ancient mysteries of the East are of no interest to us if they do not help us with our business."[16]

Hamid Bey's period of active collaboration with Yogananda was short. By 1933, he had started to drift away from the inner circle of yogoda. He remained an honorary vice president of the organization which had now been christened the Self-Realization Fellowship, but he no longer shared a stage with either Yogananda or Nerode. Still, he had clearly learned a lot in these years and had fundamentally changed his entire act. He was no longer a circus curiosity; he was a spiritual leader, billing himself as "the only Egyptian Yogi in America." In early 1933 he returned alone to Santa Cruz, where he himself gave a series of lectures on subjects including "spiritual technocracy" and "how cosmic consciousness will build your health, success, and happiness."[17]

Having left behind Yogananda, Hamid Bey quickly found a new collaborator, one who would complete his transition from vaudeville fakir to American sage. She was Harriet Luella McCollum,

an extraordinary woman who had found fame in the early twentieth century as one of America's most prominent "applied psychologists." Her childhood was the ultimate embodiment of the idealized
pioneer American dream. In the nineteenth century, her parents had
started a farm in Kansas from almost nothing, first living in a leaky
sod house made of earth and grass, then graduating to a two-room
house made of stone, where Harriet was born, before finally moving
into a wooden frame house a few years later. Her early life was hard
and uncompromising—almost a parody of the Protestant work ethic.
The children were expected to pitch in around the farm, but in return,
they were very well educated.

It was a tough formula but one that produced results. Many of the
McCollum children went on to greatness. One of Harriet's brothers,
Elmer, became a celebrated biochemist and professor at Johns Hop-
kins; another, Burton, was a successful electrical engineer. Harriet
herself studied at Lombard College in Illinois, where she became
one of the ten founding members of the women's fraternity, Alpha Xi
Delta. She subsequently married a fellow Lombard student, Charles
Gossow, who went on to become a Universalist pastor, and the couple
had two children. Very unusually for the time, Harriet McCollum not
only kept her maiden name but also handed it down to her children.[18]

After leaving university, Harriet McCollum began lecturing across
the country in something she called "applied psychology," teaching
people how to use the power of their mind to gain money and success.
The beginning of the twentieth century was a boom time for psychology. The American Psychological Association had been formed
in 1892, and by 1904 there were forty-nine psychology labs in the
country, including ones at Harvard, Yale, Columbia, and the University of Chicago.[19] Before long, psychology spread outside the walls of
the academy and into the vibrant public-speaking circuit. This new
science appeared to be offering a strange kind of magic, and crowds
rushed to hear about all the incredible discoveries being made in the
realm of the human mind.

Psychologist, in interwar America, was a vague term. It could range from Harvard professor to backstreet healer or "hypnologist." In the 1930s, the mainstream psychologist Lee Steiner ventured into the demimonde of irregular psychologists, with their mail-order degrees, grand claims, and unregulated practices. To prove a point she called up the New York City government to ask whether psychologists needed a license to practice, and the man on the other end of the line said to her: "I don't know what you mean by a psychologist, lady. Do you mean like a fortune-teller?"[20]

In the late 1910s, McCollum was at the center of this movement of popularizing psychology, touring North America, giving lectures, and running courses in this new discipline. She attributed some truly amazing things to the power of positive thinking, things that would have shocked academic psychologists. Anyone could change their appearance if they believed in themselves, she told her audiences. She started with debatable but reasonably conventional statements (fat people could think themselves thin), then moved on to make more extravagant claims—it was possible to change the color of your hair or eyes by thinking very hard. She said that people could live to the age of 150 and that the deceptively simple secret was to "tell your subconscious self not to die." Calling herself "the woman who doesn't waste a word," she spread her message of hope across America: "Anyone can make a million dollars in four years"; "nobody needs to have bodily ills"; "every woman can be beautiful." Not everyone received McCollum well. In Utah the medical association was so alarmed by her claims that people could cure illness with their minds alone that they appealed for her lectures to be banned. But there were plenty of people who were receptive to her message that "the key to health and happiness is embodied in the teachings of this new science."[21]

As a woman, she broke new ground, carving out a life for herself independent of her husband; she claimed to be the first woman ever to have spoken in the pulpit of an Episcopal church. In the 1920s, she traveled widely to preach her message.[22] At the beginning of the decade she set up a semiregular McCollum Club of Applied Psychology in Atlanta, which aimed to teach Georgians about this new area of scientific study and ran for several years. In 1922 she moved to Brooklyn, where her message reached even more people. McCollum was extremely popular in New York, where the police were known to be brought in to control her crowds.[23]

By the early 1930s, she was a veteran on the American public-speaking circuit. In 1931, she referred to herself as "the richest self-made woman in the world" (but qualified this by saying she was rich in "the only wealth that never fails"). Her applied psychology frequently accomplished miracles; in 1921 one of McCollum's pupils claimed to have been "able to cure herself of blindness through psychology." The language of "auras" and "universal vibratory waves in the ether," which would be comfortably at home in the modern New Age movement, appeared frequently in her writing.[24]

In addition to the powers of positive thinking, she insisted that a good diet, bowel cleanliness, and lots of sunlight could dramatically improve your life. Like psychology, nutrition, McCollum's other major concern, was a science in the throes of considerable flux in the early twentieth century. Today a lot of her advice seems obvious and is part of the mainstream—stay hydrated, eat whole wheat flour, avoid white sugar. Even some of her directives that seemed a little more unusual were based on up-to-the-minute scholarship, such as the advice to sunbathe nude to absorb the health-giving qualities of the sun. In the early 1920s, researchers had isolated the existence of an unusual nutrient called vitamin D. It was found in certain foods, but, curiously, it could also be absorbed from sunlight. McCollum's prescriptions to take in the rays of the sun had the backing of academic experts. Perhaps not coincidentally, Harriet's brother Elmer McCollum was an important member of the team that discovered vitamin D and the person to give the vitamin its name. Both McCollum siblings were, in a way, on the cutting edge of science, but Elmer was endorsed by the most respected institutions in the United States; Harriet was not.

When, in the early 1930s, Harriet McCollum discovered Hamid Bey, she was thrilled. Here was someone whose incredible mastery over his own body was concrete proof that positive thinking could accomplish miracles. "Never until I met Hamid Bey, have I found a man who not only is able to talk wisely but is able to demonstrate and explain," she said. "I have been convinced for years of the supremacy of the human mind . . . but this is the first time in my history when one man can prove this fact beyond a shadow of a doubt."[25]

Harriet's son, Edward McCollum, described the effect that Hamid Bey had on him at their first meeting. The fakir was refreshingly disdainful of the formalities of American society; he did not stand up to greet people and he refused to eat the food that his hosts offered him if he believed it to be unhealthy. He did not speak much but something behind this quiet man's eyes convinced Edward McCollum that he knew the secrets of the world. "Hundreds of columns have been written in the newspapers of every language concerning his apparently superhuman ability to withstand pain and bodily torture without injury. Editorial writers have referred to him as a magician. People of less understanding have branded him as a trickster. But he is certainly one of the outstanding men of the age; one of the world's giants."[26]

The McCollums were instantly charmed by the fakir, and not long after Hamid Bey had left Swami Yogananda's community, he entered their orbit. In October of 1933 Hamid Bey, this time billing himself as an "Egyptian high-priest," appeared onstage at Chestnut Street Hall in Harrisburg, Pennsylvania, to bury himself alive in front of yet another crowd. This time, though, Edward McCollum, billed as a "noted scientist," was brought out to give a lecture to the audience during his demonstration.[27]

Harriet McCollum's most important collaboration with Hamid Bey was the book *My Experiences Preceding 5,000 Burials*, dictated to her by the fakir-yogi and published under his name. It was a strange mix of autobiography, history, and religion, much of it made up of long descriptions of his personal journey to become a fakir. There were a number of fantastical tales about a hidden temple in the mountains of Upper Egypt where he learned the ways of the religion. His mind and body were trained there in a variety of ways—long sessions sitting in the so-called Dome of Concentration and lessons delivered by the temple masters. By the time the boys were in their early teens (girls were trained in a separate school but Hamid Bey did not go into much detail about it), they were learning more advanced skills, including piercing their flesh with needles, controling their heart rates, and entering the cataleptic trance that allowed them to be buried alive. To graduate from this Hogwarts of fakirism, the students had to enter the final Temple of Divine Wisdom, which was older than the great pyramids at Giza.

To reach the highest temple, the group of boys assembled at one spot on the Nile from which they swam through crocodile-infested waters to the other side. On this next bank they found the temple, where they faced their final test. They had to demonstrate their self-control by sitting beside a beautiful and fragrant flower for as long as possible. Its (highly metaphorical) scent was enticing but it was also a deadly poison if smelled deeply and the adepts needed to master themselves in order not to inhale too much of its poison. Every hour they moved one step closer to the flower. They were eventually granted symbolic rings as markers of how long they had lasted in its presence—Hamid Bey was granted seven rings. Finally, all the students were allowed to meet the Eleven-Ring Master, the highest level of master, a title granted to only one fakir in every generation. They spent an hour alone with him, during which he imparted to them his great wisdom, secrets that Hamid Bey did not print in his book.

After a long description of his fakir training, Hamid Bey's book told the story of his mission to America in 1927, attempting to bring the temple's psychic message across the Atlantic. His masters had instructed him to meet the challenge that Harry Houdini had laid down against the fakirs: "Knowing that many thousands in America are sufficiently developed and would appreciate added understanding, they decided to send someone who could prove Houdini wrong." Unfortunately, Hamid Bey said, he arrived in the United States too late. By the time he got there, Houdini had died. (Hamid glossed over the fact that, as Naldino Bombacci, he first arrived in America in May 1926 when Houdini was still very much alive.) So he spent two years touring the vaudeville circuit. This was not, he insisted, an attempt to make money or become a star. It was a necessary part of the temple's grand plan to spread their message to as many members of the American public as possible.

By the mid-1930s, Hamid Bey had learned the techniques and messages of both Swami Yogananda and Harriet Luella McCollum and was assimilating them into his old persona. What came out of this process was a uniquely Americanized fakir. He was dressed in the garb of Tahra Bey but was now giving lectures on self-improvement, nutrition, and psychology, with titles such as "Mental Science and Personal Success (How to Make Your Own Destiny)," "How You Can Become What You Want to Be," and "The Prophecy of the Pyramids."[28] The new Hamid Bey was no longer just an Egyptian fakir; he was now high priest of the ancient Egyptian Coptic Order. By the late 1930s, Hamid Bey was firmly settled in California, land of sun and New Age religious movements. In 1937, he founded the Coptic Fellowship of America from his home on Velma Drive in the Hollywood Hills, among the homes of actors and screenwriters.

Hamid Bey's organization become one of the many Californian occult movements that were circulating short pamphlets to anyone curious to learn more. The literature of the Coptic Fellowship of America was a unique product of Hamid Bey's ten-year career in America. There were exotic tales of a nine-thousand-year-old secret White Brotherhood in Egypt, the myth of Atlantis, and lessons from the Bible set alongside advice to eat healthily, focusing on green vegetables, water, and fish. He exhorted his followers to reject the lure of materialism and find deeper self-knowledge. Hamid Bey did not lose sight of his past career putting himself into a state of living death and burying himself alive onstage. In fact, he incorporated his days as a vaudeville fakir into his new message. During one of these demonstrations earlier in his life, he told his followers, he had left his trance while lying underground in his coffin. Trapped in this airless space, his powers having left him, he had almost died. In that moment, he said, his astral body had departed his physical body; he had experienced the sensation of death and survived. "Through personal experience I have learned that death is not a monster, not to be feared or dreaded."[29]

By the late 1930s, Hamid Bey had become a committed American nationalist: "America is to be the next Holy Land, and it is here that the Christ consciousness will reincarnate. Preparation must be made for this great event, and that is why the Coptic Fellowship of America has been established."[30] The Coptic Fellowship set up branches in most of the country's major metropolises, including Detroit, Chicago, Boston, and Philadelphia, as well as in smaller cities like Buffalo, New York; Harrisburg, Pennsylvania; and Toledo, Ohio. All across the country there were small groups of enthusiastic disciples to welcome Hamid Bey as he toured the country giving lectures, running classes. Sometimes he was called upon to endorse the leaders of local chapters. A visit from the master was always well received—during one trip to Ohio, a follower composed a welcome panegyric in his honor—but he could not be everywhere at once and members were often called upon to lead classes. One popular teacher was Henrietta Elizabeth Schmandt, an artist turned astrologer who went by the name Orio, the Lady of the Stars.[31]

Hamid Bey frequently told people that the Great Master back in Egypt had selected America as "the Holy Land of the future, of a New Order, and a New Race."[32] It was America where the Coptic ideals of freedom and equality were closest to being realized and America where a new spiritual age would be born. It had been only fifteen years since Hamid Bey had buried himself alive in the front yard of a suburban house in New Jersey. He had learned from the guru Swami Yogananda and the applied psychologist Harriet Luella McCollum and created a home for the fakirs in the California sun.

In the 1950s he continued to travel across America giving lectures on the secrets of a "healthier, happier, richer life" and was making extra money by selling Bey Vita–branded vitamin supplements (he did this until the FDA insisted that he stop in 1961). He was even still occasionally performing the buried-alive act—in early 1953 he appeared on a national television show where he was submerged in a coffin underwater for twenty-five minutes.[33] His Coptic Fellowship continued throughout Hamid Bey's life. After his death in 1976 a new leader took over. To this day, the Coptic Fellowship of America still exists, albeit in much-reduced form, without a permanent base, mostly delivering online lectures and broadcasting its meetings in Michigan.

Chapter 7

FUNERAL ORATION
FOR A FAKIR

TAHRA BEY STRUGGLED TO RECAPTURE HIS GLORY DAYS in the wake of his long battle with Paul Heuzé. He had tried traveling. He went to Vienna but soon moved on. He did his first tour in America, where he played at Carnegie Hall, but could not drum up enough enthusiasm to stay there longer. The program published for the show was almost apologetic: "Fakirism has not found yet a plausible, conclusive explanation, and men of intelligence continue to deny it squarely, simply because it is inexplicable." He added, hopefully, "Inability of explanation does not diminish its value."[1]

Tahra Bey had failed in the press and failed on the circus sands. In 1931, he tried the courtroom, suing Paul Heuzé for his loss of earnings. Tahra Bey was convinced that Paul Heuzé's campaign against him had irreparably damaged his career. Since the 1928 showdown, he had been relegated to small venues in nondescript suburbs—no more nights in the Théâtre des Champs-Élysées or sold-out casinos in the Riviera. Seeking redress, he summoned his lawyer, René Idzkowski, fresh from unsuccessfully defending a petty diamond thief, to demand 500,000 francs in compensation from Heuzé and the publishing house that had released *Fakirs, Fumistes & Cie*.

When the trial came before the first chamber of the Civil Tribunal of the Seine, Idzkowski delivered an eloquent speech in support of his client. The case was simple: to boost his own fame and his book sales, Heuzé had launched a dishonest and exaggerated smear campaign against Tahra Bey. The language in Heuzé's books, Idzkowski said,

Playbill for Tahra Bey's 1930 show at Carnegie Hall.

went far beyond the bounds of reasonable criticism and into defamation. As Heuzé was making money touring France as the "conqueror of fakirs," Tahra Bey's work dried up. The old venues would no longer book him and the new venues did not conform to his high expectations. In 1925 or 1926, he could easily command 10,000 to 20,000 francs per night for residencies of up to sixteen days. Now his fees were nowhere near this.

As part of his prosecution, Idzkowski tried to show that fakirism was an extremely difficult discipline. Heuzé had built his argument on the idea that anyone could accomplish these feats but this wasn't true. Sealing yourself in a coffin and being buried alive was no joke. To show this, Idzkowski alluded to the case of a fakir in Argentina who had sealed himself in a coffin for three hours and, when the lid was reopened, was discovered dead. Newspapers reported that the lid of the coffin had scratch marks on the inside where he had fought to save himself from a tragic end.[2] These *jongleries*, as Paul Heuzé had called them, were potentially fatal.

Paul Heuzé hired Maurice Garçon, a successful lawyer known for his academic expertise in historical witch trials and long experience in the finer legal points surrounding the occult. Garçon was a genuine believer in the dangers of witchcraft—not because *he* thought it was real but because others believed it was real. Even in the modern age, he saw people around him adopting endless varieties of outlandish beliefs. "Sorcery is as old as the world and will probably last as long as it does," he lamented. "What a mistake it is to think that science, positivism, and progress could have reduced the number of its adepts or their conviction."[3] He often took on cases with supernatural undertones and, in the 1920s, had made a name for himself as one of the most assiduous enemies of fake prophets, fraudulent mediums, and dishonest magicians, often participating in scientific investigations of their claims. In 1924 he had sat on the same learned panel as Paul Heuzé, examining the Italian medium Erto, who claimed to be able to produce magical lights from the spirit world. Both men, unsurprisingly, concluded that he was a fraud. Garçon, although he did not mention it during the trial, had also been one of the jury selected to adjudicate the face-off between Tahra Bey and Paul Heuzé back in 1928.

Garçon's defense of Heuzé was simple. If Tahra Bey had simply presented himself as a stage act—a magician, or a man with an unusual ability to withstand pain—there would have been no problem. But he had made bigger claims. He had told people that he knew the mysteries of the East, that he was a fakir. He even went as far as to say that he had conducted a concerted scientific study of the doctrines of asceticism. Paul Heuzé had a right to expose Tahra Bey because he was setting out to deceive. The truth was obvious: "Tahra Bey is a good magician, but he is not a fakir."[4]

Garçon was so confident that the case was baseless that he allowed himself a little time to joke at the expense of Tahra Bey, his notorious late nights spent in Montmartre's bars and his reputation for spending large sums of money to impress the high-class women of Paris. The mere fact that he was asking for the large sum of 500,000 francs proved he was not a fakir, since a fakir was supposed to renounce the material pleasures of the world. Amid this banter, he seldom let people forget that Tahra Bey was also a foreigner, an outsider in France, and potentially suspicious. "He is Armenian," Garçon remarked at one point; "he knows all the tricks and subtleties of an argument."[5]

Les Editions de France, which Tahra Bey had brought into the case because they had published Paul Heuzé's book, had hired one of Paris's top attorneys, Henry Torrès. Eloquent, charismatic, and ambitious, Torrès was not yet forty but already a rising star. In 1927, he had hit the headlines for his virtuoso defense of the Jewish anarchist poet-watchmaker Sholem Schwarzbard, accused of murdering General Petliura, the former leader of the nationalist Ukrainian People's Army. Petliura had presided over a number of bloody pogroms in the late 1910s, in which several members of Schwarzbard's family were murdered. When fate brought Petliura to Paris in the early 1920s as an exile from the Soviet Union, Schwarzbard took his chance. Armed with a picture of Petliura that he had cut from the newspapers and a small revolver, he went in search of vengeance. Schwarzbard caught up with the Ukrainian general outside a small restaurant in the rue Racine, close to the elegant Jardin du Luxembourg. To make sure it was him, he asked the man if he was General Petliura. In response the general grabbed his cane to attack. Schwarzbard fired five shots at the man he held responsible for the murder of many thousands of Jews, not stopping until he was sure his target was dead. "This is for the massacres, this is for the pogroms," he said as he unloaded the gun into the Ukrainian general.[6]

The evidence against Schwarzbard was almost comically strong. Several people had seen him shoot Petliura. He did not flee the scene, and when a policeman approached him, he gave him the murder weapon. When he was taken to the police station, he told the arresting officer, "I have killed a murderer."[7] Torrès took a brave stance, arguing that this murder was justified revenge for all the deaths that Petliura had caused. Thankfully for Torrès, the jury agreed with this unorthodox defense. Convinced that justice had been served, albeit by a slightly strange route, they did not convict, and, miraculously, Schwarzbard walked away a free man.

As Torrès stood up to speak, the fakir must have regretted his decision to bring the case. The lawyer's argument was simple but astute. Tahra Bey had brought this case as a performer—he had been damaged as a performer who earned money from his shows—not as a genuine fakir. The book had not maligned his performance skills. In fact, at several points in the book, Paul Heuzé had praised him as an excellent music hall artist. It was only as a fakir that he had been attacked, so it was as a fakir that he should defend himself. He could not have it both ways. The argument convinced several spectators. "Torrès has just delivered the fakir Tahra Bey's funeral oration," wrote one observer in his account of the trial.[8]

After virtuoso performances by some of France's top lawyers, the trial was eventually decided on a technicality. Tahra Bey had brought the case too late. In France, plaintiffs were given three months from publication of a book to bring a case, but he had waited several years. Idzkowski tried to argue that Heuzé's libel against Tahra Bey had been so egregious that it should be covered by another code, which allowed thirty years to bring a case, but the judge did not accept this argument; the three-month window should stand, so neither Heuzé nor the publishers could be found liable. The entire trial had been a waste of time and Tahra Bey was forced to pay the legal expenses.

What could have been a lucrative payout turned into another step on Tahra Bey's path to ruin. His enemies were delighted and wasted no time in their mockery. Before the verdict had even been announced, the satirical magazine *Le Canard Enchaîné* had published a parody of the events, full of the uneasy racial overtones that had long been part of this story. In it, Tahra Bey begins by swearing his oath on "the sacred crocodile head of Benares," at which he is rebuked by the judge: "We are not at the colonial exhibition." The awkward satire continues by making fun of the noticeably Jewish name of Tahra Bey's lawyer, Idzkowski, and ends with everyone in the courtroom shoving needles into their cheeks.[9]

Tahra Bey's fakir career in France was essentially coming to an end. In the depression of the early 1930s, people were less enthused by strange miracles or by portents of a brighter future coming from the East. They certainly had less money to spend on his shows, and he struggled to innovate. Rather than come up with a new act, he decided to take his old act to a new continent, South America. A few months after the trial had finished he made the long trip across the Atlantic, traveling on a Spanish passport, to bring the message of fakirism to Brazil. He installed himself in the country for over a year, writing columns in local newspapers, setting up an "institute of Tahraism" in Rio de Janeiro, and producing his own journal, *Tao: Revista Psychica*, "for the study and diffusion of the occult and psychic sciences of the East."[10] He declared, as he had many times before, that "the problem of suffering is one of the most revolutionary for human intelligence to understand." He went on to tell his Brazilian audience, "When a person claims that you can escape the tyranny of pain, they are seen as a creature that is not of this world—an angel or a devil, perhaps, but certainly no man."[11]

But he had no more luck here than in Paris. As had happened many times before, a challenger came forward to demonstrate that the fakir's skills were not miraculous, they were magic tricks. In Brazil, this opponent was Waldemar, an illusionist and member of the Brazilian Society of Magic, who had enlisted the help of another magician, called the Earl of Richmond, to assist him. For a few days Tahra Bey and Waldemar argued back and forth in the press about whether Tahra's abilities were supernatural or not. On the eleventh of April 1932, the Earl of Richmond put on a demonstration of the fakir's act in the offices of a newspaper in Rio de Janeiro, demonstrating that a magician could accomplish the feats of fakirism. A few days later he did the same onstage at the Cine-Theatro Central. It was all a very familiar story. Fleeing this hostile campaign against him, Tahra left Rio to travel through other cities across the country. He put on his show in São Paolo and the port towns of Belém and Recife, finally leaving Brazil in April 1933 on a steamer bound for France, defeated yet again.

On his return, Tahra Bey tried to reestablish his name in Paris. He announced grandly that, having spent time among the indigenous tribes of the Amazon, he had returned with more occult secrets that he wanted to disseminate. On a more mundane level, Tahra Bey had also learned a new way to monetize his psychic skills in Brazil; he could now see anyone's past or predict their future based on a few lines of handwriting. He put these skills to use for the pacifist newspaper *La Volonté*, which recruited him to answer any questions that its readers wanted to send in.[12] In a series that lasted through the winter of 1933–1934, he answered hundreds of queries on a range of subjects, including marriage, children, travel, business, and illness. He provided everyone with an answer to their questions but some of his responses betrayed the increasing bitterness of a once-great fakir whose best years were behind him. He told one of the readers, without any attempts to soften the blow: "Your illness is incurable." In response to another, who asked about a potential spouse, he gave an even more depressing response: "You will end your life in misfortune and will have a miserable old age. I advise you not to get married so you can spare another victim."[13] The unexpectedly morbid responses cannot have pleased many, and the series abruptly ended in January 1934, never to be revived.

When Tahra Bey was not in Paris, he spent most of his time in Cairo, a city that he had (perhaps) first seen when he was a rootless Armenian refugee in the early 1920s. Now, he had global fame behind him, and instead of staying in a cheap hotel near the red-light district, he stayed on the city's chic Suleiman Pasha Square in an elegant apartment, which he dubbed the Institute of Tahraism. He kept up his fakir show in Cairo just as he had in France. One Egyptian journalist visited his rooms in Cairo and described the exotic scene that greeted him as he was let in by the fakir's young servant: "The door opens and you enter a dark hall, its walls adorned with sheets of paper displaying mysterious pictures and strange shapes. On the doors are hung thick blue curtains and in the centre of the room is a large copper censer, from which the strong smell of incense rises."[14]

In this apartment, he hosted Paul Brunton, the occult researcher from England, who was working on a book about the paranormal phenomena of Egypt. Brunton was impressed by Tahra Bey's abilities and by his personal charisma, even if his best days were behind him. "His piercing, beautiful eyes are exceptionally interesting," Brunton said. "He carries himself with an unhurried ease and self-possession, a marked air of self-control, such as one always observes in really advanced fakirs. He smokes innumerable cigarettes over the course of a day." But Tahra Bey himself was increasingly jaded: "The world has forced me to commercialize my powers," he admitted to Brunton over tea, "to become an artiste when I wanted to be a scientist."[15]

In France, where he still spent most of his time, Tahra Bey was reduced to running a series of small cons and schemes to support his expensive lifestyle. He replied to questions that people sent him in the post, distributed his own horoscopes and samples of the "incense of prophecy," a substance that he claimed allowed people to access their inner mediumship, and received private clients in his offices. One of his most lucrative schemes was selling lottery tickets on which he had filled in his own predictions for the winning numbers. The French police believed that these kinds of schemes "constituted his principal occupation and the most lucrative," estimating that, through them, he was making several hundred thousand francs every year in the mid-1930s.[16] In 1937, claiming to be acting on the advice of his doctors, he left Paris for the Mediterranean city of Nice, where the air and the weather would be more conducive to his health. Here, he lived luxuriously in an elegant villa on the seafront corniche, the Promenade des Anglais, with four servants, including a valet, a typist, and a housekeeper. Tahra Bey may not have had the same public profile, but the money he made could still provide him with luxuries.

His real reason for leaving Paris, though, was probably not medical. His many years living on the edge of legality were starting to catch up with him. For many years he had been the subject of official attention and had been brought before the court a few times on minor charges. In the 1930s, he was fined for writing bad checks; official complaints had been lodged with the public prosecution charging him with "escroquerie" (charlatanry), though he managed to escape serious repercussions. In May 1937, the Ministry of the Interior, alleging that he had been "the subject of unfavourable reports," banned him from performing in casinos. By 1937, the French authorities took more interest in the complaints lodged against him. Alongside the people who had accused him of swindling them out of 15 francs, the cost of one of his pre-filled lottery tickets, two women in the Paris area each reported being swindled out of over 100,000 francs. The people who were funding his world travels were starting to rebel.[17]

His move to Nice did not take the heat off for long. In February 1938, the French government, deeming Tahra Bey's presence a threat to the national good, revoked his permission to stay in the country—as an Armenian, he was still a guest of the republic and could be expelled at any point. The fakir was not informed of the decision immediately. The revelation came later, in April of that year, when he presented himself at the police station to ask for the papers that would allow him to travel to America. Instead of receiving these documents, he was taken aside and given two pieces of bad news: not only would the office not provide him with papers, he had been officially ordered to leave the country.

Tahra Bey, who had called France home since 1925, did not meekly comply with these dictates. The outraged fakir immediately wrote to the minister of the Interior to protest, complaining that he had received no reason for this sudden decision, and he encouraged the ministry to investigate the matter further. He was convinced that there must have been some mistake. Marshaling all of the connections that he had made during the decade he had spent in Paris, he closed his letter with the names of several influential Frenchmen who, he claimed, would vouch for his good character. The list was a who's who of the French elite of the 1930s, including a former president of the Council of Ministers, Pierre Laval, and the famous war hero Colonel Picot. It is unclear what would have happened if the Ministry of the Interior had actually contacted them, whether they truly would have put in a

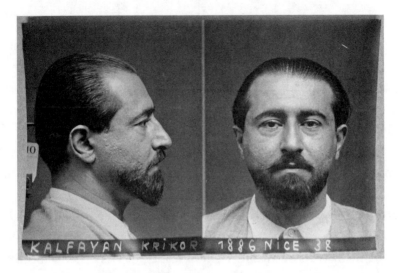

*Mugshot of Tahra Bey/Krikor Kalfayan
taken by police in Nice 1938.*

good word for Tahra Bey. Colonel Picot would not have been much help; unbeknownst to Tahra Bey, he had died the day before the letter was sent. This list of influential politicians did not change any minds at the Interior Ministry. In August 1938, Tahra Bey was told that he now had just eight days to leave the country.

Staring catastrophe in the face, he pulled out all of his old tricks in a desperate attempt to stay in France. In early September, after his deadline had expired, he went to the offices of a newspaper in Nice to deny the rumors about his expulsion order that had been appearing in the press. He maintained that the news was greatly exaggerated and that it was the result of a simple "clerical error," which had now been sorted out. Tahra Bey reassured his readers he was still practicing his psychic trade, as before, in his villa on the Promenade des Anglais.[18] A few days later, he held a party, inviting the press to take pictures of him and his friends drinking champagne. He told them that he was celebrating the cancellation of his expulsion order.

It was a valiant attempt to extravagantly ignore his problems, but the fakir soon discovered that he could not simply wish French bureaucracy out of existence. In 1938, this was bigger than just Tahra Bey. The French authorities were cracking down on fakirs across the country. A few months before, six fakirs had been brought up together in front of a tribunal on charges of charlatanry; five of the six were given fines by the judge and one was let off.[19] The police in Nice, convinced that Tahra Bey was a "swindler of a high order, whose presence is extremely undesirable in our country," were determined to put an end to his schemes. At the end of September, the order against Tahra Bey was upgraded from *refoulement* ("repatriation") to the stronger category: *expulsion*. He was arrested and, again, told he had eight days to leave the country. This time, he had no choice but to obey. After many years of creating his own reality, he was forced to bend to someone else's.

The 1930s had been a bad decade for Tahra Bey and 1938 was its nadir. Despite his expulsion from the country, he was still put on trial in absentia for selling lottery tickets at a marked-up price (which it turned out was a criminal offense in France) and was sentenced to four months in prison and a fine. He was reportedly in Italy when he heard the news and the fact that the prison sentence was commuted on appeal would offer scant comfort to the exiled Tahra Bey when he found out.[20] He found temporary respite in London, where he met Alexander Cannon, the "Yorkshire Yogi," an eccentric hypnotist and psychiatrist who had treated Edward VIII in the run-up to his abdication. Living in Kensington, Tahra Bey put on one blockbuster fakir show with Cannon's help at the Aeolian Hall on New Bond Street, but his attempts to reestablish a career were hampered by his inability to learn English. Although he later boasted that he had helped cure George VI's stammer using "oriental methods of hypnosis," there is little evidence that he had any more success in England in 1939 than he had in 1926—nor that he ever met the king or even learned to speak English.[21] Tahra Bey was again made a refugee, uprooted from his home and wandering in strange lands.

Chapter 8

"A FAKIR
IN JACKBOOTS"

IN SEPTEMBER 1939 EVERYTHING CHANGED. BRITAIN
and France declared war on Germany, and Europe, then the world,
descended into violence. The age of the gurus, fakirs, and mystics had
come to an end, replaced by an era of demagogues and dictators. As
Tahra Bey languished in London, Adolf Hitler marched the German
armies across Europe in a wave of destruction. Benito Mussolini was
trying to recreate Italy's ancient empire, and General Franco, having
defeated the Republican forces, had created his own dictatorship in
Spain. Before long, almost the entire continent would be under the
control of these strongmen.

The fakirs, mystics, and swamis of the interwar period seldom dirt-
ied their hands with real-world politics. Tahra Bey was no Nazi—
certainly not actively. He had never publicly proclaimed any political
opinion or position at all. But the more people looked, the more worrying similarities they found between the mystics of the 1920s and
1930s and the fascist dictators who dominated European politics at
the same time. Both held audiences in a seemingly magical trance.
Both used their charismatic personalities to win huge cult follow-
ings. Both made great promises of spiritual rebirth. Hitler's power to
inspire devotion from his audiences, in particular, was often spoken
about as a mystical ability. In 1933, the *New York Times* called him a
"pied piper" whose "spell" had put the German people into a "trance."
La Republique published an article saying that Hitler had a "medium-
istic power that Germany regards in the same way that a hypnotised

subject stares at their hypnotist."[1] There were even rumors that he had taken lessons from a professional hypnotist and that he had the power to put people at Nazi rallies into a genuine hypnotic trance. As one vocal critic of the Nazis wrote in 1944, "The fakirs are not the only ones who can cast a spell over the masses."[2]

In the decades since the Second World War, the occult roots of fascism and Nazism have provoked much interest and debate. Salacious stories about the occult leanings of specific figures in the Nazi Party are fodder for books, films, and video games. Rudolf Hess maintained a personal astrologer; Heinrich Himmler was a devoted student of occult sciences and Eastern religions.[3] However, whatever overt links there may have been between right-wing dictators and occult figures tended to fade away as these movements started to gain significant power. Occult groups were guided by their own aims and ideals and were usually too unpredictable to keep under control. Throughout the 1930s, both the Nazis and Mussolini's fascists launched a series of crackdowns against occult practitioners in places under their control.[4]

The career of Arturo Reghini, the man who first welcomed Tahra Bey to Rome in the hope that he might herald a new age for the city, is a good example of the complex relationship between fascists and occultists. When Mussolini first came to power, Reghini was thrilled. He was convinced that the fascist movement could be steered toward his ultimate goal of crushing the Catholic Church and reviving the mysteries of ancient paganism and Pythagoreanism. Reghini at first believed that Mussolini could be made amenable to this aim—Il Duce did spend a lot of time talking about restoring the glory of Italy's classical past. But it was not long before the political reality took control. In 1925, the fascists outlawed secret societies, striking a huge blow against the Italian occult. When the Lateran Treaties were signed in 1929, formalizing relations between the Catholic Church and the Italian state, it became clear that Mussolini would never help realize Reghini's dream of destroying the Catholic Church. He spent the rest of his life in obscurity, teaching in schools and writing occult treatises, all while under heavy police surveillance.[5]

Beyond these specific stories of occultists drawn to fascism or Nazis dabbling in the occult, many commentators at the time saw a different kind of connection between mystics and dictators that was indirect but more widespread and, perhaps, more important. The fakirs and the demagogues were diagnosed as symptoms of the same disease—the descent into irrationality and superstition that defined the 1920s and 1930s. As the old order, built on logic and materialism, collapsed, lost souls were drawn to outlandish promises and miraculous worlds, whether that was the mystics who wanted to build a new world on foundations of the occult or far-right dictators who raved about national rebirth or the "Jewish threat."

In 1935, the writer Leonard Woolf, ignoring warnings for his safety, traveled through Nazi Germany and fascist Italy. After he returned, he put his thoughts on the rise of dictators into a book that he called *Quack, Quack!* In it, he ascribed the birth of fascism to the general retreat of civilization and rejection of reason that he saw around him. Logic had been replaced by primordial fears of the unknown, belief in the power of magic, and barbarism. Woolf saw a world where the fruits of the Enlightenment had not been shared equally among everyone. Modern capitalism had created winners and losers and now the losers were in revolt, intent on destroying the civilization that had never cared about them. This backlash against the establishment could be channeled in different directions. For some people, it took the form of a "political reaction against reason, intelligence, and humanity" that led them to Mussolini and Hitler. For others, it took the shape of a "reversion to the primitive psychology of magic and superstition."[6] Woolf believed that the root cause of both was the same: a failure of civilization caused by the unwillingness of the elites to share their privileges.

Woolf was not the only person to offer this interpretation of the rise of fascism. Many of the more sober-minded philosophers of the mid-twentieth century were on his side. R. G. Collingwood railed against the "end of clear thinking and the triumph of irrationalism" that defined the fascist movement.[7] The extravagant rejection of logic and the embrace of strange metaphysical doctrines left the door open for dangerous ideas. The philosopher Theodor Adorno, in the aftermath of the Second World War, drew a direct link between the early twentieth-century occult and the rise of fascism. Followers of both phenomena shared the belief that the world of the 1920s and 1930s was irrevocably broken and they believed that the solutions that had been proposed to bring it back on track—liberal democracy, rational materialism—would lead only to further catastrophe. This was an assessment that Adorno could understand. However, he saw little value in their solutions. Both felt around for answers haphazardly, finding only vague simulacra—childish versions of the truth—which could never truly solve these problems. Fascism offered militarism, hero cults, and anti-Semitism, while followers of the occult sought answers far outside our world, looking to the stars for astrological predictions or to unseen forces of the universe that only a select few could access. Tahra Bey, Hitler, and Mussolini were all offering empty fantasies in answer to a genuine problem. "Occultism," Adorno declared, "is the metaphysic of dunces,"[8] and Hitler was, in the words of one historian, a "fakir in jackboots."[9]

As intellectually shallow as Nazi philosophy might have been, militarily it was extremely dangerous. In 1940, the armies of this jackbooted fakir occupied Paris, and the bohemian world of the 1920s and 1930s fell apart as artists and writers fled the city. Those who did not flee faced serious risks, above all Jews, who quickly became the targets of Nazi persecution. Tahra Bey's rough-and-tumble former lawyer, René Idzkowski, who had defended so many romantic lost causes in the Parisian courts, was sent to Auschwitz in September 1942. His wife had been sent a few months earlier. Edmond Roze, the impresario who had organized Tahra Bey's showdown with Paul Heuzé in the late 1920s, was transported to the death camp in July 1942. All three were murdered.

Tahra Bey's cousins, the Aznavours, who had come to Paris in the 1920s, continued to live there during the occupation. The Aznavours have gone down in history as resistance heroes. At considerable personal risk, they sheltered Jews and underground anti-Nazi militants on the run from the Germans. Their apartment near the Place Pigalle played host to a stream of political undesirables who had nowhere else to turn. There were dangers lurking everywhere in occupied Paris. There was one man in the building who was a vocal supporter of the Nazis, so they had to keep a low profile. Charles Aznavour and his sister Aida sometimes had to share a bed with a desperate refugee when the apartment was filled up. Despite these hardships, they recalled an optimistic atmosphere dominating the house, and some nights, when they thought they could get away with it, the sound of Yiddish folk songs filled their rooms.[10]

While his cousins were taking huge risks to support the fight against Nazism, Tahra Bey took advantage of the turmoil brought about by the German occupation to sneak himself back into France. The police never discovered exactly how or when he reentered the country, but at the beginning of 1942, he managed to secure an official identity card from the German authorities that allowed him to stay in France. Less than four years after he had been expelled, he was back in the city that had made him famous, with a new persona: "Dr. Kalfayan," a physician who was well connected with powerful people in the German establishment. He continued to perform occasionally as Tahra Bey, but as Dr. Kalfayan he set up a service trying to help free some of the many prisoners in German custody, for a fee ranging from 50,000 to 500,000 francs. As the Nazis began to round up Paris's Jews in the summer of 1942, his business exploded. It is not known how many times he attempted this scheme, but one particular example, from the summer of 1942, stands out as his most prominent (and unpleasant) act of the whole period—perhaps of his entire life.[11]

The story began in August 1942, when Renée Boet, a twenty-seven-year-old French woman, saw her lover, Raymond Greitzer, deported to the Pithiviers internment camp for reasons she did not understand. She insisted, perhaps truthfully or perhaps desperately, that he was not Jewish and said that she had the papers to prove it—she also noted that Greitzer had not been wearing a yellow star when he was seized, as was a requirement for all Jewish residents of Paris. Even if it was a case of mistaken identity, Boet had very good reasons to be worried. August 1942 was the height of the German campaign against Parisian Jews and trains were leaving from the internment camps around Paris to Auschwitz almost every other day carrying around one thousand people each.[12] She frantically asked among her friends and was told to visit a well-connected Red Cross ambulance woman, Catherine Raffard, who had a reputation for being able to solve problems just like this one. Raffard took pity on Renée Boet and agreed to introduce her to Dr. Kalfayan, her friend who had connections in the highest echelons of power.

Boet was taken to a bar to meet Kalfayan, who, upon hearing her story, reassured her that he believed it all. He was sure that her lover, Greitzer, had been the victim of a miscarriage of justice that could easily be sorted out. She would have to pay 500,000 francs to grease the wheels of power, but he would be able to secure this poor man's release within twenty-four hours. Dr. Kalfayan, who claimed to work at a Parisian hospital, had friends in the Vichy government. He made a show of producing a letter that the French prime minister, Pierre Laval, had sent him. This was the second time that he had used Laval's name to establish his bona fides—the first was back in 1938 when he was fighting deportation—and now Laval was one of the most powerful Frenchmen remaining in the country, at the top of the Vichy government.

Dr. Kalfayan insisted that handing over 500,000 francs was the only way to free Greitzer, but Boet was initially reluctant to hand over such a large sum to someone that she had just met. Kalfayan could see her wavering and came up with an unusual plan to convince her. At the time he was also working as an impresario for the actress Cécile Sorel, planning her upcoming tour of Germany. Kalfayan had known Cécile Sorel since the 1920s, when he was performing as Tahra Bey. When the authorities were trying to expel him from France in the late 1930s, she had (unsuccessfully) tried to intervene by writing letters on his behalf. By the 1940s, she was a legend, perhaps the best-known actress still working in the country, with undisputed fame, both national and international. When she died in the 1960s, an American obituary said that she had been "the finest French actress between Sarah Bernhardt and Brigitte Bardot."[13] She had toured the world, from New York to Istanbul, and her name was a byword for the glamour of twentieth-century French theater. Kalfayan brought Sorel into his scheme. In an attempt to calm Boet about handing over such a large sum of money he suggested that his famous actress friend could hold on to it as an intermediary until Greitzer was freed. If anything went wrong she could give her back the money, and if Boet couldn't trust Cécile Sorel, who could she trust?

To prove that he was not just inventing stories, Dr. Kalfayan personally introduced Boet to Cécile Sorel at a cabaret on rue Victor-Emmanuel III, then took them to a nearby restaurant for dinner. Over the meal Sorel played her role well. She casually mentioned her influential friends, such as Admiral Darlan, one of the most important officers in the Vichy navy, who happened to be arriving in Paris the next day and was staying in the same hotel as her. Sorel was also well connected with the German authorities at the time. She had previously performed in front of Adolf Hitler, as part of a deal that brought five thousand French prisoners back home. Her face was well known in the offices of the Nazi Propagandastaffel, where, according to the memoirs of Werner Lange, she "would often visit, almost as a neighbour."[14] After the war, this closeness to the German authorities got Sorel in trouble. She was banned from working on French stages for a year. In 1946, a letter emerged from the Gestapo archives, apparently written by Sorel in German. In it, she complained that she did not have "an apartment suitable to receive all [her] German friends," and, "in the interest of Franco-German collaboration," she asked if she could be given one of the apartments that had recently been confiscated from Jews; she suggested, as an example, one in the elegant modernist building along the Seine, 89 Quai d'Orsay, which was also home to the writer Jean Giraudoux.[15] When confronted, Sorel denied writing the letter, claiming that the handwriting was not hers. Still, it is unclear how many people that convinced. It seems very unlikely that someone would go to the trouble of concocting a letter like that, and she did not give a convincing reason why anyone would want to frame her.[16] Shortly after this she quit acting forever and retired to a convent, perhaps atoning for her sins.

In 1942, before any of these scandals were made public, Boet was reassured by the presence of this A-list star alongside Dr. Kalfayan and agreed to hand over the money. She would visit Kalfayan to finalize details the next day at the Bristol Hotel, where Sorel was staying. The Bristol was occupied Paris's most luxurious and in-demand hotel, with a client list to match: actors, heiresses, diplomats. The writer P. G. Wodehouse stayed there in 1943 after he left Germany. If there was any suitable place to hand over 500,000 francs in wartime Paris, this was it.

Boet arrived at the Bristol at three o'clock the following afternoon, where she met Kalfayan. Then they went together to take the money to his office just off the Champs-Élysées on rue La Boetie. That evening the whole group—Cécile Sorel, Dr. Kalfayan, Madame Boet, and Madame Raffard—arranged to meet at the notorious l'Aiglon cabaret to toast the deal. Even during Parisian blackouts, a few cabarets stayed open to people who were willing to ignore the 11 p.m. curfew.[17] The only way that revellers could tell whether a place was open was by the stream of people coming in and out of it. L'Aiglon was one of the seedier venues that stayed open in occupied Paris and its clientele was even seedier, described by one French jazz musician who was active as the time as a place where "the most authentic black marketeers rubbed shoulders with the most arrogant collaborationists."[18] Kalfayan would have felt at home. Unfortunately, when he and Boet turned up on the stairs outside the cabaret just before the curfew, at 10:30, they discovered that it was not open that evening. So they waited for Cécile Sorel in a nearby bar. When she finally arrived, Dr. Kalfayan informed her that the money had been safely handed over and that the plan was going ahead. Raffard and Kalfayan arranged to meet Boet the next day to secure her lover's release. It had cost Boet a lot of money, but she had reasons to be hopeful.

At midday the next day, Boet, Raffard, and Kalfayan got into a Red Cross vehicle and set off in the direction of Pithiviers internment camp. Raffard looked the part in her Red Cross uniform, wearing her medals of service. When they arrived at the camp, she went in alone to negotiate the prisoner's release, carrying the documents that Boet had provided stating that he was not Jewish. She re-emerged a short time later and explained to Boet what had happened. In the testimonies given to the police, there were two different versions of what she said. Boet insisted that Raffard gave her good news, reassuring her that everything had been arranged—the camp commandant had received a call from Pierre Laval and all that she needed to do now was wait for her lover to emerge. Raffard, however, when she was later questioned by the police, claimed that she told Boet that the Germans in the camp had not given her anything. Instead, they had told her to speak to some higher authorities, who would give her a permit to visit the prisoner, which would in turn give her a chance of getting him out. She claimed that she had explained everything very precisely to Boet and advised her to leave but that Boet had not listened to the advice.

Whatever was said, Dr. Kalfayan and Madame Raffard departed, leaving Renée Boet to wait by herself in the countryside fifty miles south of Paris, outside Pithiviers camp. As time passed and nothing happened, Boet realized that she had to take action herself. She went to see the camp commandant personally. He listened, confused, as she told him Raffard's story about Pierre Laval's phone call and his intervention to save her lover. The commandant told Boet that they had received no phone calls regarding Raymond Greitzer and explained that the people in this camp were prisoners of the Germans and not under French jurisdiction; even a call from Pierre Laval would not have accomplished anything. Boet was forced to return to Paris, leaving Raymond Greitzer in the internment camp and the 500,000 francs in Dr. Kalfayan's possession.

As soon as she got back, she went straight to Kalfayan's office to demand her money back. Perhaps realizing that she had been scammed, she even offered him 50,000 for his troubles in an attempt to put an end to the saga. Kalfayan refused, demanding a few more days to see the plan through; if they really could not get Greitzer out of the camp within that period, he said, he would return the whole sum to her. The days went by and nothing happened. Kalfayan began to make excuses. When Boet complained, he tried a new strategy. Cécile Sorel needed money for her theatrical tour in Germany, he said; perhaps Boet should consider herself a sponsor of this artistic venture. Boet turned this honor down; she just wanted the money back. Kalfayan promised that he would have the money to her by the end of the year. Boet threatened to file a complaint with the police. Kalfayan responded: "Go ahead, file a complaint. You'll regret it."

Boet was not intimidated by this threat. She went straight to the police, and thankfully for her, they took the complaint seriously. Some officers raided Krikor Kalfayan's house and found 100,000 francs under the mattress. Next, they went to his sister-in-law's house and found the remaining 400,000. They took statements from the accused—Kalfayan, Catherine Raffard, Cécile Sorel, and others— who all strenuously denied the accusations against them. A reasonably consistent story emerged in their denials. They all admitted that they had met Madame Boet and they had felt extremely sorry for her plight. Raffard had agreed to try to use her position as a nurse to enter the camp and see what she could do—simply as a favor and making no promises. Cécile Sorel, too, was happy to admit that she had met Boet and even suggested that she could talk to her friends about her predicament—but she had only mentioned it in passing and she had been sure to make no guarantees.

What about the money that Boet had handed over? It was an extremely large sum to be exchanged between casual acquaintances. All three statements (Raffard's, Sorel's, and Kalfayan's) insisted that the 500,000 francs were intended to fund Cécile Sorel's artistic ventures, not as a fee for getting Raymond Greitzer out of detention.

Kalfayan's statement said that, in the first meeting between Boet and Cécile Sorel, "we talked for the whole time about the only thing that interested us, that is, the organisation of our theatre."[19] Raffard alleged that Renée Boet harbored ambitions to become an actress herself and hoped that Sorel could help her realize this dream. Boet flatly denied this: "I never expressed any desire to sponsor her theatrical tour. . . . I never expressed any desire to act any role."

The hearing itself descended into violence at one point as one of Madame Boet's friends, who had been called in to give evidence, punched Kalfayan at a particularly emotive moment, and was fined 600 francs by the court. After listening to all the testimony, the judge eventually found in favor of Madame Boet. He convicted Dr. Kalfayan of fraud and gave him a fine of 5,000 francs and a suspended sentence of thirteen months. Raffard was given no fine and a six-month suspended sentence. Sorel escaped with no punishment—there was little direct evidence against her. Kalfayan felt aggrieved to have taken the fall for the whole scheme. He wrote a letter to the public prosecutor, claiming that he had been the victim of a scam by Sorel and Raffard. They had used him as the front man to secure funds for Sorel's vaguely conceived German tour, but they knew that the money would never really be used for this purpose. Then, when trouble inevitably came, they had pinned everything on him and escaped justice themselves. The prosecutor did not act on these desperate accusations. Krikor Kalfayan (aka Tahra Bey) had played his last card. He was now a convicted fraudster. His relationship with the great star of the stage Cécile Sorel had fallen apart. The next year he was fined 3,600 francs for using the title of doctor without proper medical qualifications. By the end of the war Kalfayan was a ruined man, his career destroyed.

As for Renée Boet and her lover, Raymond Greitzer, there appears to have been a happy ending. There are no detailed records or accounts of what happened in the months and years following this court case. His name appears nowhere on the many lists of the victims of the Holocaust (nor, in fact, in any lists of survivors). It is possible that he was not Jewish, as Boet claimed—though both his surname and his middle name recorded when he entered Pithiviers camp, Salomon, suggest that he might have been. Little was heard of him until May 20, 1950, when Raymond and Renée Greitzer appeared on the manifest of a flight from Paris to New York, listing their address on arrival as Wellington Hotel on Seventh Avenue.[20] They had survived.

Part II

GHARA'IB
WA-'AJA'IB

Human beings are naturally disposed to investigate
unexplainable phenomena; they are obsessed with
strange and wondrous things.

—Munir Wuhayba,
Secrets of the Occult Sciences[1]

~

We are living in an epoch that is rich in every
manifestation of the human spirit; a confusing
epoch, perhaps, because of the diversity
of its riches, but one which proves itself
extremely attractive.

—Irène Keramé,
La Revue du Liban, 1929[2]

Chapter 9

DR. DAHESH
TAKES THE STAGE

AS TAHRA BEY WAS DISGRACING HIMSELF IN PARIS, A new holy man named Dr. Dahesh surfaced on the other side of the Mediterranean in wartime Beirut. This new mystic was capable of impossible feats and unexplainable wonders that were less easily challenged than Tahra Bey's. In his home in the quiet Beiruti neighborhood of Musaytbeh, he welcomed guests in search of the paranormal. The room where he performed his miracles was heavy with atmosphere. "Whoever entered, felt a darkness surround them. . . . The rooms exuded fear. It was black on black; a black table . . . and a black velvet curtain embroidered with red and yellow thread." The floors were covered in thick carpets, books filled every shelf, and the walls were hung with tapestries, paintings of historical or mythical heroes, and pictures of Dr. Dahesh in mystical poses. Curios littered the surfaces, including stuffed eagles, a stuffed crocodile with an electric light bulb in its jaws, and a small wooden clock that had stopped working.[1] Within these strange surroundings, he demonstrated powers bestowed upon him from the spirit world. He conjured physical objects out of the ether, sometimes transporting them across international borders to his Beirut home, read the minds of his visitors, predicted the future, and communicated directly with the souls of the dead.

Lebanon in the early 1940s was a society in the midst of rapid social and political change, of a kind seldom before seen in its history. The first three years of the decade had seen violence and death, as power shifted hands between the Vichy government, Free French troops, and, finally, the forces of the Lebanese independence movement. By the end of 1943, as the Second World War was raging, the country was officially free from French colonial rule and starting a long project of nation building to bring its diverse population together under one flag. At the same time a very different kind of cultural revolution was taking place in Dr. Dahesh's Musaytbeh home. An influential group of the country's elite were drawn in by his incredible paranormal skills. Respected lawyers, judges, doctors, poets, and journalists were often seen entering or leaving his house. The newspapers were filled with stories about his wonders and warnings about the dangers he had brought to the country. The novelist Karam Melhem Karam, in an attempt to capture the atmosphere surrounding this new mystic, wrote that "in Beirut, it started as a whisper, then became a murmur, then a shout. The name 'Dahesh' was everywhere, 'Dr. Dahesh.' People asked, with doubt and curiosity: had the age of wonders returned? . . . There was not a living room left in Beirut—in Lebanon and Syria as a whole—that was not talking about the strange deeds of this new 'prophet.'"[2]

Many unanswered questions surrounded this new holy man. Where had he come from? What did he want? What was the source of his mystical powers? To answer these questions and to tell the full story of this unusual Lebanese sage, we must travel back in time a few decades to the 1920s, and to Tahra Bey's fakir revolution. Only once we have seen how Tahra Bey's message spread through the Arab world can we return to the 1940s and to Dr. Dahesh's spiritual revolution. In important but indirect ways, Tahra Bey was Dr. Dahesh's spiritual godfather.

After the publication of Paul Heuzé's polemical broadside, *Fakirs, Fumistes & Cie*, in 1926, the humiliated fakir had left France, tired of the constant attacks and announcing that he was returning to Egypt to bury himself alive for several years. This bold claim was not entirely untrue. He had no plans to disappear underground but he *was* bound for Egypt. At the end of 1927, he appeared in Cairo, ready to perform his act to audiences of excited Egyptians. One Arabic newspaper featured a large picture of Tahra Bey on its front page, under the headline "The Wonder of This Age Is in Egypt." Alongside the usual mix of doctors, lawyers, and journalists, curious Muslim sheikhs turned up to witness him stuff needles into his cheeks and put daggers deep into his flesh on his first major Middle Eastern tour.

After Cairo, he moved to Alexandria and then on to Beirut in early 1928. In Lebanon, he caused even more of a stir than he had in Egypt. His shows were again seen by members of the local elite—businessmen from Aleppo, racehorse owners, and newspaper editors—but they were not always so well received. During one of the performances, one member of the audience fainted and his neighbors caused such a commotion trying to attract the attention of a doctor that the show was forced to stop. Tahra Bey was annoyed that the focus had shifted from his own feats to this insignificant onlooker. Having traveled from Europe, where he made his name extoling the secret wonders of the East, he told the audience in Beirut that their behavior was "emblematic of the mindset of Easterners, who ignore serious things and get hung up on trivialities." They were so offended by this comment, which cast the entire "East" as irrational and frivolous, that they started to protest against the visitor. Some insisted that the show should be canceled immediately, and others threatened to have the whole theater shut down. Eventually, Tahra Bey managed to calm these protests, but only by reminding his audience that he too was an Easterner.[3]

Even people who did not attend his demonstrations found reasons to be angry. The Lebanese religious establishment, especially the church, felt threatened by the commotion that Tahra Bey's arrival in their country had caused. One Catholic journal complained that the so-called "liberated" and "enlightened" new generation in Lebanon had gone so wild for this fakir that they had begun to doubt the wonders of the Bible. The writer recalled young people coming up to him after Tahra Bey's show and challenging him directly. "What do you think about the miracles of Christ, the Prophets and the Saints now?"

they asked, having just seen this modern-day prophet accomplish similar miracles.[4] In the Middle East, Tahra Bey's act was exposing very different fault lines in society than it had done in the West, but in both East and West, he caused a sensation.

In the wake of all this commotion, a new vogue for fakirs swept the Middle East. In 1929, the "Persian" fakir Dr. Saro Bey came to Cairo and demonstrated his ability to disregard physical pain entirely. In one particularly attention-grabbing stunt, he had himself cruci-fied and sent pictures of himself in a Christlike pose to the press—a feat that fakirs in Europe and America had held back from in fear of offending religious sensibilities.[5] In Palestine, the psychical researcher Dr. Antoine Nahas adopted the stage name Tatar Bey and performed his own fakir act throughout the country. On one occasion he claimed to put himself in a trance-like state for several days on end.[6] Fakirs started appearing everywhere, from the theater stages to the side-shows at religious festivals.[7]

The man who took Beirut by storm in the 1940s had first caught the public's attention onstage at the Zion Cinema in Jerusalem in 1929, performing a fakir act under the name Dr. Dahesh Bey, appro-priating the Ottoman title *Bey* just as Tahra Bey had done before him. "He presses his hands on his temples in a special way and suddenly falls into a death-like state and his body becomes completely wooden," one journalist reported. "In this state, his body feels no pain and can endure powerful blows." Dr. Dahesh then proceeded to lie on a bed of nails, pierce his flesh without drawing blood, alter his heart rate, and, of course, ended by sealing himself in a coffin and burying himself alive. When the show was over, he concluded, as Tahra Bey had done, by handing out talismans infused with "a strong magnetic fluid that allow[ed] the bearer to feel things before they happen[ed]." The crowd in Palestine left this performance stunned by what they had seen.[8]

While Dr. Dahesh was far from the only fakir touring the Mid-dle East in the late 1920s, he was different from the others; from his earliest years, things had marked him out as special.[9] From very early in his life, he was surrounded by strange portents of greatness. His followers traded stories of Dr. Dahesh's early life, which, no doubt, gained much in the retelling. He was born in Jerusalem and his birth name was Salim Mousa al-Ashi—the stage name Dr. Dahesh ("Dr. Astonishing" in Arabic) was a later adoption. Depending on which source you read, his birth date was either 1909 or 1912.[10] When he was still just a young baby, an American missionary visited the house and, as soon as he entered the room, made a grand prophecy: "Your child will play an important role in the future. He will bring about great intellectual, social, and religious revolutions."[11] His parents, Shmouna and Mousa, were originally Assyrian Christian from the village of Azakh (now known as İdil) in what is today Southeastern Turkey, near the Syrian border. Before the First World War they converted to Protestantism and left their ancestral lands, spending the early decades of the twentieth century moving across the Levant in search of work, bouncing between Beirut and Jerusalem, where Salim (Dr. Dahesh) was born. During the First World War, Azakh was the scene of a long siege and now-legendary victory for a ragtag group of Assyrian forces holding out against the Ottoman armies. In 1915 to 1916, as Ottoman forces were killing or expelling the Armenians of Eastern Anatolia, they targeted the Assyrian population too. Although the family had left the town behind and did not directly experience any violence during this time, they were still marked by these events. Tahra Bey and Dr. Dahesh were linked by the suffering and genocide in Anatolia during the 1910s.

The al-Ashi family did not stay in Jerusalem very long after Salim's birth. In the mid-1910s, Shmouna and Mousa, along with Salim and his four sisters, established themselves in Beirut. By most accounts, they were living on the edge of poverty, working where they could. Salim's mother, one version claims, washed laundry in hotels, while his father picked up a variety of odd jobs. Some say that he was an employee at the city's famous American Printing Press, others that he was a cemetery guard. Soon enough, Salim gave proof of his strange powers and the great future that awaited him. When he was still a young child in Beirut, Salim developed a high fever, bordering on forty degrees centigrade. The family was so worried that they rushed him to the hospital, but the doctors could do nothing to help. His parents grew increasingly frantic as they saw his fever climb to forty-two degrees and the doctor in charge warned them that the boy was in grave danger. Suddenly, on hearing the commotion around him, the infant Salim, no more than a couple of years old, smiled and gave a quick laugh. He turned to the doctor and spoke in a clear voice: "You, poor doctor, are the one who is sick. I am in perfectly good health, thank God," and proceeded to spontaneously recite verses from the Bible in front of his astonished family.[12]

As he grew into boyhood, Salim's abilities to perform miracles became even more obvious. Once, as he was passing by an exasperated fisherman who had not caught anything the whole day, Salim stopped awhile to help, directing the poor man toward a specific spot in the water where he should cast his net. The fisherman obeyed, and as he pulled his net in, he found it laden with all kinds of fish. Salim was also apparently able to speak any language in the world without prior instruction. Friends in Beirut had once seen him walk up to an Indian man in the street and converse with him in effortless Hindi, even though he had never before shown any evidence that he spoke the language.[13]

Salim's life was completely upended in 1920 when his father, Mousa, died, leaving the family finances in a dire situation.[14] Without a primary breadwinner, his mother could not support all her children and Salim was sent to live in an American orphanage in the town of Ghazir, outside Beirut. The First World War, famine in Syria and Lebanon, and the Armenian-Assyrian genocide had created a generation of destitute children like Salim, many without parental support, in dire need of social services. Christian missionaries of all denominations—from Jesuits to Quakers—set up orphanages across Lebanon. Salim's time in one of these institutions, difficult as it must have been, gave him one of the few experiences of formal school that he would ever have and, academically, he thrived. It was probably here that he learned to read and write in Arabic. He amazed his teachers by solving complex mathematical equations in seconds, not to mention by his uncannily accurate predictions about the precise times that his mother would come to bring him treats.

However, Salim was forced to leave the orphanage after a few months and his academic potential was frustrated. The family moved to Sidon on the Lebanese coast, where he went to school for another brief period until, in the mid-1920s, the itinerant al-Ashis settled in Bethlehem, in Palestine, the country of his birth. Salim spent his teenage years here, with his mother, sisters, and extended family. As he grew up, he experimented with a range of different jobs, bringing in money where he could. Residents of Bethlehem remembered him in several different roles. One recalled him working as a shoeshine boy in a shop run by another Syriac Christian. Another remembered him running a small stall in Bethlehem's central Manger Square that rented and repaired bicycles. Salim's employment did not lift his family out of poverty, and money remained a problem, as demonstrated in 1926 when he was briefly arrested for the nonpayment of debts.[15] It was a hard-knock existence but one that helped form his later character. "I am a child of real life," he used to say, referring to his education on the streets rather than in schools.[16]

Through this financial hardship, he continued to perform miraculous feats in Bethlehem just as he had done in Beirut. At the age of thirteen, his aunt crept into his room late one night to see him conjuring a magical light out of thin air that allowed him to read in the darkness—although his education had been cut short, Salim remained bookish. There were stories that people had seen him walking on water at Solomon's Pools, just outside Bethlehem, stunning the townsfolk who sat nearby. The famous Palestinian writer Jabra Ibrahim Jabra, who had known Salim as a child, recalled in his memoirs that locals in Bethlehem during the 1920s used to call him "Salim the Magician because of the wonderful tricks he performed in evening parties to entertain the elders of the town."[17]

These mystical abilities would soon rescue his family's fortunes. By the end of the decade, Salim was moving toward the big time and was demonstrating his supernatural powers onstage, touring Palestine and the neighboring countries with a new magic act. His earliest documented performance was in November 1927 at al-Nasr Cinema in Amman, Jordan. He was still using his given name, Salim al-Ashi, but his show was otherwise very similar to the one he would soon put on in Jerusalem as Dr. Dahesh Bey. The performance took many elements from Tahra Bey's fakir act: he slept on a bed of nails and hypnotized various animals, then, after an interval, went on to read the thoughts of the audience, and closed one section with a burial alive.[18]

Two years later, he was ready to put on the show closer to home. In 1929 Dr. Dahesh stepped onto the stage of the Zion Cinema to perform his fakir act in Jerusalem. He was starting his career in a country that was facing an unprecedented form of political turmoil. The rise of Dr. Dahesh's mystical persona owed much to Tahra Bey and global fakir fever, but it also came against the backdrop of a very specific set of anxieties and troubles. Since his birth, Palestine had been entirely transformed by a series of events brought about by the First World War and the collapse of the Ottoman Empire. In the early 1920s, the British had taken control of administering Palestine. In line with the 1917 Balfour Declaration, they had been charged by the League of Nations to "secure the establishment of the Jewish national home" in Palestine, though they had no similar obligations to the Palestinian Arabs.[19]

Jewish immigration to Palestine exploded in subsequent years. Between 1919 and 1931, the Jewish population of the country tripled, from around 56,000 people to 175,000. In 1944 the British government estimated that there were around 554,000 Jews living in Palestine[20]—in other words, the Jewish population multiplied tenfold in the space of thirty-five years. The local Arab population, who had been freed from Ottoman control, now found themselves struggling to negotiate between British rule and a growing Zionist movement that showed little will to accommodate them. It was a clear recipe for political strife. As tensions rose between the Jews and Arabs of Palestine, violent incidents became increasingly common.

The year 1929 has been dubbed by one historian "Year Zero of the Arab-Israeli Conflict," the moment when the tensions that had been rising for a number of years would first spiral out of control.[21] This year marked, in some interpretations, the point of no return for Jewish-Arab relations. Just days after Dr. Dahesh finished his first performance at the Zion Cinema, disputes arose about competing rights of Jews and Muslims at the Western Wall of the Temple Mount. In the early twentieth century, the area surrounding the wall was not a large open plaza, as it is today. It was hemmed in by the houses of the predominantly Muslim Maghribi Quarter. The 1920s saw increasingly bold attempts by members of Palestine's Jewish population to assert their religious rights to one of Judaism's most sacred spots. The Western Wall also had a certain, albeit much smaller, religious significance for Muslims. Beyond these religious concerns, this site also took on enormous national significance. For many Jews, it became an emblem of their national rebirth; for Arabs, the increasingly confrontational attempts to assert control over the wall were seen as an encapsulation of a larger project of replacement. The disputes over this one specific place took on much larger significance and tensions boiled in the late 1920s, which eventually turned into era-defining riots.

The spark that ignited everything came in August 1929. A small group of Jewish activists marched to the Western Wall, staking their claim to the area, carrying flags and singing the Zionist anthem, "Hatikvah." They delivered a few speeches and chanted slogans including "The wall is ours," but on that day the protest ended without incident. It was in the subsequent days that these events at the wall took on more symbolic importance. The Ashkenazi chief rabbi of Palestine, Avraham Kook, gave an interview in which he suggested clearing parts of the Maghribi Quarter to allow better access for Jews to the Western Wall. This ominous statement, as well as reports in the press that exaggerated the significance of this small march, provoked fears that Jewish groups were trying to seize control of this contested site. Arab Palestinians held counterprotests and, amid significant British mismanagement, the situation turned bloody. Jewish and Arab communities turned on each other and the violence lasted for over a week. By the end of the disturbances, official figures put the dead at 133 Jews and 116 Arab Palestinians. In one incident now known as the Hebron Massacre, the bloodiest event of the summer, over 60 Jews were killed.[22]

Palestine of the 1920s, with the collapse of the Ottoman Empire, the subsequent British colonial presence, and the political turmoil that it brought, was a place infected with anxiety and fear—perhaps more so than anywhere in the world. A country buffeted by uncertainty and worry like this was an obvious breeding ground for the supernatural. It is no surprise that a miracle worker like Dr. Dahesh rose to fame at this time, as if willed into existence by the chaos. Over the decade before he arrived in Beirut, Dr. Dahesh would navigate the ever-changing and evolving Middle East, in Palestine and in Egypt, creating a mystical persona to fit the modern Arab world and taking the fakir act in radically new directions.

Chapter 10

THE MYSTERIES OF
MAGNETIC SLEEP

WHEN DR. DAHESH STEPPED OUT ONSTAGE TO PERFORM his fakir act he was not dressed in long white robes or a headdress; he wore a Western suit with a white shirt, a bowtie around his neck, and a handkerchief in his pocket. His hair was neatly trimmed, and instead of a beard, he had an elegant moustache. In press photos he wore a medal on his lapel. Dr. Dahesh was crafting his image for the Arab world, where the "mysteries of the East" were considerably less exotic than they were in Europe. He had no tales of fathers handing down the secrets of fakirism to their sons or talk of mysterious psychic unions. This was not unusual. Even Tahra Bey had toned down his Easternness when he came to Cairo in 1927. He did not claim to be a fakir from Tanta; instead, he told people that he had been born in Istanbul and studied modern medicine. When asked about his fakir's robes, he said that he wore them in homage to his great teacher, the Bedouin Sheikh al-Falaki.[1]

In Cairo, Beirut, or Jerusalem the occult came dressed in different clothes than it had worn in Paris. Dr. Dahesh was no traveler from the East. For him, fakirism was a small step on the way to a much bigger goal. He promised people a different kind of marvel: "modernity." Soon after his first show at the Zion Cinema, he started appearing onstage with his sister, Yukabed, who took the stage name Antoinette, alongside him as his hypnotic "medium." Dr. Dahesh embraced hypnotism, a phenomenon that, in the early twentieth-century Middle East, was the mirror image of fakirism.

Dr. Dahesh would demonstrate the wonders of hypnotism to audiences by putting Antoinette into a trance and showing the incredible abilities that she manifested under his hypnotic power. These phenomena were vividly described when the two paid a visit to the offices of the Jaffa-based newspaper *Filastin* in the 1930s. The newspaper, in a glowing article, described how Dr. Dahesh "put his medium into a hypnotic trance, placed a handkerchief over her eyes and had the audience ask her questions which she answered with complete accuracy." The questions posed were not just any questions; they were about things that no ordinary person could know the answer to. During this display, the newspaper's managing editor wrote a message on the back of a pack of cigarettes, which he held in his hands. He then asked the blindfolded Antoinette what he was holding. She answered in perfect detail, "You have a packet of Ottoman cigarettes in your hand, with 15 cigarettes left in it and you have written the name al-Hajj Tahir Qurman on it." Her answer was exactly right. Another member of the group who had gathered in the offices for the display then asked a vaguer question: Would he ever marry and, if so, whom? She confidently told him that he would soon be happily married to a woman from Gaza—a prediction that pleased him. No one there could explain how Antoinette could have known these things.[2]

Dr. Dahesh was not the first person to demonstrate the powers of hypnotism to the people of the Arab world; its history went back many decades to the late nineteenth century, a time of huge intellectual curiosity and development in the Middle East when scholars studied and translated the latest global developments in science and culture. This period, known as the *nahda* in Arabic, was a time of intellectual renaissance. Fueled by a rapid expansion of Arabic-language printing, this was a golden age for novels, plays, political manifestos, and philosophical treatises. Learned journals disseminated the scientific or intellectual developments that were occurring across the world. Soon, whatever happened in Paris, London, New York, and Berlin became common knowledge in the capitals of the Middle East. The possibilities of a new world were opening up before their eyes. "The marvels of science are innumerable, they serve us in everything: in our personal lives and our home lives, in our national awakening, in the class struggle and in the revolutions of all peoples," declared one optimistic writer in the early twentieth century.[3]

Modern hypnotism first entered the Arab world in the late nineteenth century as part of this deluge of knowledge. Since the late 1870s, scientists in Europe had been seriously investigating the medical potentials of the hypnotic state. Hypnosis had a slightly embarrassing history in Europe, having first been popularized in the eighteenth century by the eccentric showman Franz Mesmer, who conducted his experiments dressed in a purple cape and waving a wand. It had developed a reputation closer to magic than science, but in the nineteenth century, a series of French doctors began a new wave of research into the controversial science. Jean-Martin Charcot at the Salpêtrière Hospital in Paris and Doctors Liébeault and Bernheim in Nancy explored the uses of the practice in the treatment of psychological ailments. They appeared to produce good results by putting patients into a hypnotic state.

The work of Charcot and others attracted considerable attention well beyond the borders of France. By the 1880s, hypnotism was being discussed in scientific circles in Britain, Germany, and Italy. In 1885 a young Sigmund Freud spent several months working at Salpêtrière Hospital and returned to Vienna with a fascination about hypnotism. The first Arabic scholars began exploring the European hypnotism boom around the same time, and by the 1890s a small community of hypnotic scholars had formed.[4] They mostly started by translating studies into Arabic—*hypnotism* was rendered in Arabic as "magnetic sleep"—then, by the early years of the twentieth century, they were writing their own treatises on the subject.

The first major Arab proponents of this miraculous new science were medical men. As early as 1902, one doctor who said he was trained in Paris and Istanbul set up a clinic in Cairo advertising free hypnotherapy services for the poor.[5] The chief medical officer of the Cairo governorate, Dr. Mohammed Rushdy, emerged as one of hypnotism's most vocal and enthusiastic cheerleaders. When he was not busy with his day job, monitoring the city's public health and attempting to contain potentially devastating cholera outbreaks, his time was taken up with the study and practice of hypnosis.

After several years of research, reading, and experiments, Rushdy released a book on the subject in 1913, which he entitled *Hypnotism and Its Marvels*. It was a paean to the progress of modernity, of which this science was just one part. In the introduction, he listed the wondrous advances that the world had seen in recent years: trains and boats that could travel huge distances, the discovery of the role of microbes in causing disease, and the creation of the telegraph to send messages across hundreds of miles in the space of seconds. However, as far as he was concerned, "the most wondrous of all these modern discoveries has been the use of hypnotism for the benefit of humanity."[6] Rushdy believed that the technique could be used to cure a range of psychological problems, from cocaine addiction to compulsive masturbation, from constipation to nervous diarrhea. Rushdy even claimed that hypnosis could prevent people from feeling pain and be used as a form of anesthetic during surgery.

Fantastical medical outcomes like this were only the perceptible results of an even stranger underlying phenomenon. Rushdy observed that there was something about what happened to people when they were put into a trance, somewhere between waking and sleeping, that was unlike anything science had ever encountered. It was as if hypnosis could access a hidden level of human consciousness where the ordinary rules of nature no longer applied. Rushdy had read accounts of people knowing things under hypnosis that they had no awareness of when awake; he read about one session in which a man was able to write in Spanish while hypnotized despite not being able to do so when conscious. He had also heard that it was possible to plant ideas into people's heads while hypnotized that they unconsciously took into their ordinary lives. In his book, Rushdy told the story of a Cambridge student who was incorrigibly lazy, incapable of study and dedicated only to dance halls and cabarets. After one session of hypnosis, in which he was told to take his work seriously, his entire personality was altered and he became a diligent and studious young man.

When Rushdy began to experiment by himself, he achieved even more astonishing results. He hypnotized an anonymous young woman in Cairo and began to test what she could do when in a trance. He found that, under hypnosis, she acquired abilities that no conscious person in the world possessed, abilities that were almost supernatural. In one sitting, observed by several doctors, he organized a test of her skill. Once she was in her sleeping state, eyes closed, he handed her a silver cigarette case and instructed her to tell the observers what was inside it. "Cigarettes," she said at first—a pretty reliable guess. Then he asked her to give a little more detail and she obliged: there were six cigarettes in the case and also some money "but not of silver or of gold." Rushdy opened the case to reveal six cigarettes, just as she had said, and a five-pound banknote. In the next sitting she demonstrated even more amazing skills. As a panel of doctors surrounded her, one of them secretly hid something in his hand. Then all the doctors held out their hands in front of them and asked her to identify the hand that concealed something. She quickly picked the correct hand, then, when asked what was inside, she correctly said, "A ring." Next, she held the hand of one of the doctors and he asked her to tell him what he was thinking. Somehow, by osmosis, the hypnotized woman was able to tell the doctor that he was thinking about going on a trip; the doctor confirmed that this was correct.[7]

As hypnotism became more widespread in the 1910s, people began to worry about the extent of its powers. Too much about it was unexplained. Frankly, it seemed weird and potentially dangerous. The control that hypnotists wielded over their subjects was too powerful: there was no telling what they could make people do once they had put them into a trance. There were worries, for instance, that people could be made to sign contracts without even knowing they had done it. Hypnotism seemed to exist on a strange plane between science and magic.

At the beginning of 1913, Mohammed Rushdy was called to lend his expertise to a particularly disturbing trial, which confirmed many of the skeptics' worst fears about this new science. A fifty-six-year-old Syrian doctor practicing in Cairo, Fadlallah Ibrahim, had been charged with hypnotizing a girl who was working as his assistant and then raping her. The girl was fourteen when she was sent to work at the doctor's house in the spring of that year, under the impression that she would be helping him with his patients. But instead, her father alleged, he had put her into a trance, then had sex with her.[8]

The prosecution had a very strong case. Not only had the victim lost her virginity while staying at the doctor's house, something confirmed by medical examination, she had also contracted gonorrhea, a disease that also afflicted the accused—surely more than a coincidence.[9] The doctor needed to mount a robust defense to turn the judges against a fourteen-year-old girl. To help, he had hired one of Cairo's best lawyers, Mohammed Abu Shadi, who, a few years later, would go on to become president of the Egyptian Bar Association. In Egypt, it was a common threat, among those in the know, to say that they would shoot you and then hire Mohammed Abu Shadi to defend them in court—this way they would never be found guilty.[10] If there was anyone who could help this doctor, it was him.

During the trial, Abu Shadi tried to paint the doctor, Ibrahim, in the best possible light. He reminded the court that his client was in an honorable profession and that, in his twenty-two years of practicing, including hypnotism, he had never been accused of anything like this. Continuing in his repetition of the standard litany of defenses in a case like this, Abu Shadi noted that Ibrahim had a wife and that she was very beautiful, giving him no reason to sleep around. Abu Shadi made some counteraccusations of his own too: the girl was a fantasist whose father, a very poor man, had tried and failed to marry her to Ibrahim as a second wife.[11] The doctor claimed that he had innocently been using hypnosis in an unsuccessful attempt to cure the girl of her compulsive lying and delusions, but her father, annoyed that his marriage proposal had not worked, launched a false accusation of rape against him. As for the sticky matter of the gonorrhea, one of the prosecution's big pieces of physical evidence, Abu Shadi insisted that the disease was very prevalent in Egypt—perhaps as many as one in ten people in the country had it. There was no reason to think that she had necessarily contracted it from sex with the doctor. Abu Shadi suggested that she may have acquired it from an infected wound, implying that her family lived in filthy conditions where she could have caught all kinds of diseases. He even told the court that the girl had probably given the doctor's wife gonorrhea after they had shared a menstrual towel that was not cleaned between uses and that the wife might have then passed it on to her husband.

These lurid details, however, were not the center of the case; it was the doctor's hypnotic powers. When he put the girl into a trance, he had complete control over her and, inexplicably, when she was conscious she had no recollection of what had happened to her. This made taking a statement from her rather difficult. The judges discovered that if she was in a hypnotic trance, she was suddenly able to say what had happened to her. So they called on the services of Egypt's leading hypnotism specialist, Dr. Mohammed Rushdy, to demonstrate some of the incredible powers of this science.

Rushdy, in front of the whole court, put the victim into a trance using his own tested method, which had served him well before this. He sat his subject on a soft velvet-covered chair, with himself sitting opposite, touching his knees to hers, staring into her eyes and holding her hands until his reached the same temperature. Rushdy then repeated a series of complex motions—wrapping his arms around her body, holding his hands on top of her head with his fingers locked together, running his hands around her body without ever making physical contact—until her eyes got heavy and she sank into a hypnotic trance. At this point, Rushdy demonstrated that the subject was totally compliant to his will, making her stand up, sit down, raise her arms and lower them. He told the court that, at the end of the trance, he could tell her either to remember what had happened to her or to forget it.

Unlike many European doctors who used hypnotism, Dr. Rushdy

made no attempt to downplay its powers or reassure people that some of the wilder stories about it were exaggerated. In fact, it was quite the opposite. Rushdy was eager to demonstrate some of the more unusual phenomena that could happen while subjects were in a trance. He pressed his watch against the middle of the hypnotized girl's forehead, so there was no way that she could see it, and asked her to tell the time. Somehow, despite not being able to see, she read the hands accurately and announced their position to the court. He then moved the hands to read a different time and pressed it against her stomach; again it was out of her sight and again she could tell where both hands were pointing. Rushdy then proceeded to set up further experiments, sitting people on chairs behind her and getting the girl to say what they were wearing on their heads, for instance. Even Mohammed Abu Shadi seemed interested. Rushdy encouraged him to get involved in the experiment, setting up a trick similar to one that he had experimented with previously. Rushdy instructed Abu Shadi to put something in his hand and close his fist. The hypnotist then told the girl to guess what it was. She immediately said, "A gold ring," and when Abu Shadi opened his hand, she was proved to be right.

After these demonstrations, Rushdy was questioned by the court about the intricacies of hypnosis as a science and the details of the case. He said that he believed the girl's story and confirmed that if the doctor had been able to hypnotize her, he could have made her do anything he wanted, even submit to rape without any memory of it ever happening. This trial was becoming the showcase for a powerful new science. Hundreds of people who had been following it in the newspapers turned up, partly to hear the verdict but also "to hear about the mysteries and wonders of hypnosis that made up such a big part of this case."[12] The prosecution did not hold back in their closing statement. The doctor, they said, "had condemned this poor girl to lose the most precious thing in her life and to be denied her future," and warranted harsh punishment.[13] The defense, despite their best efforts, did not manage to convince anyone of the doctor's innocence; he was found guilty and sentenced to seven years in prison. In the process, hypnosis acquired a dangerous mystique. Who could tell the limits of this new science's capabilities or the potential threats that it posed?

In 1926, the controversial story of hypnotism in the Arab world moved into a new phase. Over a decade after the headline-making trial, a mysterious stranger who called himself Dr. Salomon Bey arrived in Cairo, claiming to be able to accomplish incredible things through the power of this science. What Tahra Bey was to fakirism, Dr. Salomon Bey was to hypnosis—a strange mirror image of a fakir. He was the first Arabic-speaking hypnotist to demonstrate the science in front of large theater audiences. Dr. Salomon said that he had come from Naples and first learned the practice of hypnotism at the age of ten. He boasted of three years spent studying medicine in Brussels, during which time he had performed his hypnotism act in front of the king and queen of Belgium. Accompanied by his medium, Emile, he demonstrated miracles to the people of Cairo. Dr. Salomon could put Emile into a trance and make him perform marvels: while hypnotized and with a blindfold over his eyes, he would reveal the secrets of the future, answer questions whose answers he could not possibly have known without supernatural help, read the minds of the audience and the contents of sealed envelopes.

Dr. Salomon cultivated a distinctly European persona, with sharp Western suits and academic credentials from Belgium. He adopted generalized European affectations, interspersing his conversation with French words. There were those who believed his European-ness was exaggerated or perhaps even invented. He had claimed to be from Naples, but during one court case in Jaffa, brought by Dr. Salomon against a member of the audience who accused him of faking his skills, it was revealed that he was "an Arab from Damascus" and that his medium, Emile, was his brother.[14] One journalist, who believed that he had discovered the truth of his origins, was irritated by his European cosplay: "If I see you again, Salomon the Syrian, why not speak to me in the language of your father and grandfathers," he said, "and wish me a good morning in Arabic? Leave behind all this 'bonjour,' 'bonsoir,' and 'au revoir.'"[15]

Dr. Salomon sitting on top of his medium, Emile.

Despite these attacks, there were good reasons for Dr. Salomon to play up his attachment to Europe and the West; they sold well in the Arab world of the 1920s. Over the course of several decades a powerful cocktail of colonialism and capitalism had brought huge change to the Middle East. Western culture was suddenly everywhere and the politics of the region was dominated by European power or European structures of power. Even those who fought to reject the West's political power could not escape its cultural power. Everywhere, people were reading European novels, watching European plays, eating European foods. Many members of the new generation, coming of age in the 1920s, went wild for anything new that came across the Mediterranean. Opponents of this trend lamented the faddish, often superficial, embrace of the West but they could not hold it back. The narrator in Tawfiq al-Hakim's influential autobiographical novel set in the 1920s, *Sparrow from the East*, lamented this generation's rejection of their own culture. "Today, there is no East," he said. "In its place there is a jungle and in it are monkeys sitting on trees dressed in Western clothes."[16]

Dr. Salomon, combining the fashion for Europe with the marvels of modern science, quickly became a sensation and drew curious audiences across Cairo. In 1926 he even entered the world of high politics when invited to demonstrate his abilities at the headquarters of Egypt's popular Wafd Party, the country's most significant anti-colonial organization led by one of its most revered figures, Saad Zaghloul. The Wafd had been subject to severe political repression over the past few years. In 1924, the British governor general of Sudan, Lee Stack, had been assassinated in Cairo, and the British government blamed Saad Zaghloul and his Wafd Party—if not directly for committing the deed, then for inciting others to take violent action against them. Zaghloul had been forced to resign as prime minister and the party were stripped of power. They were anxiously awaiting an election at the end of May 1926, which they hoped to win.

When Dr. Salomon stepped out before the members of the Wafd, people posed him a succession of political questions, which he dutifully answered with the help of his medium, Emile. They were asked about the fate of two members of the Wafd Party who had been imprisoned on political charges, and Emile said that they would soon be released (he was correct). The group then asked who would form the government after the next election and Emile responded that it would be Saad Zaghloul (he was correct that the Wafd Party won the election but, largely due to British interference, Zaghloul did not become prime minister). After these optimistic predictions, Dr. Salomon performed some more hypnotic marvels, which later became standards of the Arabic hypnotic act. He put a watch into a small wooden box and told the assembled politicians to concentrate very hard on a specific time. When he removed the watch from the box, he revealed that its hands had magically moved to read that very time. Next, he put Emile in a trance and covered his eyes so he could not see, then asked everyone in the crowd to write a message on a piece of paper. Using the power of hypnosis, Emile was able to read what was written on the notes: "Long Live Egypt" and "Long Live Saad."[17]

With a seal of approval from the country's most beloved politician, Dr. Salomon and Emile climbed the ladder of paranormal fame. They kept a set of rooms at the Gloria Hotel on Cairo's Emad al-Din Street, opposite many of the city's best cabarets, where they welcomed visits from anyone wanting to ask questions about their future. The two brothers were soon a regular feature in the newspapers, on the night-life stages of the Middle East, and at the private parties of the elite, amazing audiences with what they dubbed "wonderful deeds that no human mind could imagine."[18] Dr. Salomon shared a stage with the country's most famous nightclub singer and actress, Mounira al-Mahdeyya; the Grand Egyptian Masonic Lodge gave him a gold medal in recognition of his abilities; the police enlisted him as a consultant in their investigations; and before long, people started refer-ring to him as "the Miracle of the Twentieth Century."[19]

Dr. Salomon also traveled across the region, demonstrating the modern marvels of hypnotism to excited audiences in several differ-ent countries. In Beirut, the Interior minister went to see him per-form. When he went to Amman it was reported that Jordan's ruler, the emir Abdullah, personally welcomed him.[20] In 1931, Dr. Salomon traveled to Palestine, where his Jerusalem show attracted all echelons of society. At a time when religious differences were becoming more pronounced, Jews and Arabs both came together to welcome this new star of the Arab world. According to one attendee, writing in the *Pal-estine Bulletin*, there were "Jews in Shtreimels and collarless chalutzim [Zionist pioneers] in shorts" alongside "Arabs in kafias [*sic*] and tar-bushes, men, women, and children." News of the unbelievable show soon spread across the city. "Those who weren't present know all about it, everybody has at least one friend who was there and Jerusalem is talking," wrote the astounded journalist.[21]

Dr. Salomon was popular across different religions and social classes from the highest to the lowest. In Akka, an Orthodox Chris-tian social club invited him to give three performances at the Zahra Cinema, before audiences of local dignitaries and school students. Isaaf al-Nashashibi, the eminent scholar of Arabic language, litera-ture, and culture, invited the young hypnotist and his medium to give a demonstration at a party he was holding in his recently constructed, luxurious Jerusalem villa. Dr. Salomon also took walk-ins from ordinary members of the public, charging twenty-five piastres for his services—about five times the price of an average cinema ticket—and attracting enthusiastic clients. Among the many people who used his supernatural services was the famous Palestinian oud player Wasif Jawhariyyeh's brother Khalil, who paid Dr. Salomon to identify the person who had stolen money and some important documents from his office.[22]

Dr. Salomon and his flurry of hypnotic activity had lit a path for Dr. Dahesh and others to follow. As the 1920s came to a close, many hypnotists appeared—Dr. Hawawini Bey, Dr. Edward al-Uqsuri, Dr. Salam al-Hindi—and all had successful careers of their own, but Dr. Dahesh was the most successful. In the years after his first Jerusalem appearance in 1929, Dr. Dahesh and his medium, Antoinette, developed their hypnotic powers until, in the spring of 1931, they were ready to demonstrate them in Egypt, home of Arabic hypnotism. They moved into the Gloria Hotel, the same hotel where Dr. Salomon had welcomed visitors in the mid-1920s. On March 15, 1931, billed as the "Miracle of the Twentieth Century" just as Dr. Salomon had been a few years before, Dr. Dahesh put on a demonstration of his powers at the Printania Theatre, in the heart of Cairo's entertainment district.[23]

As late as 1931, he was still performing many of the classic elements of a fakir show—piercing his flesh with needles, lying balanced on two swords as someone broke a stone across his chest, burial alive.[24] However, these were the last days of this fakir act. He had come to show the people of Egypt that he was a master of hypnosis. Bringing his sister-medium, Antoinette, onstage and putting her into a trance, he instructed her to read the minds of specific audience members. These mind-reading skills disturbed and amazed the crowd far more than any of the physical feats that Dr. Dahesh displayed in his fakir act. One member of the audience, allegedly worried that Antoinette would be able to read a secret letter that he had stashed in his pocket, begged her to stop the demonstration before she reached him.[25]

Shortly after this stage performance, Dr. Dahesh paid a visit to the offices of a local newspaper. There he demonstrated his mastery of the secrets of hypnosis to a group of important writers, politicians, and religious figures, just as he had done the previous year in the offices of the *Filastin* newspaper in Palestine. He showed this important group of people things they had never seen before. His most impressive feat, a seemingly unique innovation on his part, was his ability to call Antoinette on the telephone while she was back in their hotel and put her into a hypnotic trance. With Antoinette hypnotized on the other end of the line, he passed the telephone receiver among everyone present and, through the power of hypnosis, she was miraculously able to see what was happening in the room. At first, she told the group exactly what Dr. Dahesh was looking at as he was speaking. After that, the telephone was passed to a member of the small audience, and without anyone giving her clues, she was able to name the man holding the receiver. During a lull in the proceedings, someone else started playing with their business card. Dr. Dahesh told them to ask Antoinette what they were holding in their hand, and, through the telephone wire, she was able to read out the name written on the card. Dr. Dahesh and Antoinette were pushing the limits of hypnosis's power. Now, the medium did not even need to be in a room to observe what was going on. They left the editor of the newspaper convinced that hypnosis was a "true science, not a magic trick."[26]

Dr. Dahesh spent a few months in Cairo, where he set up a small business for private hypnotic consultations and quickly gave up any pretensions to being a fakir. He invited the public to visit him at the Gloria Hotel anytime between 10 a.m. and 2 p.m., and promised to reveal the answers to all their questions. "Through the medium of hypnotism," his advertisements declared, "you can learn any secret: business—marriage—love—travel—the verdict in court cases— anything you want to know."[27] If his later stories are to be believed, he proved a big hit among Cairo's chattering classes, counting two of Egypt's biggest film stars among his clients—Bahiga Hafez and Mary Queeny—as well as some well-connected members of the aristocracy.

In the summer of 1931, Dr. Dahesh returned to Jerusalem full of stories of his Cairo adventures and boasting about his list of elite clients, including members of the royal family like the famously wealthy explorer Prince Youssef Kamal.[28] Back in Palestine, he set up offices to take private clients and continue his supernatural calling. His location frequently moved in the early years of this decade—sometimes near the post office, sometimes on Princess Mary Avenue, and other times on Mamilla Street, not far from the Jaffa Gate—but these changes of address did not stop curious Jerusalemites from consulting him and Antoinette. Dr. Dahesh and his sister were willing to use their powers to provide answers to any questions their clients desired, from lost items to travel plans, romantic relationships, upcoming lawsuits, or recurrent illnesses, for a fee.

His clients came from a wide cross section of society, across religious and class divides. On one occasion, for instance, a young Jewish woman called Mazal paid him a visit to ask for predictions about her future (but she could not afford the price and the spirits did not comply). On another day, he received a visit from the Muslim Mohammed Khattab, who had come from a village near Jerusalem looking for his wife's stolen coin-embroidered headdress (*shatweh*), which Dr. Dahesh managed to deliver to him. One visitor was so impressed with the skills on display that he felt pushed to send a letter to the press informing people that he had witnessed Dahesh "perform miracles . . . which baffle the mind and confound any scientific explanation."[29] In the early 1930s, a hypnotic fever descended on the Middle East.

Dr. Dahesh and Antoinette usually worked as a team. One newspaper in Palestine published an article describing a typical visit to his offices in the 1930s. The client, wanting to find out the secrets of their present or future, was taken to a waiting room decorated with "strange pictures" and posters displaying stern warnings to beware of charlatans and quacks—there were a lot of people out there who might want to cheat you. While the visitor was sitting in this waiting room, Dr. Dahesh told them to write down their questions and to hand them to one of his assistants. After a short time, the client would be ushered into the dark "medium's room," which was hung with heavy black curtains and decorated with more images apparently designed to "provoke fear in the soul of the [already anxious] visitor." Completing the morbid scene, on the table sat a real human skull. Once the client had adjusted to their surroundings, Dr. Dahesh hypnotized his medium into a trance—her eyes closed as if she were asleep. Before answering the visitor's questions he would give some demonstrations of the abilities that his hypnotized medium possessed. This usually meant asking the visitor to take something out of their pocket and then asking the medium, whose eyes were closed so she could not see, to say what it was. In her trance, Antoinette could miraculously sense things in a client's hand, from handkerchiefs or cigarettes to pocket watches or pens. The client was usually now suitably impressed and was then allowed to ask the question that they wanted—about their health, love life, financial affairs, or future prospects—and Antoinette would reveal the answer from the secret realm of hypnotic mysteries.[30]

Sometimes, though, Dr. Dahesh eschewed a medium and put himself directly in a trance. One medical doctor paid him a visit in the early 1930s to test out his outlandish claims and asked Dr. Dahesh to read his thoughts. Dr. Dahesh closed his eyes and put his hands on his temples for around a minute. Then he responded, tersely, "You are thinking of an expensive ring that was lost about three months ago." The doctor was stunned; there was no way in the world that Dr. Dahesh could have known about that ring. He had not told anyone. Then, Dr. Dahesh went further. He told the doctor to reach into his pocket, and as he did, his hands felt something that had not been in there before; it was the very same lost ring that he was just thinking about. "I was completely amazed," he said. "How can you explain a miracle like that?"[31]

Chapter 11

THE SPIRITUAL
SCIENCES

THROUGHOUT THE 1920S, PEOPLE STRUGGLED TO UNDER-
stand the marvels of hypnotism demonstrated by Dr. Dahesh, Dr.
Salomon, and their mediums. By the beginning of the 1930s, one
dominant hypothesis emerged that tested the limits of conventional
science. Hypnotism, it was theorized, was an observable manifestation of the power exerted on our world by the spirits of the dead.
Hypnotism was just one part of the larger and even more extraordinary doctrine of Spiritualism—a belief system that had emerged
in mid-nineteenth-century America and spread rapidly throughout the world in the following decades. Modern Spiritualism was a
broad church, encompassing many philosophical and religious traditions, but at its heart were two central beliefs: firstly, that the soul
had an existence independent of the body and survived after it died;
secondly, and more importantly, that in the right circumstances the
souls of the dead were able to communicate with and even influence
the physical world. For much of the late nineteenth century people
tried to prove these assertions, experimenting with different methods
to contact the dead—from séances, in which a medium was possessed
by the souls of the dead, and automatic writing, where the power of
the spirit took a medium's hand and made them write a message, to
more technologically driven methods like spirit photography, where
ghostly apparitions showed up on photographic prints after they had
been developed.

Scholars of the paranormal in the Arab world were convinced that the abilities demonstrated in a hypnotic trance proved both the central assertations of the Spiritualist creed. Firstly, hypnosis demonstrated that the human soul existed independently of the body. When put into a trance, a medium's physical body was unconscious, but somehow they could still perceive things in the outside world, answering questions about the time shown on a clock they could not see or the contents of a sealed box. The only explanation for this was that their disembodied spirit was still, in some way, conscious while their body was asleep, peering into places that their eyes could not see. Their spirit gathered answers to questions that were posed and fed them to the medium's body while they were in this trance state. One Egyptian Spiritualist concluded that hypnotism offered proof that "a human being is not just material but that it has a secret spiritual element separate from its physical body. . . . If it did not have this, then you would not see the kind of amazing spiritual phenomena that happen when a person is in a hypnotic state, with all their physical senses and feelings suspended."[1]

Secondly, according to Dr. Salomon's more radical Spiritualist explanation for his medium's powers, hypnosis proved not only that the human soul survived death but that it was possible for us to communicate with it in the afterlife. He told people who asked him about the secrets of his powers that Emile, while in his hypnotic trance, was making contact with the world of the spirits. As an example, he recounted the story of one of the many visitors to his Cairo hypnotic practice: a young man who had lost a valuable treasure. The man did not give his name, nor did he say what this "treasure" was, but once Emile had been put into his trance, he knew not only the man's name and what he was looking for (a wooden box filled with money that his dead father had left him) but also its precise location (underneath the third window on the right in his house). Once Emile had come out of his trance, they all went to visit the man's house and the treasure was immediately discovered in exactly the place where Emile had said it would be. There was no way that Emile's spirit alone could have known these details. Dr. Salomon rationalized that Emile's spirit must somehow have communicated with other souls in the spirit world, who had given him the information he needed.[2]

As early as 1923, one young scholar of hypnosis had published a how-to guide in Cairo that claimed to be able to teach people to "learn this art without a teacher." Spiritualism featured prominently in the text. Just nineteen pages in, he instructed people in a technique that would allow the spirits of the dead to inhabit the body of a medium in a hypnotic trance. Once the medium was asleep, he told his readers, they should light sweet-smelling incense to attract pleasant spirits, write incantations on the medium's right hand, say a bismillah, and call upon the spirits to appear. If they had done everything right and if both the medium and the spectators were pure of body and soul, then a spirit would inhabit the body of the hypnotized subject.[3]

By the end of the 1920s, hypnotism formed an important wing of a larger and thriving Spiritualist movement in the Middle East. Since the beginning of the twentieth century scholars had been investigating this new science coming from the West. In the popular press and cultural journals, more and more articles appeared, written by a variety of authors explaining and examining concourse with the spirits and giving translations of Spiritualist works written in European languages. Readers wrote in to ask questions about the subject, which were answered in detail. As one journalist wrote at the time, "One hardly flips through a periodical these days without coming across what is called in European languages 'Spiritism' or the science of spirits."[4]

Many different intellectual movements in the Arab world were attracted to the new study of Spiritualism that was making its way into the learned societies of the West. The earliest Arabic pioneers of Spiritualism were not secular scientists, they were devout Muslims who saw this new doctrine as an exciting way to prove the central tenets of their own faith, most notably the survival of the soul after death. Mohammed Farid Wagdy, one of the first scholars in the Arab world to study the doctrine in earnest, made his religious motives very clear. This new science, he believed, could "establish countless tangible proofs for the existence of the soul and the truth of its immortality, establishing which was previously a difficult obstacle lying in the path of religion."[5] Wagdy, who was part of a new movement of Muslim scholars, coming of age at the turn of the century, that wanted to prove not only that Islam was compatible with modernity but that it was the ideal belief system for the modern world. Reforming intellectuals tried to purify Islam from what they saw as the superstition and ignorance of the previous centuries and return it to its pristine early state. Science and logic were two great weapons in their battle to revivify the religion. Scholars like Wagdy studied natural and physical sciences, attempting to show both how modern science confirmed and bolstered many aspects of the Quran and how the discoveries of the past decades could be used to advance the Muslim world.

One of the most vocal proponents of this Islamic-scientific revolution was the Muslim sheikh Tantawi Jawhari. Born in 1862, he had been educated in the late nineteenth century at al-Azhar in Cairo, one of the most respected institutions of Islamic learning in the entire world. His education was unquestionably rigorous, but the style of teaching favored rote memorization above debate or discussion and the syllabus had changed very little over the centuries. Jawhari was stifled in this atmosphere. "The student at al-Azhar has freedom but it is a limited kind of freedom—it is the freedom of a fish in a tank," he later joked.[6] He became increasingly convinced that religious insight would not be found by repeating dry academic texts but by contemplating the glory of the world around him. God had created the heavens and earth and He could be found there too. Jawhari found joy in leaving Cairo for the Egyptian countryside, where he would meditate on the wonders of nature, smelling the flowers and tasting fresh fruits. He had Quranic support for these views; he was fond of pointing out that there were 750 verses of the Quran dedicated to nature and the universe but only 150 about *fiqh* (Islamic jurisprudence). So why were the teachers at al-Azhar neglecting the natural sciences and focusing on *fiqh*?

As Jawhari studied the world around him, he also saw the incredible feats that Western technology had accomplished in recent years. He saw the trains that traveled the length of Egypt, transforming life for millions of people, and he began to study the science that had made them possible. First, he began to teach himself, reading works in English by leading scholars, including John Lubbock, with whom he later unsuccessfully tried to start a correspondence.[7] Then, in his twenties, Jawhari moved to a new institution called Dar al-Ulum— "the house of sciences." It had recently been created in Cairo to take the most promising students from al-Azhar, teach them about the secular topics that they had not learned in their religious education, and send them out to become teachers in Egypt's new state schools. As Jawhari studied science, history, geography, and physics in more depth, everything he had thought for years was confirmed. The books that he was reading, from Darwin's theory of evolution to modern astronomy, "which Europe boasts to us about, were the same things which I had been thinking about in the fields, the same things to which the Quran dedicates 750 verses."[8]

As Wagdy and Jawhari, two of the most prominent Islamic reformers of the early twentieth century, scrutinized the discoveries of modern science further, they soon happened upon the growing field of spiritual sciences. In labs across the world people were conducting elaborate experiments to examine the claims of Spiritualists in controlled settings and test whether they had any basis in science. Mediums were put under observation, hooked up to various machines, and told to demonstrate the unusual things that the spirit world could do. Islamic scholars, reading about these experiments in Cairo, were thrilled to see that modern science was examining one of their most foundational beliefs—the survival of the soul after death. The immortality of the soul was fundamental to Islamic metaphysics so, again, Western science was merely repeating what the Quran had already established many centuries before. Jawhari was not threatened by these scientific studies in the West, but he did feel that they were missing the necessary religious element. In 1919, he published the first major study of Spiritualism to be written in Arabic, *al-Arwah*

(The spirits). In it he argued that, as Muslims whose faith in the after-life was strong, he and his colleagues had "more right to this knowl-edge than Westerners."[9] Jawhari spent much of the 1920s attending séances and conducting his own research into this new science. In 1936, he published a book whose central premise had been revealed to him by the departed soul of the caliph Harun al-Rashid.[10]

Religious faith, however, was not the only reason for people in the Middle East to study Spiritualism. For a generation of secular Arab intellectuals, the new doctrine also spoke to one of the most impor-tant and divisive issues of their age: the apparent divide between East and West. The new generation of the 1920s and 1930s had grown up under the shadow of colonialism and rising Western influence. One of their primary concerns had been to find their place as "Easterners" in a world that was increasingly dominated by the West and a West-ern version of progress. One common response to this solution was to create a simple dichotomy: The West is materialistic, and the East is spiritual. The West has science, and the East has religion.

Many intellectuals from the Arab world started to take pride in their supposed spiritual superiority. In 1933, the historian Ahmed Amin argued that, whereas the West surpassed the East in many things, the East was clearly more developed than the West when it came to belief in a world beyond perception, divine inspiration, and an inclination toward spirituality.[11] The author Tawfiq al-Hakim became particularly well known for his interest in this topic. His novel *Spar-row from the East* is the most detailed exploration of this theme. In it, he recounts the travels of a young Egyptian called Muhsin, a char-acter based on al-Hakim himself, to Paris in the 1920s. In the final chapter, Muhsin meets a dying Russian man who expresses the most uncompromising version of this apparently defining cultural differ-ence. "The West takes pride in its science, its discoveries, its products, and its inventions. But what value do they have compared to the great discoveries of the East? The West has discovered the earth, but the East discovered the heavens," he declares in one of his monologues.[12]

The appearance of modern "spiritual sciences" upset the rigid dividing line that had been constructed between East and West in the 1920s and 1930s. If the West was scientific and the East was spiritual, then who had more rights to the scientific study of the spirit? Was it Eastern or Western? The Spiritualist-hypnotists like Dr. Salomon and Dr. Dahesh, part Eastern and part Western, exploited these ambiguities that made Spiritualism such a topic of fascination in the twentieth-century Arab world. Secular Westernized youth and traditionalist Muslim sheikhs alike eagerly studied this new doctrine.

In Palestine, where Dr. Dahesh was based for most of the 1930s, Spiritualism arrived later than it had in Cairo; it was not until May 1932 that an Arabic Spiritualist circle first appeared in the country, formed in Haifa, on the shores of the Mediterranean. It was the brainchild of wealthy Iraqi polymath Michel Minni, a cosmopolitan man of the world, who had grown up in Baghdad and spent much of his early life traveling. He had studied theology in Rome for ten years and lived in Paris for four years before returning to Baghdad to work in trade. After amassing a sizable fortune in Iraq, he took a job for the Ottoman Bank, moving to Istanbul, then Beirut and, finally, Haifa, where he planned to spend his retirement. Minni had first discovered Spiritualism during his European travels and spent much of his subsequent life studying the doctrine. In the early 1930s, as he passed his final years in the seaside town of Haifa, he decided that it was finally time to set up a group of his own. He made an application to the government and, after several months waiting, was granted permission to form Palestine's first Arabic Spiritualist organization, which he christened Najah—"success."

Minni's unusual retirement project quickly attracted attention in Palestine. In November 1932, a journalist paid a visit to report on this new group's activities. He arrived no doubt expecting a room full of unhinged fanatics, but was pleasantly surprised to find himself in the company of some of the most refined members of the country's rising bourgeoisie—people of "fine manners and respectable station," including a pharmacist, a doctor, several poets, and other writers. Probably the most famous person present was the Syrian poet, politician, and journalist Khayr al-Din al-Zirikli, a long-standing enemy of French imperialism in the Middle East who was living in Palestine while on the run from authorities in Syria. The crowd were exclusively male, but the visiting journalist was struck by the religious diversity of the visitors and the harmony on display at this Spiritualist circle, especially in the context of the inexorably rising tensions in the country. Spiritualism, which did not demand that its followers renounce their previous religious beliefs to join, had always had a reputation as an open and inclusive movement. Minni's circle was no different. "They accepted all religions," the visiting journalist noted. "So, you can see among them Muslims, Christians and Jews. Every member is free to have their own religion since they believe that all faiths go back to one thing, God, and that they all command good deeds and forbid evil. The association's motto is love for all humanity."

This was not an interfaith study session, though. It was an earnest attempt to communicate with the spirits of the dead. Once everyone had gathered, a poem composed for the occasion had been recited, and sweet treats had been circulated, the circle's medium, Louis Minni, went into a trance and tried to bring messages back from the other side. In front of him sat a card with the alphabet printed on it. After a while, his hand began to move, selecting certain letters to spell out words, in a way not very dissimilar to a Ouija board. Slowly sentences formed and great spirits from the past began to communicate: the French leader Napoleon Bonaparte and one of his generals, Michel Ney, the Spiritist Allan Kardec, and the recently deceased Palestinian writer from Haifa, Jamil al-Bahri. The journalist who was present found the experience a little strange but kept an open mind. After all, he reasoned, science had made great progress recently, with telegraph, radio, and other things; it was not so ridiculous to think that it could also help us contact the spirits of the departed.[13]

Among the many people who gathered at Michel Minni's circle was the young Dr. Dahesh, making his name as a man with access to great secrets from the unseen world.[14] His interest in the paranormal, and specifically hypnotism, had drawn Dr. Dahesh into the world of Spiritualism since at least 1930. He had spent several years conducting personal research into the spirit world and, by the end of 1932, he was a vocal advocate of the doctrine. He told people: "I have not neglected a single book that investigates hypnosis, the summoning of spirits or the occult sciences." Some of "the greatest men of the West," he said, had witnessed the truth of Spiritualism, including Arthur Conan Doyle, author of the Sherlock Holmes novels and one of the doctrine's most famous proponents. He explained, as others had before him, that hypnosis opened a door to the spirit world, and he even said that he had used it to summon the soul of his dead father. Dr. Dahesh was invested in the progress that Spiritualism was bringing to the modern world, breaking down one of the most fundamental barriers of humanity—that between life and death. He knew that there were skeptics, but he asked them, "How many inventions and discoveries do we use today which were not trusted when they first appeared?"[15]

Dr. Dahesh also brought a friend and protégé with him to Michel Minni's circle; he was the committed new Spiritualist from Hebron called Abd al-Rahim al-Sharif. This young man was working as a civil servant in the Palestinian courts and had been introduced to Spiritualism by Dr. Dahesh in the summer of 1930. In al-Sharif's own account of events, he had been reading an article about Spiritualism in a newspaper and contemplating the strange wonders of this new science, when Dr. Dahesh walked up to him. This was not the first time al-Sharif had met Dahesh and he knew that the hypnotist was the right person to ask about paranormal matters like this. In response to al-Sharif's questions Dr. Dahesh just smiled, shook his head, and said, a little haughtily, "Do you really want to join our spiritual ranks, brother? . . . Take my advice and concern yourself with something easier."

But al-Sharif refused to be turned off by this attempt to rebuff him and insisted that he wanted to learn the secrets of the occult.

"Is the spirit really eternal?" he asked.

"Yes, and every spirit inhabits a certain level in the spirit world, based on the actions they accomplished before they crossed over," Dr. Dahesh replied.

However, Dr. Dahesh preferred deeds to words and decided that the best way to explain this complex subject was to demonstrate some spiritual phenomena. By this point, a small group had gathered around the two men. Dahesh asked around the audience for a one-pound note, instructing the volunteer to put their signature on it and note down its serial number. Then he ripped it up into tiny pieces, put those pieces in someone's hand, and told them to close it into a fist. A few moments later, he told them to open their fist and they revealed the note had been reassembled as if by magic, bearing the same signature and serial number. When the stunned audience asked Dr. Dahesh how this seemingly impossible feat was done, he replied that it was a clear demonstration of the power of the spirits. To give further proof, he commanded the spirits to remove a nearby picture from the wall (it suddenly flew off its hook and onto the ground) and then to put it back up again (the picture rose through the air and returned to its resting place).

Some people might have taken these undeniably impressive displays as magic tricks but Abd al-Rahim al-Sharif believed in Dr. Dahesh's more grandiose assertion that the phenomena were tangible proofs of the power of the spirit realm. By the end of the day, he was convinced that "people's spirits are eternal and exist in this world, though material things have little control over them. They see us and we do not see them but they are in constant contact with us."[16] Excited to discover more about the powers of the spirit world, he became a devoted student of the psychic sciences and was so assiduous in writing articles on Spiritualism for the Palestinian press that he earned himself the nickname "the Arthur Conan Doyle of the East."[17] For al-Sharif, this new movement coming from the West was not simply a shortcut to impressive party tricks; it was an entire way of life. He made utopian promises about its potentials to his readers; according to his writings, Spiritualism, as well as opening "a line of communication between the Earth and the Sky" and revealing "the secrets of eternity," would bring countless moral benefits. "Spiritualism is the easiest and shortest path to paradise," he said, since it "teaches us what evil is and how to keep it far away from us."

When al-Sharif observed Michel Minni's Spiritualist circle, he was unimpressed. It all seemed so amateurish and he dismissed the whole venture as "having no scientific basis."[18] The young enthusiast for Spiritualism chose to follow Dr. Dahesh and his marvels instead, and together they would spend the next years spreading their message, forming a new quasi-religious brotherhood. Al-Sharif was convinced that the miracles of this new movement had the ability to change the world. As his entreaties reached a crescendo, he declared: "When Spiritualism is universal, righteousness will be universal, woes will be banished, wars will end, hatred will leave humanity, and peace will reign."[19] These two men foresaw a bright future in Palestine.

Chapter 12

JINN, CHARLATANS, AND MIRACLES

WHEREVER YOU WENT IN THE MIDDLE EAST AT THE beginning of the twentieth century, you would have heard about countless examples of old-fashioned miracle workers—Muslim, Christian, or Jewish—surviving into the modern age. In a cave in Syria, outside the town of Saydnaya, lived a mystic known for casting love spells using wax dolls and helping young people woo the objects of their desires. In early 1930s Baghdad, a tall, thin, middle-aged Jewish man claimed that he was the promised Messiah who would put an end to war and usher in an age of global unity. Shut up in one small room, he performed miracles and went for weeks without food or water.[1] In Egypt, the miracle-working Sheikh Salim al-Tahtawi, seemingly able to manipulate the fabric of the universe itself, was a major celebrity. He could make objects magically appear from faraway cities and teleport himself at will, mysteriously disappearing from locked rooms and reappearing calmly walking on a nearby street.[2]

Hypnotist-Spiritualists like Dr. Dahesh and Dr. Salomon claimed that their skills were rooted in modern science—mystical sages performing wondrous deeds were more associated with the traditional practices of the past than with progressive modernity. However, although they would have been unwilling to admit it, they were, in many ways, heirs to this much older tradition of charismatic, miracle-working holy men. In fact, the feats of Dr. Salomon, Dr. Dahesh, and the other hypnotists were particularly indebted to one particular practice in the Middle Eastern occult world: jinn summoning. Since pre-

Islamic times, belief in the existence of mysterious elemental beings called jinn (singular: *jinni*) had been part of Arabic-speaking culture. They are mentioned several times in the Quran, where it is told that King Solomon harnessed their power to create his palace and even included some in his royal court. But the jinn have proved very hard to categorize. They are beings that inhabit our universe but exist on a separate plane from us and have a unique nonhuman essence. The Quran says that humans were created from "sounding clay moulded from black mud" and the jinn were formed from "smokeless fire." Beyond this, much about them is unclear, from the basic (how many exist, how long they live, whether they are good or evil) to the complex (whether they have their own prophets that are different from human prophets, whether they can enter paradise). Throughout the history of Islamic civilization, scholars have debated their precise nature, but few, if any, have denied their existence altogether. Perhaps the closest analogy is angels in the Christian tradition—few dispute that they are canonical parts of Christian faith, but beyond that simple statement, countless interpretations exist.

In Middle Eastern popular culture, the jinn were the subject of constant fascination. Folklore across the region is filled with wondrous stories of jinn, hiding in caves or dark spaces, playing tricks on humans, or shape-shifting into the form of wild animals. Ibn al-Nadim's *Fihrist*, a vast bibliography assembled in tenth-century Baghdad, which attempted to list every book the author could find any information about, mentions many stories of the jinn, which were circulated during Baghdad's golden age, including the publication of poems written by jinn and tales of the love affairs between humans and jinn. Up until the twentieth century, there were reports that Islamic jurists permitted the marriage of a human man to a jinni woman.[3]

Sober, scholarly voices since the Middle Ages have tended to pour cold water on these colorful tales of wonder. The jinn, many have said, are not just invisible tricksters; they are a complex race of creatures that humans cannot easily understand. The historian Ibn Khaldun, for instance, did not give in to flights of fancy. He asserted that the verses about the jinn were among the "allegorical" or "ambiguous" parts of the Quran, which covered subjects like angels, the afterlife, and the nature of God, "the knowledge of which God has reserved to himself."[4]

This confusion and mystery surrounding the nature of the jinn created the perfect breeding ground for entrepreneurs who could claim to have special knowledge of these enigmatic beings. Throughout the Muslim world, professional jinn summoners had long plied their trade, often operating somewhere on the fringes of acceptability. They promised to use the occult powers of the jinn to help people in this world. One of the most comprehensive descriptions of their activities comes in the thirteenth-century CE work *The Book of Charlatans* by the Syrian scholar al-Jawbari. In it, he claims to expose the scams and schemes of all varieties of thirteenth-century tricksters, from false prophets to quack doctors, and he dedicates one lengthy section to jinn summoners, who used a variety of tricks to convince people they were making direct contact with the jinn. Al-Jawbari, a resolute skeptic, described the most common way that these mystics spoke to the jinn: a process called "striking the mandal." This magical practice involved a series of preparations. The summoners lit incense, drew a circle in the sand, produced a reflective surface like a bowl of water or a glass vessel, then prepared to call upon the jinn. What happened next varied considerably depending on who was performing this ritual. Usually, the summoner recited some kind of religious formula or incantation, then waited for a miraculous sign to materialize showing that one of the jinn had arrived—it was common, for example, that the reflective surface used to summon the jinni would shatter. If the summoner was skilfull and had created the right atmosphere of mystery and magic, then the audience would be ready to believe anything they heard. Some jinn summoners used shortcuts to achieve this result, like putting marijuana in the incense, which helped the assembled crowd see visions of armies of jinn marching toward them. Others brought in accomplices, on whom they performed fake exorcisms. These summoners often found credulous marks among the medieval public; al-Jawbari's book warns readers that some even swindled women into sex by pretending to be physical manifestations of the jinn. These jinn summoners remained a popular part of Middle Eastern folk culture long past the medieval period, and the practice of striking the mandal continued well into the twentieth century. One article published in 1926 in an Egyptian journal described the process to its readers in considerable detail, in a way that sounded strikingly close to al-Jawbari's tales of jinn summoners in the thirteenth century. It required a shiny surface, which could be a glass but could also be something as simple as an oiled fingernail, and a "seer," usually a child, whose eyes would be covered with a handkerchief. The sheikh would light incense, dim the lights, and strike the ground with a cane, reciting incantations. The jinn would then appear, endowing the young "seer" with the knowledge they sought.[5]

Even in 1948, a Lebanese psychic researcher, who wrote a book on the occult practices in the Arab world, was still able to personally meet people famous for striking the mandal in Syria, Lebanon, and Egypt. One from near Baalbek, in Lebanon, had told him that he had met with seven kings from the jinn world in a cave and they had told him that the jinn were split into seventy different groups, each of which was further divided into seven thousand tribes. Another, from Saydnaya, in Syria, walked around perfumed with mastic and carrying incantations written on paper decorated with bright colors. A summoner from Cairo had shown him a way to call upon the jinn by hanging talismanic papers from a date palm.[6]

These jinn summoners offered a valuable service, providing answers to important questions that the general public had about their lives. Worried people would consult them about their future, about pressing decisions that they had to make, about illnesses, or about more mundane things, like the location of items that they had lost. There was, of course, no guarantee of the veracity of the answers, but people craved an answer from a higher power even if its reliability was debatable.

Like other occult practices in the Middle East, the practice of jinn summoning was spread across the region's different religious groups.

A visitor to Cairo's Jewish quarter in 1910 described someone trying to find the identity of a thief who had stolen a bank note from a local shop. They used a classic version of striking the mandal to get their answer:

> At last a wizard was sent for, and, in the same room where I was entertained, he practiced his black art. He had a tumbler of water brought to him, into which he emptied a phial of some black mysterious liquid. Then he ordered a little girl of about ten years of age, whom he covered with a large black shawl, to look into the water and tell the audience what she was seeing. After some minutes of tension and suspense, the girl commenced her tale. The shop was revealed before her eyes. She saw the master and all his employees. She saw two boys, one dark and the other blonde. The wizard then ordered the little girl to speak to the boys and interrogate them in regard to the missing bank-note. She did so and elucidated the fact that the boy with the fair hair was the culprit.[7]

In the age of modernization in the early twentieth century, the region's young, bourgeois intellectuals were trying to mold their countries for the new era that was on the horizon. Europeans in the Middle East frequently disparaged its culture as backward and claimed that most of the Arab world was not ready for self-governance. For those in the Middle East who had internalized this negative attitude, practices like jinn summoning or striking the mandal were seen as embarrassing relics of their superstitious past and became the subject of considerable suspicion. This old form of the occult was holding the nation back, stifling the national renaissance that was in progress. In the 1930s, the full force of the modern legal system was turned against these folk practitioners. It is impossible to read the Arabic press of this time without stumbling across court reports about alleged charlatans exploiting naïve victims with the power of the jinn. One of the most infamous trials of the entire interwar period involved an Egyptian gang who swindled a recently widowed woman out of large sums of money by convincing her to marry Shamhurish, one of the kings of the jinn. The press went wild for the story, dubbing it "the Shamhurish case" and filling their pages with accounts of the trial. *Al-Ahram*, Egypt's biggest newspaper, even also published a small pamphlet to accompany their coverage, which anyone following the trial could buy for just two piastres (less than half the price of a bottle of beer in a good cabaret). So many of the elements of the case appealed to the 1930s audience—a pathetic victim, a devious group of scammers, both sexual and supernatural intrigues—that it soon captured the public imagination. It also had the added element of a clash between the modernity of the legal system and the traditional practice of jinn summoning.[8]

Through police reports, witness statements, and cross-examinations, a bizarre and melancholy story emerged. Regina Giuliotti, the victim, was originally from a European-Jewish family and had come to Cairo as a young woman in the late nineteenth century in search of a new life. In many ways, hers was an exemplary tale of success. In 1904, she married Oreste Giuliotti, a successful Italian medicine importer and owner of a small chain of pharmacies in Cairo and Alexandria. In the 1910s and 1920s, she lived a life of wealth and comfort in Cairo. In 1927, Oreste retired and sold his business, planning to pass the last years of his life in travel and relaxation. The first thing he did was plan a trip to his native Italy. Nervous about her husband's trip, Regina decided to consult the jinn to see what they advised. For at least a few years before then, she had been visiting Egyptians who claimed to be able to communicate with jinn. Her first documented experiments in this world occurred when her husband was involved in a court case. Regina, worried about the outcome, had decided to visit a local seamstress, Zeinab al-Najjar, who claimed that she could summon the powerful jinni "Sheikh Ali" to reveal the result of the case in advance. Regina paid the seamstress a small fee and received reassurances that her husband would be victorious. The jinni's prediction proved correct, convincing Regina of the power of the jinn, and she resolved to consult Sheikh Ali on other important matters in her life.

Before this important trip to Italy with her husband, Regina went to Zeinab's house to consult Sheikh Ali. The jinni warned her that danger was lurking in Europe and that she should not, under any circumstances, make the journey. Regina, not wanting to tempt fate, followed the jinni's advice and stayed home as Oreste left Egypt. Some months later, he made it back to Cairo safely, his trip apparently having passed without incident. However, shortly after his return, he started showing signs of illness; then, all of a sudden, he inexplicably lost his sight. Regina believed that Sheikh Ali's prediction was coming to pass and that this calamity was further proof of the jinn's power. In the last years of the 1920s, she was a frequent visitor to Zeinab, bringing gifts for the jinn, in the hope that they might intervene to cure her husband's ailment.

But nothing worked. In spring of 1931 Oreste died and Regina was left alone. She was bereaved, with strong faith in the prophetic abilities of the jinn, and possessed of a considerable fortune bequeathed to her by her husband—that is to say, she was the perfect target for a scam. The jinn summoners saw their chance and a larger business grew around her. The seamstress Zeinab al-Najjar, who had been summoning Sheikh Ali for a small fee, needed to expand her operation. She said that Sheikh Ali had moved from Egypt to Mecca and could not be contacted anymore. She recommended that Regina try to talk to another woman, Nazla Abdullah, who had the power to reach many other jinn (and, it was revealed at the trial, formerly employed Zeinab as a domestic servant). In autumn of 1931, Nazla Abdullah turned up at Regina's door dressed in black, saying that the jinn were mourning the loss of her husband and wanted to speak to her.

Regina let this visitor in and gave her coffee, begging to hear what the jinn had to say. At first, Nazla was reluctant and said that she would have to come back later. Regina was forced to accept this, but insisted that Nazla return the following day to summon the jinn for her. The next day Nazla demonstrated a new method of jinn summoning, which would become very familiar to Regina over the ensuing months. After leading her into a darkened room, Nazla closed the doors and instructed Regina to put on a blindfold. Incense filled the space and Nazla called upon the jinn. Unlike in earlier instances of striking the mandal, when the power of the jinn was materialized but their words were not heard, now the voice of Sheikh Afifi, a new jinni, addressed the assembled company directly. (In the trial, it was alleged that Nazla materialized this voice by some form of ventriloquism, but the prosecution could never prove it.)

This disembodied voice told Regina that she had been possessed by an afrit, or malignant jinni, and that she needed to be exorcised. This was a complex process but she agreed to undergo it, giving Nazla the hefty sum of twenty Egyptian pounds, to buy incense, candles, and other unnamed necessities. Once she had acquired everything required, the ritual could begin. The first night was just a preparation. Nazla wafted incense over Regina, then told her to light a candle and sit beside it until it had burned out. That was all for now. For the next night, Regina was told to dress in white and procure three chickens. Nazla slaughtered the three chickens above the head of the blindfolded Regina, dripping their blood on her to exorcise the spirit of the afrit. After this ceremony, a new visitor appeared. This time it was the voice of a king of the jinn, Abd al-Rahman Shamhurish. He informed Regina that she was no longer possessed, though he warned her that if she told anyone what had happened over the past two nights, she would be burned to death by the power of the jinn.

After this successful ritual, the demands that the jinn put upon Regina kept increasing. Nazla, who was working with two men—her second and third husbands, according to some newspaper reports—seemed to be testing how far she could push Regina. First, the jinn asked for money to go to a religious festival in the Nile Delta, which Regina willingly provided. As things progressed, their demands became stranger. They asked her to install a new elevator in the building in downtown Cairo that her late husband had left her in his will. This seems to have been a simple attempt to make some extra money.

The gang claimed that the elevator would cost 1,000 Egyptian pounds and Regina gave them the whole sum, but they proceeded to do the work for a much lower price, cheerfully pocketing the difference.

In their most ambitious scam—and the one that got the most attention in the press—they convinced Regina to marry Abd al-Rahman Shamhurish. It was a difficult feat to accomplish and they had to move slowly, advancing in small increments. At first, Shamhurish began to replace Sheikh Afifi as the main voice coming from the world of the jinn. Around this time Nazla and her gang were also becoming increasingly involved in Regina's life. They helped her niece Jeanette, who lived in Egypt, marry a pianist named Cesar Hoffberg, removing her from Regina's life. Then they convinced Regina to move into a house together with them, putting her completely under their control. Once they had isolated her, Shamhurish began to make a series of ever more difficult demands. First, he told Regina to fast for Ramadan. Then, he forbade her from meeting any other men because it made him jealous. Seeing her comply with these requests, Shamhurish instructed her to convert to Islam, and she obeyed, taking the name Fatima al-Nabawiyya. Regina was from a Jewish family, had married an Italian-Christian, and was now converting to Islam. Over the course of a few years she had moved chronologically through the three Abrahamic faiths. Once Regina had shown herself to be totally obedient even to the more extravagant demands of the jinn, Shamhurish took the next step. He asked her to marry him.

Regina was taken aback; why would a jinni king want to marry her, an old widow who had been married to someone else for three decades? But Shamhurish insisted that he was serious, and, apparently flattered, Regina accepted. The wedding, held in the Delta city of Tanta, was a lavish affair, attended by all the different kings of the jinn. Regina was blindfolded but she heard the proceedings as they happened. Mohammed, the king of the Ethiopian jinn, and his wife, Negma, were there, as were Regina's old acquaintances Sheikh Ali and Sheikh Afifi. She also heard the voice of her husband-to-be. The next night, dressed from head to toe in white, she signed the marriage contract. The marriage was consummated shortly after. Regina put on her blindfold, filled the room with incense, and lay in bed. The reports gave no further details. "Here we refrain from publishing details of this indecent assault," said one.[9] This was, after all, a rape.

After the wedding, Nazla Abdullah's gang kept the scam going for as long as they could. They convinced the newly wed Regina to sign over her house in a *waqf* (religious endowment) in her new husband's honor—Nazla and her associates would, of course, be the ones to administer the finances. Over the course of two years Regina had given them an estimated 5,000 Egyptian pounds in cash and a house worth 14,000. She had lost so much money that she was forced to borrow almost 1,000 pounds from her nephew and to move into her servant's house in Giza just to survive. The court reports do not reveal the precise moment when the scales fell from her eyes or what made her realize she had been tricked. Her niece had already made a complaint to the police, but when they interviewed Regina, who was in the gang's thrall, she initially denied that she was being exploited. But by the end of 1933, she realized that she was being swindled. In early 1934 legal proceedings began against Nazla and three of her associates, including Zeinab, the woman who had first introduced Regina to Sheikh Ali the jinni.

In 1935, the case came to trial. "There was a charged atmosphere yesterday as the audience gathered for the trial of the Shamhurish case," the first report began. "The strange stories, immoral tragedies, and comic eccentricities of the case have captured everyone's imagination and the courthouse was so full of people that there was hardly room to move."[10]

When police investigated the case, they revealed that Nazla Abdullah's gang had been running a much larger operation and had preyed on other victims. Alongside Regina Giuliotti was an Egyptian couple who had lost their son and turned to the gang for help. Nazla had somehow managed to get her hands on (or forge) two letters from the young man that had been sent from Paris and Switzerland, proving that he was alive. Having given the family false hope, they proceeded to ask for sizable gifts of money for the jinn, which they allegedly spent on nights out in theaters and cabarets, buying expensive bottles of champagne.[11]

After several long days of proceedings, the lawyers for the prosecution summed up their case in extravagant style. "This trial has shown us dark times of the worst kind," they claimed. "Barbarity has been enacted in its most despicable form. In this case, we have seen civilisation committing suicide, humanity killed in its cradle. The accused were like hungry wolves hunting a gentle lamb; they ate richly of her flesh and drank deeply of her blood."[12] The defense had little to offer in return. Rather than prove that they had a genuine ability to summon the jinn, they tried to claim that Regina Giuliotti had concocted the whole story because she regretted giving away the building she owned. But the sheer number of witnesses against them and the strength of their testimony made the protestations appear shallow. Nazla Abdullah was sentenced to five years in prison, though there was not enough evidence to convict her accomplices. As the trial closed, she wept in the dock and kissed her son before being taken away.

This was one of Egypt's most high-profile trials of the mid-1930s, generating newspaper coverage for years—there were even rumors that it was going to be turned into a movie, though it never was.[13] Still, despite the prosecution's assertion that this was a crime like no other, the Shamhurish case was, in actuality, just one in a series of remarkably similar incidents happening at the same time. The press in the 1930s was full of references to different holy men or women allegedly swindling people out of money by claiming to have contact with the jinn. As Nazla Abdullah's trial was being covered in the newspapers, another tale of jinn summoning came to light, this one known as the "al-Sayyid Maymun case." The accused in this instance was the head of an (invented) ancient Sufi sect called the Asaadi Naqshabandi, Khalil Asaad al-Madani, who managed to convince several highly influential people, including a number of former government ministers, that he had the power to summon the jinn. He was eventually brought to trial on charges of swindling his followers and was sentenced to two years and three months' hard labor for his crimes. But, perhaps due to the sentiments of his powerful victims or because there was not the salacious sexual angle, it did not receive as much coverage as the Shamhurish case.[14]

A few years later, police conducted a raid on the house of Mohammed Ibrahim Ahmed, who was well known in his Cairo neighborhood for embodying the spirit of a jinni queen, "Sheikha Zahiyya." He would dress in women's clothes and host people at his house, where he would reveal hidden secrets from the world of the jinn. When police entered, they rounded up a group of thirty-seven women attending an event that he had organized, but he escaped without a trial.[15] Jinn-summoning cases were not limited to Cairo, either. In Damascus a sheikh swindled several different women by claiming that the jinn could reveal to him the location of secret underground treasure. He even convinced one woman that a mouse that she had killed was a jinni in disguise and that the jinn were demanding blood money for their brother, as well as funeral expenses. When he was eventually brought to trial, he was sentenced to a year and a half in prison.[16]

The Spiritualists and hypnotists like Dr. Dahesh and Dr. Salomon who had appeared in the Arab world since the beginning of the twentieth century had an uncomfortable relationship with these jinn summoners. They advertised themselves as the modern products of cutting-edge science, completely anathema to these suspicious, "traditional" practices, which were at best a backward superstition and at worst a dangerous scam. The hypnotists claimed a different heritage, vaunting their qualifications from European institutes and the modern scientific basis of their skills. They separated themselves from the folk practices that were increasingly a target of public and legal scrutiny, protecting themselves with an exotic, modern veneer. There were almost certainly gender and class elements running underneath this. The hypnotists were well-educated, respectable men, whereas many jinn summoners were women from poor backgrounds. In spite of all this, it is hard to ignore the striking similarities between hypnotists and jinn summoners; the former could barely have existed without the latter. The structure of their shows alone closely mirrored the more traditional practices that they eschewed. The way that they hypnotized their mediums, often blindfolding them, and got them to answer questions about the unknown was remarkably similar to descriptions of striking the mandal. There was really just a hair's breadth between Dr. Salomon and the "magician" who visited that Jewish household in Cairo in the early twentieth century to identify a thief. Beyond the mechanics of the shows themselves, it is also clear that people consulted hypnotists like Dr. Dahesh for the same reasons they used jinn summoners—to see into their future, to identify thieves, or to locate lost items. The hypnotists, despite their modern garb and their foreign qualifications, were fulfilling a long-standing need for answers to unknowable questions. By selling themselves as hypnotists, they had found a niche that allowed them to escape some of the attacks directed against jinn summoners. This was modern science, not ancient magic or superstition.

Sometimes it worked. One writer who saw Dr. Salomon in Palestine was convinced that "a young man filled with enthusiasm for the psychic sciences" could not be a swindler.[17] But to their detractors, hypnotists and jinn summoners were hardly different; they were all charlatans. The Arabic word for a charlatan was *dajjal*—"deceiver," "swindler," or "quack"—and it was thrown around extremely frequently in the interwar period. Whether as dashing and villainous characters in popular plays and novels or as the subject of frantic public debates, these dangerous figures were everywhere.[18] One newspaper article in 1934 tried to inform potentially naïve readers about all the different types of *dajjals* they might encounter during their day-to-day lives in Egypt. Not just jinn summoners, who made up the largest group of *dajjals*, but many others besides: Spiritualist healers, astrologers, and more. The author of this article about the dangerous fraudsters operating in the 1930s, unconvinced by the modern veneer of Dr. Salomon and Dr. Dahesh, also took aim at hypnotists—or, as he called them, "those people who add the title Doctor to their names."[19]

Chapter 13

"THE DANDY OF
THE SPIRIT WORLD"

BY THE EARLY 1930S, DR. DAHESH HAD BROUGHT together various paranormal doctrines that were circulating in the Arab world and was in the process of creating a unique mystical persona for this modern age. He had become, by that time, Palestine's most in-demand Spiritualist-hypnotist, working as a private consultant for anyone needing assistance from the spirit world. As the decade continued, Dr. Dahesh kept moving forward, changing himself from a showman into a spiritual leader and creating his own brand of Middle Eastern occult. He was no longer interested just in the new field of psychic sciences but in creating a new world. Through 1933 and 1934 he gathered several "spiritual brothers" around him who swore oaths to serve this mission. One of his earliest followers was that young Spiritualist from Hebron, Abd al-Rahim al-Sharif, who had attended Michel Minni's séances in 1932. The small group also included other illustrious members of Palestine's rising middle class. There was a doctor, the owner of a hotel in Petra, and the son of a recently deceased businessman from Bethlehem's prominent Kattan family. These were thoroughly modern men, drawn in by new promises of the supernatural. By the end of 1934, Dr. Dahesh's small group numbered nine people.[1]

The day-to-day workings of this spiritual brotherhood were opaque to outsiders. The best available sketch comes from a later account by Abd al-Rahim al-Sharif, who described something very close to a commune, or perhaps even a cult. The group, which lived under one roof either in Jerusalem or Bethlehem, were held together by Dr. Dahesh's charismatic leadership and his ability to harness the miraculous powers of the spirit world. All of the disciples in this "brotherhood" were men and they were all asked to take a vow of celibacy.[2] Together, these men pursued spiritual perfection through a series of practices and beliefs that are not entirely clear.

In September 1934, Dr. Dahesh convinced one particularly illustrious "brother" to swear an oath to this small but elite group. This new recruit was Mutlaq Abd al-Khaliq, a poet from Nazareth in his early twenties who, by the time he joined Dr. Dahesh's movement, already held a prominent place in Palestinian cultural life. By the age of twenty-five, he had written a historical opera, set in the time of the caliph Omar Ibn al-Khattab, produced a growing corpus of romantic, mystical, Sufi-inspired poetry that had been published in several well-regarded periodicals, and worked as an editor in many of the country's most important newspapers.

In the mid-1930s the influence of Dr. Dahesh started to show in Abd al-Khaliq's work and his brotherhood's occult concerns appeared more centrally in his poems, as he became increasingly fascinated by the metaphysical. In the year after he joined Dahesh's group, he published a number of spiritual poems in *al-Difaʿ*, a Jaffa-based newspaper with one of the highest circulations in Palestine. He composed an ode in praise of the divinity, who "revealed the world of invisible secrets." In one of his poems from the period, entitled "Talismans," Spiritualist themes about life after death and other worlds began to appear. He mused cryptically on "the riddle of mortal life and the secret of eternity, far out past death."[3]

Dr. Dahesh, as well as being a spiritual leader, was starting to dip his foot into the vast ocean of poetry himself. Even though he had received only around a year of schooling, he began to compose a series of highly wrought poems. His first works appeared in the Palestinian press in the early 1930s. One of his earliest published works appeared in September 1933, when a newspaper printed his verse eulogy of the recently departed Hashemite king, Faisal I, who had died of a heart attack while still in his forties. Dr. Dahesh was distraught at the loss of this young Arab hero who had already achieved so much but whose soul was now "wandering in the world of visions and dreams."[4] The next year he published a short metaphysical ode entitled "On the Deathbed," heavy with eschatological messages about the promise of a future golden age. The verse overlaid optimistic visions of a future where "shepherds play intoxicating, simple tunes on their lyres" with Dr. Dahesh's sadness about his own lost love.[5]

Much of Dr. Dahesh's poetry had a vein of sadness, anger, or bitterness like this running through it, alongside its mystical messages. Although he was still young, Dr. Dahesh had been through many things in his short life—he had lost his father as a young boy, had been forced to travel the Middle East in attempts to avoid a life of poverty, and had worked demeaning jobs to support himself and his family. In his poetic outpouring, the pain and feelings of betrayal behind his onstage persona showed themselves. Dr. Dahesh, it appears from his early writings, was a deeply damaged romantic, who dreamed of casting off the iniquities of our damaged world and finding a pure promised land.

In 1936, Dr. Dahesh and Abd al-Khaliq, the two spiritual brothers with literary ambitions born within a few years of each other, produced their first official collaboration: a book-length work entitled *The Sleep of Death, or In the Embrace of Eternity*. Arabic poetry was notoriously difficult and grammatically complex; Dr. Dahesh may have felt embarrassed about his lack of schooling and untutored knowledge of the form and so asked for the help of a professional poet. For this book, Dahesh prepared the prose text and Abd al-Khaliq versified it for publication. The result was an epic poem—evocative but sometimes confusing and marked by Dr. Dahesh's harsh sensibilities. Insofar as there was a plot, it was a tragic love story, set in Egypt, featuring a central male character clearly inspired by Dr. Dahesh himself, and his idealized lover, Diana. After their passionate affair, which leads to the birth of a baby girl, the young male hero dies in the flush of love. Shortly after, his beloved Diana, overcome by her grief at this loss, commits suicide on his grave.

It was, in part, a story of the eternal power of love. The text was full of impassioned declarations of devotion and lyrical evocations of the metaphysical world in which their love lives forever. It was also an angry lament against the corruption of the physical world and the impossibility of perfection within it. For Dr. Dahesh, to live well it was necessary to transcend humanity; the material world was irrevocably fallen, and the flesh was a prison. The book was filled with Dr. Dahesh's characteristic mix of romantic idealism and his feeling of betrayal in the face of reality. In the closing scenes of the story, the couple's daughter, who has survived them both, appears at their grave begging her parents to come back and take care of her. Her entreaties are left unanswered. The narrator ends by apologizing to his reader: "This was a tragedy that contained only misery, failure, and vengeance."[6]

Dr. Dahesh released *The Sleep of Death* in an initial edition of one thousand in the spring of 1936. It was a curious artifact, unlike any other books released at the time, and Dr. Dahesh had spared little expense putting it together. Its front cover featured a striking reproduction of *Marguerite au Sabbat* by Pascal Dagnan-Bouveret—a painting of a haggard, topless woman clasping a dead baby—with the book's title emblazoned across her chest. The back cover was a picture of him theatrically hypnotizing Antoinette with the words "the secrets of hypnosis" written across it in Arabic. He had hired professional calligraphers to write the text, which was set inside an intricately designed frame on each page, and had commissioned the Italian-Egyptian artist Mario Morelli to produce fifty new drawings for the project. Alongside these, he included several reproductions of Western paintings: sensuous images of frolicking nymphs, bucolic nature scenes, and some well-known masterpieces, including a section of Botticelli's *Venus* and a full reproduction of Waterhouse's *Hylas and the Nymphs* (this latter painting was removed from display at Manchester Art Gallery in 2018 to prompt conversation about its highly sexualized depiction of the young nymphs.)[7]

The Sleep of Death, an aesthetically striking work, stood out on the bookshelves of Palestine. One reviewer enthused that it was "the first book to be published on Eastern presses in such a beautifully and skilfully printed edition."[8] Another said that it was so elegant it looked like "it was made of banknotes."[9] The poem received extensive coverage in the press, bolstering Dr. Dahesh's mystical persona and further reinforcing his image as a holy man. "We know the author as an exceptional hypnotist, and an amazing Spiritualist," wrote one reviewer. "He is a strange young man in every way," he continued, "and his book is also strange, like him, in every way."[10]

Financially, however, *The Sleep of Death* was not a success. It did not sell enough to warrant a second edition, and the costs of the original production of one thousand copies must have been enormous— one reviewer estimated that even if every copy had sold, Dr. Dahesh would still have made a loss.[11] However, as a piece of publicity, it was extremely effective. This charismatic young hypnotist and Spiritualist was now a writer, a philosopher, and a mystical sage. This book was a crucial part of this new persona and he used it on his journey to occult celebrity, mixing in important Palestinian literary and cultural circles. Dahesh gave copies of the book to friends, followers, and influential people. He even sent one to the hypnotist Dr. Salomon, who called it one of the best and most amazing books he had read.[12]

Hisham Sharabi, who in later life was an internationally respected Palestinian academic, vividly remembered meeting Dr. Dahesh one afternoon in the late 1930s. Dahesh had come to Sharabi's grandparents' house in Acre to deliver a copy of *The Sleep of Death*. Although Sharabi was only a young boy at the time, this event remained imprinted on his mind for many years. As any near-teenager might have been, he was struck by the unusual book that Dr. Dahesh had brought, especially the pictures of scantily clad nymphs that appeared on its pages. He was more struck, though, by the visitor himself, his strange aura, "his piercing eyes, and the atmosphere of silence and tension that enveloped him." Entranced by Dr. Dahesh, the young boy reached out to shake his hand and was taken aback to discover that it was cold as ice to touch.[13]

Shortly after the publication of *The Sleep of Death*, as Dr. Dahesh's fame was rising, Palestine descended into violent political turmoil unlike any it had seen before. The year 1936 marked the beginning of what Palestinian Arabs called the "Great Revolt" against both Zionism and British colonialism, which came to define the 1930s. Events had started in April 1936, with an outbreak of Arab-Jewish violence, followed by a general strike that lasted six months, and continued attacks on both Jewish and British targets. The British responded by bringing fresh troops into the country, whose presence eventually managed to bring about a tentative truce in October 1936. The British commissioned a report, headed by Lord Peel, to propose a new future for Palestine.

The commission's findings were published in the summer of 1937 and recommended that Palestine should be divided, with different parts assigned to Arabs and to Jews. The Arab parties rejected the proposal immediately and the country was engulfed by further violence. The British response was swift and forceful. They exiled Palestinian leaders, tried lower-ranking rebels in military courts, interned others in a concentration camp set up in Acre, and imposed a de facto state of martial law. British reprisals against Palestinians were often violent and disproportionate, targeting people who had done nothing at all—after Palestinian attacks on the British, they ransacked villages, burned houses, and killed civilians. At the same time, Palestinian society was turning on itself—rebels attacked their fellow countrymen, and some Palestinians became collaborators with the British. Dr. Dahesh's cynical view of the material world was appearing more and more justified. By the end of the revolt around 5,000 Palestinians were dead—3,800 killed by the British and 1,200 killed by their own side.[14]

Dr. Dahesh himself remained aloof from the grave political developments of the 1930s. However, his most acclaimed disciple, Mutlaq Abd al-Khaliq, vigorously embraced the Palestinian national cause. He became part of what the writer and political activist Ghassan Kanafani later referred to as a "wave of nationalist poets who inflamed the whole of Palestine with revolutionary awareness and agitation."[15] In 1937, the poet had joined forces with Wadi al-Bustani, a veteran lawyer, nationalist activist, and Indologist. Al-Bustani had been active in the Palestinian national movement since the early 1920s and in June of 1936 had published a pamphlet attacking the British mandate, its denial of political rights to Palestinians, and its refusal to recognize them as an independent nation.[16] Around a year into the Revolt, the young poet Abd al-Khaliq had teamed up with al-Bustani to organize a campaign for the release of Palestinian political prisoners held by the British.

In November of that year, Abd al-Khaliq was driving to visit al-Bustani and discuss their next steps. But on the way, his car was hit by a speeding train and the poet died instantly. His funeral the next day in Nazareth was attended by illustrious friends and colleagues. Large numbers came to say their farewells; not only had he been young and talented, taken from the world at the age of just twenty-seven, he was also a martyr of the Palestinian cause. Poets, newspaper editors, and other admirers sent their tributes. His "spiritual brothers" were especially distraught. Abd al-Rahim al-Sharif addressed his departed friend with words of reassurance: "Your pure soul will always flutter above our heads. So, rest easy in your bed, knowing that we will not forget you." Dr. Dahesh, too, wrote an emotional message: "My heart breaks when I remember the nights we spent together," he said. "Your absence has brought me a grief which will not disappear until I depart this life which is so filled with evils and iniquity."[17]

In the final years of the 1930s, Dr. Dahesh also lost another follower in unusual circumstances, which had no connection to political events. Tawfiq al-Asrawi, the hotelier and tour guide of Petra who had embraced Dahesh's spiritual message in 1934, renounced the material world in a dramatic fashion. He gave away all his belongings and went to live as a penniless hermit in Jordan's Wadi Musa, where he died shortly afterward.[18]

However, for Dr. Dahesh, the dramatic political upheaval of the late 1930s in Palestine and the deaths of two of his spiritual brothers were the prelude to the total collapse of his movement, in a series of events that would shake the holy man to his core and force him to leave Palestine forever. In 1937, Dr. Dahesh's youngest spiritual brother, Victor Kattan, and his mother, Farida, went to the police, alleging that Dahesh had been using his supernatural powers to swindle them out of large sums of money. The picture that they painted was not one of a mystical holy man with a grand message for humanity but of an unscrupulous charlatan. Farida Kattan had first met Dr. Dahesh while he was working as a hypnotist for hire in Jerusalem. She was the widow of a Bethlehemite businessman, Youssef Kattan, who had died a few years earlier, leaving her and her children a sizable inheritance. By the early 1930s, Farida Kattan was very wealthy, very vulnerable, and willing to do almost anything to contact her lost husband.

Some years after Youssef Kattan's death, Farida found her way toward the doctrine of Spiritualism. In search of answers, she visited the offices of Dr. Dahesh, where the dead spoke to the living. He organized several séances to receive messages from her husband's spirit, during which worrying details about Youssef's existence in the next world emerged. The bad news was that his soul was confined to an unpleasant part of the spirit world; the good news was that Farida could help by giving Dr. Dahesh money to buy incense, which he would use to placate hostile spirits. According to Farida's later accounts, Dr. Dahesh exploited her loneliness and her credulity for several years. Throughout the 1930s, she ended up spending money on a succession of different supernatural items or services: she bought talismans to protect her from evil spirits; things began to go missing from her house and she paid the spirits for their return. In total, by 1937, Farida had given Dr. Dahesh over 3,000 Palestinian pounds—essentially her entire inheritance and also the equivalent of around ten years' salary at a mid-to-low-ranking desk job.[19]

Farida's teenage son, Victor, followed his mother into Dr. Dahesh's spiritual embrace. The young man, who turned eighteen in 1933, became an enthusiastic student of this new guru and an official member of his spiritual brotherhood. Victor became utterly devoted to Dr. Dahesh, perhaps even more so than his mother. One event stood out as a turning point in his relationship to Dr. Dahesh and the point where he became an integral member of the brotherhood. While Victor was on a business trip in Sudan, he received a disturbing letter informing him that Dr. Dahesh's body had died and that his corpse was lying lifeless in a coffin. Fortunately, the letter continued, Dr. Dahesh's spirit remained alive in the body, but Victor was the only one who could bring him back to life. He immediately rushed back to Palestine to discover that everything he had read in that letter was accurate: Victor found Dr. Dahesh's body lying in a coffin, just as described, surrounded by a worried group of disciples. Victor anxiously followed a set of instructions that he had been given to revive his spiritual leader; he recited incantations over Dr. Dahesh's corpse, and gradually, as "spiritual fluids" entered Dr. Dahesh's body, he miraculously returned to life. The brothers had just witnessed a resurrection, and at that moment, Dr. Dahesh was, in Victor's words, "raised to the ranks of the gods in the eyes of those present."[20]

After Dr. Dahesh's fakir-esque resurrection from a cataleptic state, Victor moved deeper into the brotherhood's embrace. They lived together in a communal house. Victor officially became a member of Dr. Dahesh's legal family when he married Antoinette, Dahesh's sister and medium. However, for Victor Kattan, as for Farida, this spiritual brotherhood did not come for free. Over the course of their association, Victor also handed over a large part of his own 4,000-Palestinian-pound inheritance to Dr. Dahesh. Both mother and son were in the thrall of this miracle-working holy man and paid good money to be close to his miraculous powers.

It would be years before the Kattans came to believe that they were being duped by Dr. Dahesh and it is unclear exactly what caused their revelation—whether there was a single moment of clarity or a slow process of realization. Eventually, in 1937, Victor reported Dr. Dahesh to the police for thousands of pounds' worth of fraud. The police started an investigation into his activities and gathered some compelling evidence. The Kattans handed over a set of handwritten diaries composed by Dr. Dahesh from 1933 to 1935 that chronicled his misdeeds. Dr. Dahesh's other disciples turned against him too. Abd al-Rahim al-Sharif, who had once been his most devoted servant, betrayed Dr. Dahesh to give testimony against him in the legal proceedings.

As the police net tightened, Dr. Dahesh fled Palestine, leaving behind the country of his birth forever. With the defendant absent, no formal legal proceedings could ever get off the ground and Dahesh never faced a formal trial. Instead, both sides took to the press to present their evidence before the unreliable court of mid-twentieth-century public opinion. Their arguments became long, drawn out, and labyrinthine in their complexity, with no impartial judge to rule on their merits. The version of events told in this book up to this point largely comes from accounts given by Farida and Victor Kattan in the press. Full of anger at having been exploited, they sent letters and articles to numerous publications, telling their side of the story.

Victor's mother, Farida, was particularly wounded. In May 1938, she published one emotional and detailed account of her accusations in an article entitled "Ladies, Beware of Charlatans." She called Dr. Dahesh "the worst charlatan this era has known," who preyed on the women of Palestine like a wolf on the prowl. He had a pattern, she claimed: he targeted rich women who had recently suffered tragedies like the loss of husbands or children, then cheated them out of their fortunes. To protect himself, he accumulated *kompromat*—pieces of incriminating information that he could use as blackmail material at a later date: "If he gets a woman in his clutches, he employs every trick he can . . . to make her trust him and give him her secrets, then he leaves her sad and desperate, with no hope of revenge because he continues to hold those secrets over her."[21] To Farida, it was very simple. Dr. Dahesh was a deceitful charlatan, who had made his way through the women of Palestine, taken their money, and left them broken and broke. A few years later she dubbed him "the dandy of the Spirit world."[22]

Naturally, Dr. Dahesh disputed this version of the story. From the safety of Beirut, he took to the press to defend himself. He had hired a lawyer and told people that he was ready to bring cases against the authors of any defamatory articles, as well as any newspapers that published their libelous accusations. He wrote open letters alleging that the Kattan family were spreading "fake news" because they had a vendetta against him. Their lawsuit in Palestine was a simple act of revenge. In Dr. Dahesh's version of events, he had caught Farida having a steamy affair with his associate the Spiritualist Abd al-Rahim al-Sharif. He had been so scandalized by their relationship that he kicked the lovers out of their shared spiritual house and told them never to come back. In revenge, they were trying to smear his name in the press and in the courts. He also categorically denied having stolen any money from the Kattans. In fact, he said, the opposite was true; Victor Kattan owed *him* 2,000 Palestinian pounds, and he sent copies of two promissory notes to the press to prove it.[23]

Dr. Dahesh did not blame Farida Kattan for these attacks on his reputation. He believed that the articles written against him had not come from her; they had been concocted, "circulated by my enemies, hiding behind a woman's name." The man that he blamed was Abd al-Rahim al-Sharif, his former partner in Spiritualism, who had ended up betraying him. The falling-out was extremely acrimonious and Dr. Dahesh would never forgive his former friend. In 1938, he sent a list of accusations against his former partner to a magazine in Egypt. Dr. Dahesh accused al-Sharif of a huge variety of sins: he had stolen a government dossier and burned it, he had lied about being poor in order to get his daughter a free scholarship, he had spied on his fellow Palestinians for the British during the past years of intense political violence, and he had routinely exploited credulous women for his own nefarious ends.[24]

In the decades to follow, Dr. Dahesh never forgot Abd al-Rahim al-Sharif's betrayal, nor did he stop his attacks against him. He labeled him a traitor, a charlatan, a crook, and a thief. In the 1940s and 1950s, Dahesh and his supporters still boiled with rage against his erstwhile companion, abusing him in their publications long after the dust had settled on this feud and long after they had forgotten about the Kattan family themselves. It must have angered them to see al-Sharif rise in prominence throughout his life. After the Kattan affair, al-Sharif went to law school and subsequently progressed through the ranks of the Palestinian legal system to become a judge. After the Arab-Israeli war of 1948, he became an influential figure in the Jordanian-controlled West Bank. In the early 1960s, he was made governor of the city of Nablus and in 1964 he briefly served as minister of the economy in the Jordanian government, his former forays into Dr. Dahesh's mystical philosophies long forgotten.[25]

Back in 1930s Palestine, Dr. Dahesh's protestations of innocence and his accusations of libel did nothing to diffuse the controversies. To his detractors, his absence was evidence of his guilt. One anonymous critic addressed him directly in the press: "An honest, innocent man does not hide in the dark like a venomous insect in its lair," they said, asking, "if you are really blameless, as you claim, why not come back to Jerusalem and defend yourself?"[26] But he never did.

Chapter 14

THE RISE AND FALL
OF DAHESHISM

AT THE END OF THE 1930S, DR. DAHESH LEFT BEHIND the scandals of Palestine and moved to the fashionable port city of Beirut, a few hundred miles to the north. Accompanied by his mother and his sister, Antoinette, he started a new life for himself in Lebanon, where he began demonstrating his incredible paranormal skills to a fresh audience. From his house in the south of Beirut, Dr. Dahesh experimented with new and inexplicable miracles. He was no longer just hypnotizing Antoinette to help people find lost items; he was able to read people's minds, conjure objects from thin air, and communicate with the dead. These wonders, combined with his aura of mystery and personal charisma, soon won him a small but influential coterie of disciples among the country's intellectual elite.

Beirut at the close of the 1930s was a very different city than the one that Dr. Dahesh had left as a child in the early 1920s. Then, it was recovering from war and famine, hosting desperate refugees from a genocide in Anatolia; now, it was a fashionable holiday destination for wealthy travelers from across the Mediterranean and the Arab world. Over the course of the 1930s, Lebanon had made a name for itself as both a tourist destination and a center for international trade. Beirut, nicknamed the Tinted City after the distinctive paint tones used to color its buildings, attracted pleasure seekers with its famous cabarets and cheap champagne.[1] In the mountains of the country's interior, ski resorts appeared, catering to a rising number of winter sports enthusiasts, turning Lebanon into a California on the Mediterranean.

It was against this backdrop that Dr. Dahesh reached the peak of his fame and influence, far exceeding his Jerusalem years. It was here that he preached a new religious message of "Daheshism" and became a twentieth-century prophet. The story of this movement in the early 1940s is full of controversy and competing allegations. The most detailed picture of it can be found in the reminiscences of the poet Halim Dammous, who filled the pages of newspapers and journals across the Arab world with stories of miracles and wonders, meticulously documenting every unexplained phenomenon that Dr. Dahesh produced. From the 1940s onward, Dammous dedicated his entire life to Dr. Dahesh, writing poems about the new holy man and taking on the role of "historian of Daheshism."[2]

Halim Dammous had first encountered Dr. Dahesh in 1936, shortly after the publication of *The Sleep of Death*, Dahesh's debut poetry book. Both men were spending the summer in the hills above Beirut, in the popular holiday destination Souq al-Gharb. Dr. Dahesh, visiting from Palestine, was a regular guest at the Farouq Hotel in town, an intimate establishment with high-ceilinged rooms that boasted views across olive groves to the city of Beirut in the distance. Dammous, almost fifty years old at the time, had careers in business, publishing, and the Ottoman civil service behind him. Best known for his intellectual work and as a familiar face on the Lebanese literary scene, he had published a mix of poems, plays, short stories, and literary criticism—even a dictionary of colloquial Arabic. In 1936, when he came to summer in Souq al-Gharb, Dammous was not quite a household name, but he would have been well known to anyone with an interest in contemporary Arabic literature.[3]

In that summer of 1936, as Dammous walked around the central square in Souq al-Gharb, he heard people discussing the mystical celebrity Dr. Dahesh, who was staying in town. There was a lot of talk that the Spiritualist guru would be putting on some public demonstrations of his miraculous abilities. Dammous, who, like many others, had read accounts in the newspapers about Dr. Dahesh's activities in Jerusalem, worked hard to secure a coveted invitation to one of the evening performances. The details of what transpired that night are unclear. In his later account of the event, Dammous did not mention precisely what miracles Dr. Dahesh demonstrated that summer in the hills above Beirut—it seems likely to have involved hypnotism and Spiritualism. However, he did report that he was utterly stunned by what he had seen. He left the show muttering to himself: "This wonderful, noble man possesses a supernatural, spiritual power."[4] For weeks after the performance, Dammous thought of little else besides the miracles of Dr. Dahesh. At first, he remained cautious about jumping to conclusions. He did not doubt the marvels that he had seen but he was also very well aware of the accusations of charlatanry and fraud that had been leveled against Dr. Dahesh. Dammous did not know whether to believe his senses or his logic. As the months passed, he managed to put his curiosity to one side and continue with his life, though Dr. Dahesh's name never entirely left his mind.

Several years later, on May 12, 1942, Dammous attended a lecture in Beirut organized by a literary society and given by a Youssef al-Hajj, a minor Lebanese poet and former freemason turned ardent anti-freemason, on the subject of Spiritualism and communicating with the dead. Al-Hajj's lecture was dominated by anecdotes of Beirut's newest and most talked-about Spiritualist, Dr. Dahesh, and stories about his abilities to communicate with the dead. Al-Hajj had recently dropped in on Dr. Dahesh's house, he said, to find him in the middle of a séance during which he had made contact with the soul of the Lebanese poet Kahlil Gibran. Gibran, who had died around ten years previously, was considered one of the great Arabic poets of the twentieth century, a leading light in the movement that had brought spiritual romanticism into Arabic verse, and as Dr. Dahesh convened with his soul, he revealed a new work to the audience, entitled "Fog." Al-Hajj read out this posthumous text during his lecture, and Dammous, who was listening intently, found unmistakable echoes of Gibran's style. It seemed genuine.

This lecture reawakened something in Dammous. Two days later, he awoke at 5 a.m., possessed by a strange desire to visit the mystic. As if in a trance, he made his way over to Dr. Dahesh's villa in Musayt-beh, where, surrounded by richly patterned rugs, strange paintings, and taxidermied animals, he had a series of experiences that would change his life. The first phenomenon that Dammous witnessed that morning was also a test of his own pure intentions. Dr. Dahesh entered the Spiritualist trance that often preceded his miracles—he was using Antoinette as a medium less and less at this point—and Dammous stared in curiosity. Then, magically, 2,000 Lebanese lira (around $10,000 in today's money) appeared in the house, conjured from the spirit world. The group of attendees at this séance gazed in amazement at the huge sum that had suddenly appeared among them. Slowly, one of them offered to give Dammous the entire amount. The symbolism was clear; in his moment of induction he was being asked to choose between material and spiritual wealth. After some thought—2,000 lira was a lot of money—he rejected the sum. At that moment, a spirit manifested itself in Dr. Dahesh's body to congratulate him for passing the test.

For the rest of the day, Dammous stayed in the company of Dr. Dahesh and his disciple Youssef al-Hajj, whose lecture he had seen just a few days before. These three men ran errands together in Beirut. They got on a tram to visit the offices of a Lebanese magazine, but soon after they got on, Dr. Dahesh stopped and told them that they should turn back home—the son of the magazine's owner had just died; Dr. Dahesh could sense his spirit as it left his body. The three men stepped off the tram and found a phone to call the magazine's office. The person on the other end of the line told them what Dr. Dahesh already knew: the owner's son had died and he would not be accepting visitors. When they returned to the villa, Dr. Dahesh performed his final miracle of the day—it was one of the classics. He handed Dammous and al-Hajj each a glass of water, and as they took a sip they found that it had been transformed into a very drinkable wine.[5] What Dammous saw on that day left him in no doubt of Dr. Dahesh's powers. "I saw, I touched, I heard, and I believed," he later said. On that day, his soul "awakened from a deep and heavy sleep, emerging to the dawn of a new spiritual age."[6]

Over the next two years, Dammous witnessed Dr. Dahesh perform at least 135 separate marvels for which he could find no explanation. Some appear to a sceptical reader like run-of-the-mill magic tricks, but others were genuinely incredible. Dammous described how Dr. Dahesh had healed the sick; summoned the spirits of the dead, like those of Plato, the classical Arabic poet al-Maari, or the biblical figures Noah and the prophet Elisha; read people's innermost thoughts; and conjured a variety of physical objects from nowhere, including lost books and jewelry. His pet birds would seemingly die and then come back to life at his command. Some of the miraculous phenomena almost defied description. On one occasion, Dr. Dahesh managed to materialize a strange being from another dimension before Dammous's eyes. This was not just an object or even an animal. The creature, which appeared in a haze of smoke, standing before them "with a red face, fiery eyes, fast speech, and a strange appearance," had its own consciousness. Dammous said that at first it spoke in an incomprehensible, alien tongue, but after Dr. Dahesh put his hand over the creature's mouth and drew a sacred sign, it started to speak perfect Arabic: "I am an inhabitant of one of the worlds that cannot be seen by human eyes," it told them. "Many thousands of years ago I was an inhabitant of your world and I endured the thing you call 'death,' which is really just moving from one world to another." The spirit told them that the secrets he had to tell them would take many hours to explain and fill many volumes, but unfortunately he had to depart their world soon. He did tell them one thing, though: that everyone has a material body that inhabits our world and a spiritual body that has its abode in the spiritual world. Before he left, the strange red-faced creature told Dammous about the vast superiority of the spiritual world to the world where he lived.[7]

These examples of Dr. Dahesh's miracles were just the tip of the iceberg. Halim Dammous saw things that he could barely believe.

"From 1942 to 1944 we saw the secrets and wonders of the spirit," he said, "which make the power of the atomic bomb look like a mere candle before a blazing sun."[8]

Dr. Dahesh, however, was not only a miracle worker; he also had aspirations to launch a new spiritual revolution, after the failure of his first Palestinian brotherhood. In the spring of 1942, he started to preach the message of Daheshism, a new doctrine for a new age. It was a belief system in large part based on the charisma of its leader, but with a number of other doctrines included. To outsiders, it appeared to have been stitched together from an array of different traditions—one contemporary observer called it a "mix of Bahaism and Buddhism."[9] To its adherents, it was a world-changing message of enlightenment and coexistence. Any attempt to define what Daheshism was must answer one thorny question: Had Dr. Dahesh just created a whole new religion or was he simply advancing a set of philosophical-spiritual ideas? Was he a new Jesus Christ or just a new Thomas Aquinas?

Daheshism certainly had many of the hallmarks of a religion. Its followers had many of their own unique dogmas and creeds, the majority of which seem to have emerged from the cradle of Spiritualism, hypnotism, and the early twentieth-century occult that gave birth to Dr. Dahesh himself.

Daheshists, for instance, believed in multiple different worlds, in the separation of the soul and the body, and in the power of the spirits. Perhaps their most fundamental metaphysical belief was the existence of things called *sayyals*, or "spiritual fluids," which governed the functioning of the entire universe—from communication between humans and spirits to cell reproduction in the physical world. Different abstract concepts—both good and evil—all had their corresponding sayyals. There was a sayyal for justice and a sayyal for oppression; a sayyal for generosity and a sayyal for stinginess. Every soul had three hundred sayyals, which determined its character. Frustratingly, this crucial concept was also notoriously difficult to grasp. A later Daheshist wrote that "the final spiritual reality of the sayyal defies man's imagination, experience and rationale. It is far beyond our conceptual ability to understand it, or even express it fully in words."[10]

The idea for these "fluids" or sayyals, which formed such a central part of the Daheshist metaphysics, almost certainly had its roots in Dr. Dahesh's days as a hypnotist. The concept closely mirrors the concept of animal magnetism pioneered by the godfather of hypnotism, Franz Mesmer, who argued that all living beings were connected by a mysterious "universal fluid."[11] Arabic studies of hypnosis took up this terminology in the early twentieth century, making frequent references to a "magnetic fluid" (*sayyal maghnatisi*), which was transferred from the hypnotist to his medium during the trance. From as early as 1929 Dr. Dahesh had adopted this terminology, handing out talismans suffused with this "magnetic fluid," which he said gave people the power to sense future events.[12] In the early 1940s, he appeared to be taking this specialist term and reapplying it to the whole of existence. Daheshism also had its own unique set of practices, much like a religion. In the 1940s, Dr. Dahesh continued to produce talismans assiduously, though by this point, they were much more sophisticated than before, carrying prayers and requests to higher powers. These talismans were exchanged among the followers of Daheshism and were believed to have spiritual powers. Copies of several of them survive and they all have a similar form; they are illustrated by a five-pointed star at the center surrounded by a series of cryptic letters. At the top, they have an invocation to God, to the spirits, or to some other entity—two preserved versions include invocations to a guiding spirit known as the Great Raymond.

The identity of this "Great Raymond" has confused outside observers. One researcher in the 1940s, who found two talismans bearing the spirit's name, guessed that it was invented.[13] However, this figure was probably an example of Daheshism's debt to his research into Spiritualism. The Great Raymond seems very likely to have been a reference to British Spiritualist Sir Oliver Lodge's most famous book, *Raymond, or Life and Death*, which describes his attempts to contact his dead son Raymond. Lodge's work had become very popular in

Arabic Spiritualist circles by the early 1930s and the name Raymond would have been known by most enthusiasts of this new philosophy in the Middle East. It is almost impossible that Dr. Dahesh, who had read so much on the subject, would have been unaware of Lodge's work—Halim Dammous certainly knew of it.[14] Perhaps this Raymond who featured on the Daheshist talismans was the name of a spirit guide inspired by Oliver Lodge's book.

Despite all these religious elements, Daheshism very seldom advertised itself as a new religion. For the most part, its followers did not publicly refer to it with the word *religion*, usually opting for the slightly vaguer term *message*. Members were not asked to formally convert and were free to keep practicing their own religions if they wanted. One of the central tenets of Daheshism, and certainly its most easily understandable, was the belief in the fundamental unity of all creeds. Its disciples believed that they could bring an end to bigotry, chauvinism, and sectarianism if they could unite every faith under one banner.

This radical anti-sectarian message helped Dr. Dahesh to flourish in early 1940s Beirut in a way that he never managed in Palestine. In Lebanon, there was a significant audience for any movement that could break down religious barriers. Since the 1920s, when the country was first officially recognized as a separate country from Syria, people had been debating what made it distinct as a nation. One answer that came up again and again was that it was defined, above all, by its religious diversity. Lebanon was the great bastion of the characteristically Ottoman "confessional" system, where Maronite Christians, Greek Orthodox Christians, Armenian Christians, Shia Muslims, Sunni Muslims, Druze, and Jews all lived alongside each other. The 1932 census of Lebanon counted eighteen distinct sects. Any successful Lebanese state would have to manage this diversity very carefully. The country's first constitution, written under the French mandate, stipulated that the parliament should have equal representation of Christians and Muslims and proportional representation among the confessional groups. In 1943, when Lebanon won its independence from France, this slightly vague directive was made more specific in something known as the National Pact. This agreement—informal but faithfully implemented—stipulated that the president should be a Maronite Christian, the prime minister a Sunni Muslim, and the speaker of the house a Shia Muslim. It also established a proportional system in parliament, by which the ratio of Christian to Muslim lawmakers was set at six to five. This agreement was a genuine attempt to give the country's different sects a stake in its future, but it was imperfect in many ways, not least in cementing the importance of religious creed in the political arena above all else.

As politicians struggled to perform this complex religious balancing act, Daheshism preached a simpler solution—bring all religions together into one movement. Dr. Dahesh told his adepts to look outside their own religious traditions for answers; he told Christians and Jews, for instance, that the Quran contained many truths that they should follow. No religious doctrine should be written off by narrow prejudices. Most of Dr. Dahesh's followers in these early days were Christian. In their attempts to prove their commitment to the cause many gave themselves Muslim names. Halim Dammous started calling himself Hassan, after the early Muslim poet Hassan ibn Thabit, who had been a companion of Prophet Mohammed. Some Christians were disturbed to see Dr. Dahesh's Christian followers promoting the teachings of the Quran with such fervor and started to speculate that Dr. Dahesh's new message was, in fact, a covert attempt to convert Christians to Islam.[15]

Opposition like this from established religious communities did little to dent the message of Daheshism, which was offering something completely revolutionary and something very attractive to forward-looking Beirutis. This new message for a new era would avoid the mistakes that religions had made in the past. Daheshism had no priests, did not call anyone an unbeliever, and respected all humanity. One outside observer, commenting on its appeal, noted that "this new religion is different from the others because it does not have their terrible history. . . . Unlike Islam, Christianity, and Judaism, no one who opposed it has been killed."[16] Dr. Dahesh's astonishing feats combined with this unorthodox religious message quickly attracted the attention of the mainstream press. Everyone was talking about this new holy man—either because they had seen him personally or, more commonly, because they had heard about someone who had. Some were confused that so many people were flocking to this strange hypnotist.

In the summer of 1942, Daheshism gained its highest-status adept, the painter and poet Marie Hadad. Halim Dammous may have been a well-known writer, but Marie Hadad came from Lebanese aristocracy. Her father, Antoine Chiha, had founded one of Beirut's most illustrious banks. She was related to people across the highest echelons of Lebanese politics, and her brother, the writer and intellectual Michel Chiha, was instrumental in drafting the Lebanese constitution of 1926 and intimately involved in the creation of Lebanon's entire sectarian system of government. Her sister, Laure, had entered the inner sanctum of Lebanese politics when she married Bishara al-Khouri, a Maronite lawyer and politician educated in Paris who, in 1943, would become the first president of post-independence Lebanon and who was the architect of the National Pact. Al-Khouri, "short in stature but commanding in presence," was considered by many to be Lebanon's "most accomplished politician."[17] Marie Hadad's family tree read like a street map of central Beirut.

Before she met Dr. Dahesh, Hadad had led a life of creative pursuits that was reasonably common among women of her class. She, however, had been more successful than most, winning international acclaim as both a visual artist and a writer. In 1933, she had exhibited her paintings at a solo show in Paris's prestigious Galerie Georges Bernheim. Her canvases—impressionist still lives, intimate Lebanese landscapes, and evocative portraits of Bedouins—were displayed at galleries in Paris, Beirut, London, and New York; one is still in the renowned collection of the Musée d'Orsay. In 1937, with her reputation as a painter cemented, she demonstrated her literary talents when she published *Les Heures Libanaises*, a prose poetry collection featuring nostalgic reminiscences of her childhood. This first foray into literature was well received in the French press. One reviewer observed that Hadad, "having proved herself as a painter," was now showing herself to be "happily gifted as a writer."[18]

Dammous, since his conversion to Daheshism, had been bombarding all the writers he knew with incessant talk about his new guide's spiritual message. Marie Hadad was just one of the people he targeted, and after some initial skepticism, she eventually relented and agreed to visit Dr. Dahesh's house. She arrived together with her husband, George Hadad, to observe some of this new holy man's spiritual powers. Dr. Dahesh, who must have known that these were important visitors, put on an exciting display. After bringing them into his séance room, he told George Hadad to think of anything in his house that he wanted. George, without saying anything out loud, selected a piece of ceramic-ware that lay shut away inside a locked chest in his reception room. As he was thinking about this innocuous item, the exact same piece of ceramic materialized in his hands, as if it had escaped the locked box by magic and traveled all the way to Dr. Dahesh's house in the blink of an eye. This was not a grand miracle, but there was no logical explanation for how Dr. Dahesh had accomplished it. The Hadads left their first meeting with Beirut's most talked-about prophet both confused and amazed.[19]

Over the following weeks, Marie Hadad went back to visit Dr. Dahesh several times to observe his skills even further. She recorded one incident in her journal that had particularly affected her. She had come to Dr. Dahesh's house, part of a group of people who had gathered to witness the displays of his powers. At this séance, one unnamed woman (another recent convert to Daheshism) made an offhand comment about her chastity and purity to everyone present, boasting that she was living a clean life and never conducted inappropriate relationships with young men. As soon as she had finished her proud speech, Dr. Dahesh questioned her claims. She swore to God and all the prophets that she was telling the truth. Dr. Dahesh then told her to look at the ceiling, and as she did a roll of film mysteriously fell to the ground next to her, conjured from the spirit world.

Dr. Dahesh quickly had the film developed in his darkroom, and as the attendees gathered round to examine the results, they saw sixteen images of this supposedly pure young woman naked and in a compromising position with one of those young men whom she claimed to spurn. The woman (who was referred to simply as "B" in the account), when confronted with evidence of her transgression, fell to the ground in shame and pledged to everyone there that she would live a clean, moral life.[20]

Just as the magical appearance of 2,000 lira and the changing of water into wine had first convinced Dammous, this unusual evening of Spiritualist slut-shaming left Marie Hadad with no doubt about Dr. Dahesh's miraculous powers. After this summer she witnessed many more marvels, like the spirits conjuring money into the pocket of an orphanage manager or a tiny bottle of expensive perfume growing to one liter in size. Hadad and her husband soon became two of the most devoted and passionate adherents of this new sage.

Unlike the jinn summoners, whose victims were often desperate, with few other places to turn, Dr. Dahesh's disciples were rich, well educated, and high profile. The involvement of so many prominent people worried skeptical observers, who saw him as a potentially dangerous influence on the country. It was not long before comparisons were made between Dr. Dahesh and the famous holy man Rasputin, whose influence over the tsar and his family in early twentieth-century Russia had been a global scandal.[21] One newspaper concluded that at least a few of Dr. Dahesh's followers, who were well educated and well respected, must be working a scam with him—surely, they could not all really believe these outlandish things.[22]

Marie Hadad's embrace of Daheshism, in particular, was a boon to the movement, but it brought powerful enemies. Her wealthy and politically influential family were worried about her strange new beliefs. A vocal campaign emerged, calling on the government to end Dr. Dahesh's activities, which Hadad suspected was orchestrated by her relatives. As early as September 1942, tongues started to wag about the dangers of Daheshism, and articles appeared in newspapers urging Lebanon to institute an anti-charlatanry law in response.[23] In 1943, the authorities obliged. When the new Lebanese penal code was promulgated, it contained one article that hung threateningly over Dr. Dahesh and his new creed:

> The practice of Spiritualism, hypnotism, divination, chiromancy, cartomancy, and all practices related to the occult are punishable, on first offence, with a fine of five or ten lira. The clothes and instruments used will be confiscated. In the case of reoffence, someone found guilty can be imprisoned for up to six months and fined up to 100 lira. Furthermore, foreigners can be expelled from the country.[24]

In the same year, the police officially began to investigate Dr. Dahesh's activities and brought several of his most devoted followers in for questioning. They tried to find out why this new celebrity had come to Beirut and what he wanted. Perhaps aware of the allegations of stealing money that had been leveled against him in Palestine, the police were particularly interested to know how Dr. Dahesh supported himself in Beirut. The Daheshists all told the police the same thing: Dr. Dahesh had amassed a considerable amount of money performing as a hypnotist in the 1930s and he lived a simple existence, the cost of which he could easily cover through his savings. They were adamant that his Spiritualism and demonstrations of supernatural wonders were done out of selfless love of humanity, not for financial gain.[25]

The police do not seem to have been persuaded by the Daheshists' answers during questioning. They remained suspicious of this strange man and the supernatural control he seemed to hold over Lebanese society. In 1944, they moved against Dr. Dahesh. Later Daheshist sources recount the events in minute detail, describing the arrest as part of a concerted government effort to destroy this nascent religious movement, with force if necessary. The Daheshists believed that this conspiracy reached as high as the president of Lebanon, Marie Hadad's brother-in-law Bishara al-Khouri, and that it constituted "the crime of the twentieth century."[26] On the morning of August 28, 1944, the wheels were set in motion for Dr. Dahesh's demise. He was in a car driving back to his house, in the company of George Hadad and another Daheshist disciple, Joseph Hajjar. As the group pulled up outside the villa and were about to step out of the vehicle, they spotted a conspicuous gang of eight armed men, brandishing weapons and awaiting their arrival. Dahesh and his comrades did not intend to stay around and find out what these intimidating thugs were looking for; they drove straight past without stopping. Once they reached a safe distance, they made straight for the nearest police station to report this suspicious and threatening activity. The officers at the station met their statements with bizarre, dismissive laughter and claimed that it was too early in the morning to do anything about it. This reaction immediately seemed very strange to the Daheshists. The policemen were so contemptuous, in fact, that Dr. Dahesh and his friends concluded that they must have been given orders from high up to ignore them.

Unwilling to go back home, where the gang were still waiting for them, the men went on to the house of the local police commissar, whose address they knew, but found that he, too, was reluctant to do anything to help. Their entreaties grew increasingly frantic and vigorous, followed by threats to bring a lawsuit; finally, the high-ranking officer relented, agreeing to accompany Dr. Dahesh back to his house. When they arrived at the villa, the Daheshists claimed, they saw the police commissar give a subtle wave to the men in the gang, proving their suspicions that these events had been part of a coordinated plot against their leader. However, they had managed to create such a scene that morning and gather such an audience that it was impossible for the gang to do anything to them without several witnesses. They had avoided violence and could breathe easily, for now.

In the immediate aftermath of this incident, which Daheshists claimed was an assassination attempt, Dr. Dahesh faced further dangers. The commissar advised him to go to the police station and give evidence against the suspects who had been waiting outside his house that morning. Dahesh followed the commissar's instructions but soon came to regret it, when he discovered that he had been sent into a trap. Immediately after his arrival at the station, Dahesh was arrested, put in chains, and sent to al-Raml Prison on the outskirts of the city. The controversial mystic was held in prison for thirteen days without charge, languishing in a cell. On the night of September 9, his final night in captivity, the prison warden summoned him and told him that he was free to go. But Dr. Dahesh was suspicious; he could not understand why they would suddenly decide to let him out of prison in the middle of the night. He refused to leave his cell and insisted that he would wait until the morning. The authorities dragged the now-frantic Dr. Dahesh to the warden's office. By this point, Dr. Dahesh was convinced that he was going to be killed and that Marie Hadad's relatives were responsible, especially her brother-in-law Bishara al-Khouri. He had flown too close to the sun, and as he left he told his cellmates that if he died his blood would be on al-Khouri's hands. However, when he reached the warden's office, Dr. Dahesh was not killed. He was told again that he was being released and was informed that, for his own safety, he would be given a police escort back to his house. However, soon after leaving the prison and stepping into the car, he discovered that this had been a lie. The Lebanese authorities were not trying to kill him (at least not anymore), but they did not want him in the country either. A few days earlier, Bishara al-Khouri had signed a decree ordering his exile, claiming that "Dr. Dahesh's presence in Lebanon has caused a disturbance and is threatening public safety."[27] Inside the car that was supposed to have come for his protection, he was violently beaten, then taken to another police station, where he was beaten again. Finally, after a nine-hour drive, during which he was bound and whipped, he was dropped off in Aleppo, over the Syrian-Lebanese border. Dr. Dahesh's enemies had succeeded; the new prophet had been expelled from Lebanon.

The man whose miracles had stunned Beirut and who had started his own radical religious movement found himself bloodied and bruised, at the mercy of the Syrian authorities. Syrian police were at first unsure what to do with Dr. Dahesh. He had not committed any crime so they could not arrest him, but they did not want to let him go free in their country either. After some debates, they decided to take him to the border with Turkey and send him across into potentially hostile territory, washing their hands of the problem. Sending Dr. Dahesh across an international border during wartime—even into a neutral country like Turkey—put him at considerable risk. Shortly after this moment, Dr. Dahesh dropped off the grid, his precise location unknown to all but the inner circle of his followers. For the next few years, he wandered the Middle East, writing and corresponding with his disciples from hiding.

Back in Beirut, Daheshists, shocked by the persecution of their leader, were left in a state of panic and disarray. The government started to investigate Dr. Dahesh's followers alongside the prophet. In January of 1945, the campaign against Daheshism claimed its first life. Marie and George Hadad's daughter, Magda, who was also a fervent Daheshist, locked herself in her bedroom, put a gun against her head, and pulled the trigger. When the family finally managed to get the door open, they found her lifeless body lying on the floor. Her father did not know how to react and declared simply, "This was the will of God." The bereaved parents took their daughter's body to the town of Jounieh, where they held a small ceremony with their fellow Daheshists; newspapers reported that they had adorned her coffin with Daheshist symbols and forbade any Christian priests from saying a final prayer over her body.[28]

People sought explanations for this tragic suicide. Magda's parents blamed their family members, who had launched so many attacks against their faith. Magda, they said, had been determined to take revenge after the exile of her prophet. She plotted ways to kill her uncle, Bishara al-Khouri, whom she blamed just as her parents did. She went as far as to acquire a gun that she could use to shoot him. According to the Daheshist version of events, Dr. Dahesh, in his exile, heard about what was happening and immediately wrote to the young girl to dissuade her from taking this drastic action. He told her that murder was against the principles of Daheshism and that she should not sully herself with a crime as serious as that. Anyway, he told her, al-Khouri would get his comeuppance without her intercession—divine justice would run its course.[29]

The teenage Magda Hadad obeyed Dr. Dahesh's orders, but she remained in a state of extreme psychological anguish over what had happened. She shut herself away in her room and brooded over the impending demise of Daheshism. Caught in a cycle of depression, she could see no way out except suicide, and eventually, Magda turned the gun that had been intended for the president of Lebanon on herself. Her parents were devastated by the loss but also fired up by their belief in Dr. Dahesh and their feeling that they and their movement had suffered a great injustice. After holding the Daheshist funeral, Marie Hadad directed her ire toward her family. She wrote an excoriating letter to her brother, Michel Chiha, venting her anger against the relatives who had betrayed her: "The purest girl in the world has killed herself in protest at your crimes. . . . This dear girl has shown you the greatest example of heroism. And you are the reason for her death."[30] Dahesh's enemies, though, had other explanations for her suicide; they claimed that more sinister things were going on. Michel Chiha himself, according to Marie Hadad, spread rumors that Dr. Dahesh had been having an affair with the young girl and this had been the real reason for her suicide. Apparently, during her autopsy the corpse was even treated to the indignity of a virginity check, something that added another layer of damage to her mother's psyche.[31]

One Palestinian newspaper printed an even more gruesome and far-fetched story, which demonstrated the high levels of sensationalism and fabulation surrounding Dr. Dahesh in the mid-1940s. It reported that Dahesh had been using Magda as a pawn in one of his vicious schemes and that, far from trying to dissuade her from assassinating her uncle, he was the one who convinced her to do it. However, the reckless plan to murder the president was quickly discovered by the police and Dahesh was forced to call it off. In the aftermath, worried that Magda might crack under the pressure of questioning and reveal the details of his plot to the authorities, he persuaded her to commit suicide. He even convinced her that he would use his mystical powers to resurrect her corpse once the heat was off them, and they could continue to live as they had done before. According to this journalist, writing in 1946, the Hadad family continued to believe Dr. Dahesh's story long after Magda's funeral and were still waiting for their prophet to bring their daughter back to life.[32]

In the space of a few short years, Dr. Dahesh had risen to heights he had never seen before. Using his miraculous abilities, he had won followers and caused a sensation in Beirut. His promises of a future without religious persecution or intolerance struck a chord in the multifaith society of 1940s Lebanon. Dr. Dahesh's charisma and his Spiritualist wonders astounded some and terrified others. With success came suspicion and, in the space of a few years, Daheshism had faced growing public hostility, a government crackdown, the exile of its leader, and, finally, the death of one of its youngest members. In early 1945, the movement that had burned so brightly looked as if it was on the edge of extinction.

Chapter 15

BLACK BOOKS AND
THE ARAB RASPUTIN

MOST ACCOUNTS OF THE EVENTS OF THE EARLY 1940S—
the rise of Daheshism, the plots against its prophet, and his exile—are
told from the perspective of Dr. Dahesh and his followers. However,
there were many dissenting voices, too, and since the early 1940s,
occasional articles had appeared in the press denouncing Dr. Dahesh
and his movement. However, in 1945, after Dahesh's exile, the dis-
senters went into overdrive. A group of opponents calling themselves
the Anti-Charlatan Front, committed to discrediting Dr. Dahesh and
his movement, stepped up their campaign against him. This small
but influential association of writers, journalists, and intellectuals led
a war of words against the occult threat that reached the very top of
Lebanese society. They were only seven men, but they were very vocal
and adamant that Dr. Dahesh was not a new prophet, nor did he have
miraculous powers—he was a skilled manipulator who had worked
his way into the elite through scams and trickery.

As the Second World War was coming to a close, the controversies
surrounding Daheshism filled the Beiruti rumor mills. In 1945 alone,
three members of this anti-Dahesh vanguard published book-length
exposés of his group. Two of these works seem to have completely
disappeared, not available in any library catalogues nor for sale in any
bookshops: *The Truth about Dr. Dahesh* by the Spiritualist and magician Mounir Wuhayba and *Who Is Dr. Dahesh* by police chief Colonel
Elias al-Mudawwar. The final and most influential of them, which
survives in only a few copies, is *The Devil's Deputy, or The Great Char-*

latan: Dahesh by the Iraqi journalist Youssef Malik. This 268-page compendium of charges against Dr. Dahesh is unlike the other two; it was written by a disillusioned former supporter of the Daheshist movement who had an intimate knowledge of its workings.

Malik, a writer and newspaper editor based in Beirut, had first met Dr. Dahesh in the summer of 1942, after being persuaded by weeks of pleading from Halim Dammous. At this point, Dr. Dahesh was still a new curiosity on Beirut's cultural scene and Malik was intrigued by the apparently inexplicable feats that he demonstrated. Over the next year, he attended many séances in Dr. Dahesh's house and saw some impressive phenomena. At one, Dr. Dahesh, while in a trance, manifested 200 Lebanese lira from the spirit world, which at this point was one of his reliable staples. Soon afterward, he did something more impressive. Pointing to a specific spot on one of his bookshelves, he instructed a follower to bring a book down. As the dutiful Daheshist took a volume off the shelf and showed it to the crowd, Malik noticed that it was his own copy of the Bible, which he had last seen sitting in his own house. During another séance, Dr. Dahesh again impressed Malik. He handed over a blank piece of paper that he instructed Malik to fold up and hold tightly in his fist so no one could tamper with it. After a few minutes, he told Malik to unfold the paper. When he did, it was no longer blank but magically contained a personal note written by Dr. Dahesh.

Youssef Malik was on track to becoming an enthusiastic Daheshist by 1943. He even began to work on English translations of several works written by Dr. Dahesh, who had not given up his literary ambitions even as he was preaching his new religious message. In the early years of the 1940s, he published a poetic reworking of the Song of Songs as well as a new take on Dante's *Inferno*, his 1944 epic *Jahim* (Hell). Malik set to work on the latter text, which he said was "the most difficult and most enjoyable book" that he had ever translated into English. During the process, he came to admire Dr. Dahesh's writing. "I have not found anyone writing in Arabic who could describe the lower reaches of Hell in such a wide-ranging, long-lasting, awe-inspiring way," Malik commented.[1]

Soon, though, Malik started to ask some uncomfortable questions. He was confused why Dr. Dahesh needed his translation services at all, when it was well known that he could use the power of the spirits to translate one language into another. As he thought about it more, he started to pick holes in Dr. Dahesh's Spiritualist phenomena. The feats that had impressed him at first could be explained away as magic tricks. The note from Dahesh that had appeared on the folded piece of paper was accomplished by invisible ink, which appeared when heated by his tight grip. The Bible that had appeared at the séance had not manifested by a miracle. He remembered that Dammous and Dahesh had visited his house a few days before and must have taken the opportunity to purloin it from his bookshelf.

Malik came to the conclusion that Dr. Dahesh was not a miracle-working holy man but a dangerous con artist. He began work on his long denunciation, *The Devil's Deputy*, which gathered together as many allegations against Dr. Dahesh as he could find, from the salacious to the humdrum. Malik interviewed a huge number of people, from Dahesh's alleged victims and his hardened enemies to those who appear to have been just casual acquaintances. He talked to the wives and family of Daheshists—anyone who could provide any incriminating information about Dr. Dahesh. He even tracked down Abd al-Rahim al-Sharif and the Kattan family, who gave an in-depth account of the scandal in Palestine, providing several original documents to back up their assertions.

In amassing as many different crumbs of evidence as he could, omitting no potentially damaging detail, Malik produced a bloated and incredibly complicated book. The experience of reading *Devil's Deputy* is, very often, one of confusion. There was little attention to chronological or thematic order, as everything that could be used to discredit Dr. Dahesh was inserted, seemingly at random. Copies of Daheshist talismans and the words of Daheshist prayers sit alongside anti-Daheshist poems written by his detractors and long accounts of his scams. One more unusual exhibit is a short note in which Dr. Dahesh apparently admitted to masturbating while thinking of the good-looking sister of one of his friends. Even though the handwriting was unclear, spread strangely across the paper, Malik considered it an incontrovertible accusation.[2]

Malik believed that this book would stand as a damning indictment of Dr. Dahesh and his followers. In his introduction, he laid down a challenge to any who disagreed: "I have put this book before the people. . . . I have no weapons—not even a stick—my address is well known to these cowards and I am ready to meet them, one-on-one or in a group, in any place of their choosing, so that they know the power that I derive from my faith in God to confront the tricks of their 'prophet.'"[3] Sifting through these different charges reveals some very disturbing accusations and evidence of deep research. Dense as it might have been, this book contained many things that were hard to deny.

One consistent accusation across almost all of the anti-Dahesh literature of the 1940s was the charge of sexual impropriety. Dr. Dahesh had been dogged by these insinuations for many years. There were constant rumors that his 1931 trip to Egypt had ended in a scandal of a sexual nature. The introduction to a recently published reprint of *The Sleep of Death* has suggested that he was expelled from the country for conducting an illicit affair with a woman in the royal court, after being invited to give a hypnotic demonstration in the palace.[4] Malik, aware of the rumors that swirled around, attempted to collect as many stories as he could about sordid events happening at Dr. Dahesh's house. There was a "holy room" in the villa that only believers could enter, and which was used to hold Spiritualist séances. Malik claimed that this also doubled as a space where Daheshists could bring women to "satisfy their worldly desires."[5] On one occasion, he recounted, the young son of a prominent Daheshist believer walked into this holy room to find Halim Dammous sitting beside a woman whose dress was pulled over her head. Malik also included troubling reports that this activity was not always consensual; one woman said that Dr. Dahesh took her into his holy room, then attempted to grab her and kiss her, until she fled his advances.[6] Even after he had released this book, Malik continued to publish accusations against Dr. Dahesh. In 1946, he claimed to have come across a small note in Dr. Dahesh's hand that talked about having sex with one of his devotees: "The poor girl thinks I love her, but I only love her body," Dahesh allegedly confessed in this mysterious document.[7]

Malik was not the only person to repeat stories like these. One newspaper in Palestine produced a report on Dr. Dahesh entitled "The Arab Rasputin," which claimed he often used these sexual encounters to get material for blackmail. According to this article, "he lured people into scandalous positions, then took photos and threatened to publish them or to show them to members of their family. Or he would lure them into writing [compromising] letters which he could also keep to threaten them with later."[8] If true, this gives a very different perspective on Marie Hadad's story of Dr. Dahesh exposing the lies of a supposedly pure and virginal young woman in the summer of 1942. By the mid-1940s, accusations of this nature were so prevalent that they appeared in a short article in *Time* magazine, which recalled that when Dr. Dahesh was "at the top of his vogue, in 1944, the souks (bazaars) of Beirut peddled many a rumor of orgies in his modern villa in the Mazraa section of the city."[9]

Daheshists could, of course, dismiss these stories as sordid rumor-mongering—exactly the kind of thing that gets said about any spiritual group that might challenge the status quo. Yet Dr. Dahesh's own writings sometimes betrayed an uncomfortably lax attitude toward sexual relationships. In his book *The Memoirs of Jesus of Nazareth*, written in the early 1940s, which claimed to relate a previously unknown narrative from Jesus Christ's early life, he appeared to endorse the right of religious prophets to have sex with many different women. Twice in the course of this noncanonical tale, Dr. Dahesh's text asserted that prophets who had sex outside of marriage were not deemed by God to have sinned. King David slept with Batsheba, wife of Uriah, but was judged to have lived a pure life; King Solomon kept a harem of many hundreds of concubines and was not criticized for it. Quite the opposite: "The concubines who filled the palaces of King Solomon greatly benefitted spiritually by their presence alongside this wise prophet."[10] It is not hard to see how this endorsement of prophetic promiscuity could lead to exactly the kind of things described in Youssef Malik's book and elsewhere.

The Anti-Charlatan Front could not stay silent in the face of this injustice. Dr. Dahesh was using tricks and lies to exploit his followers. Most believed that he was a simple con man, using magic tricks that he had learned over several years to confound Beirutis and take their money. However, another explanation, hinted at in the title of Youssef Malik's book, hung worryingly in the background. Perhaps these miracles were not magic tricks. Perhaps they were genuine products of a more dangerous spiritual world. This man who had described the inner depths of Hell so accurately might have come up from its depths to visit an infernal punishment on the credulous people of Lebanon. If Dr. Dahesh was not a con artist, could he be a devil? The Anti-Charlatan Front were not taking any chances.

The Daheshists responded fiercely to these campaigns against them. Marie Hadad swiftly took up her pen to defend their spiritual leader. Returning fire in kind, she attacked Dr. Dahesh's enemies in a series of pamphlets, which included four books of "documents" claiming to expose the lies and treachery that had led to his downfall. The first dealt with the beginnings of Bishara al-Khouri's plot against Dahesh in the days before he ascended to the presidency; the second covered al-Khouri's time in power; the third described the events leading up to Dr. Dahesh's arrest and its aftermath; the fourth and final book of documents told the story of Dr. Dahesh's life in exile.

The preeminent work that she produced during this crisis period was her "black book," *J'Accuse*. Taking its name from Emile Zola's famous open letter about the arrest of the Jewish military officer Alfred Dreyfus in the late nineteenth century, it immediately cast Dr. Dahesh as a man persecuted and discriminated against for his religious identity.

This moment was a test for the newly independent Lebanese Republic's ability to handle controversial debates about freedom of belief and freedom of expression. In the case of Dr. Dahesh, it seemed to be failing. As soon as an unorthodox religious figure emerged, he was violently exiled and very nearly killed. If independence did not bring more freedom, what was the point of it?

Hadad's text went on to level a series of charges against specific Lebanese politicians, policemen, and public figures. Above all, she singled out that great enemy of Daheshism, Bishara al-Khouri, whom she called "a savage wolf dressed in the clothes of a suckling lamb."[11] She turned this into a political matter as well as a religious one. In his fevered campaign against Dr. Dahesh, Hadad said, al-Khouri had revealed the true nature of his rule. He had abused the rights of Dr. Dahesh's followers, illegitimately used his political power to meddle in the legal system, and violated the constitution by exiling a Lebanese citizen. (Dr. Dahesh's supporters were insistent that, despite not being born in Lebanon, Dr. Dahesh had Lebanese citizenship thanks to his residency in the country during the breakup of the Ottoman Empire. Whether this is true is not exactly clear.)

J'Accuse also aired a string of potentially damaging accusations against other members of Bishara al-Khouri's family: She accused his son Khalil of using a government train to smuggle hashish into Egypt and his brother Fouad of using dodgy government ties to make millions in the cement business. She attacked government ministers for taking cuts from the proceeds of illegal gambling houses and skimming off profits from smuggling operations.[12]

For the Daheshists, 1945 to 1946 was their moment of truth, the last chance to save their prophet's mission. They had to show the world that their spiritual mission was genuine, or else it would all have been for nothing. This led to some rather frantic behavior. Some were so fervent in their defense of their leader that they ran into their own trouble with the authorities. Halim Dammous briefly spent time in prison for his activities. In July 1945, Marie Hadad was confined to a mental asylum for several months, where she claimed to have been confined to one large room with thirty other inmates. Daheshists insisted that Hadad's confinement was another way for the government to persecute them. This apparent mental health measure was just imprisonment by another name. There is good evidence to back up these claims; in the remarks sections of her intake records at the asylum there are only two words written: "Not Insane."[13]

Many neutral observers were left confused in the face of the violent denunciations, insults, and accusations of bad faith that dominated the debate on both sides. One Egyptian journal, in its review of Youssef Malik's *The Devil's Deputy*, threw up its hands and admitted that it could not find any independent method to weigh up the claims of either party; one said that Dahesh was a new prophet, the other that he was the criminal of the century. "The supporters [of Daheshism] seem insane in their exaggerations, while its opponents seem like extremists in theirs."[14]

This did nothing to make the Daheshists temper their campaigns. Instead, they increased their propaganda for the new creed outside Lebanon and across the Middle East. Marie and George Hadad reminded people that unity of religions, which formed the basis of their movement, could create a wonderful new world, free from the sectarian clashes of the past. They had personally sent a telegram to the pope, officially leaving the Catholic church because they believed that it had played a hand in the attacks on Dr. Dahesh. Organized religions, as far as they were concerned, were hotbeds of bigotry and division. "One of the goals of Daheshism," the couple explained, "is to destroy religious extremism in the hearts of all. . . . We are ready to use our money and our souls to redeem the founder of the Daheshist creed."[15]

However, it was Dammous, the poet, not the Hadads nor even Dr. Dahesh, who was the most prominent face of Daheshism in the mid-1940s. The Saint Paul to Dr. Dahesh's Jesus, the Nathan of Gaza to Dr. Dahesh's Sabbatai Zevi, Dammous became, according to one old friend, "more of a Daheshist than Dr. Dahesh himself."[16] In 1946, he embarked on a consciousness-raising tour of the Arab world, where he told audiences about Daheshism, its core principles, and the many struggles it had been through over the past years. He spent the last years of his life enthusiastically spreading the message throughout the Arab world.

The first major stop on his tour, after a brief visit to Dr. Dahesh's former hometown of Jerusalem, was Cairo, the most important cultural center of the Arab world. In the Egyptian capital, Dammous gave lectures on spiritual topics and met influential people to tell them the good news of Daheshism.[17] He tried to convince publishing houses in Egypt to produce editions of Dr. Dahesh's works and visited the offices of some of Cairo's most important journals, where he attempted to convert their editors to Daheshism. He rhapsodized about Dr. Dahesh to anyone who would listen. One morning, at the Continental Hotel, he spent two hours detailing the beliefs of Daheshism and the miracles of Dahesh to a young English journalist, telling him, among other things, how Dahesh had once miraculously brought a dead pigeon back to life and had summoned the spirit of his cousin who had drowned many years before in South America.[18] In talks and interviews, Dammous enthused about the new world order that Daheshism would bring and its message of the unity of religion. He promised that the world was close to realizing "a global brotherhood to unite the cross, the crescent, and the star of David."[19]

The next year, Dammous found himself in Aleppo, where he stood up in a mosque after the imam's sermon to recite a poem and tell the congregants about the marvels of Daheshism. It was becoming a habit of Daheshists to spread their message in mosques. A few months before, the young imam Ahmed Kuftaro (who later went on to become grand mufti of Syria) was giving a sermon in Damascus's Yalbugha mosque when an unnamed group of young Daheshists stood up and extolled the pro-Muslim stance of their leader. "They said that Dahesh had told them about the virtues of the Prophet and explained to them the exalted lessons of the Quran."[20]

News of Dr. Dahesh spread as far away as the Arabic-speaking diaspora of Argentina, where the writer Jubran Massuh proved sympathetic to their cause and used his monthly journal, *al-Mukhtasar*, as a venue to host their arguments. For Massuh, this was, in large part, a matter of religious freedom. He was disturbed that the newly independent Lebanese state was cracking down on a minority religious movement so early in its life. The Lebanese constitution protected freedom of both speech and religions and Massuh asked in his journal: "If the state protects many different religions, why should it not protect one more?"[21] He even went as far as to personally write to the prime minister of Lebanon, Riad al-Solh, complaining that the treatment of Dr. Dahesh was against the spirit of justice and freedom that the new Lebanon ought to embody.[22]

Massuh had some other interpretations of his own to explain the hostility against Dr. Dahesh. He insisted that it was rooted in a latent inferiority complex among his fellow Arabs, who believed that the West was the only source of modern enlightenment. People were desperate to copy anything that came from the West and rejected anything they saw as Eastern. Dr. Dahesh, he said, "has committed a crime that we cannot forgive: he is a son of our country. If his philosophies had come from a French or Italian priest, some English or American missionary, we would have received them happily. . . . But because they are coming from the mouth of someone born under our skies, speaking in Arabic, he is a 'charlatan' and a 'fraud.'"[23]

For every sympathizer like Jubran Massuh, there were many others who were unpersuaded by Dammous's enthusiastic proselytizing and did not see it as an issue of religious freedom. Many of the poet's old friends were put off by this new fervor for Daheshism; it seemed that Dammous talked about nothing else anymore. He bombarded one Iraqi newspaper editor, whom he had known for years, with constant requests to publish articles and poems about Dr. Dahesh. The editor, slightly embarrassed about the whole situation, did not want to disappoint his old friend, nor did he want to publish paeans to a strange new religion in his newspaper. He deftly sidestepped any responsibility, telling Dammous that he was worried about potential reactions

from religious conservatives and blaming the overly cautious government censor, who would not let him publish them.[24]

Amid this frantic proselytizing across the Middle East, Dr. Dahesh
himself remained in hiding and only his closest followers knew his
precise location. Sometimes reports emerged that he was in Aleppo;
others said that he was in the deserts of Iraq. No one could be sure, as
he was no longer making public appearances. He chose to communicate in writing instead, corresponding with his followers and compos-
ing new works of literature, heavy with moral and spiritual messages.

In 1946, Dr. Dahesh published the most significant work of his
entire life, *Memoirs of a Dinar*, which he wrote in the space of just
one week. Its narrative conceit was simple: it was the story of a piece
of gold that was mined around the turn of the century, then minted
into a coin, and sent to travel the world as currency. As this coin
passed from hand to hand, it witnessed the depravity of a fallen society: greed, imperialism, injustice, the hypocrisy of the clergy, and the
faithlessness of women. The heavily moralizing tale, like much of Dr.
Dahesh's oeuvre, is filled with bitter laments at the corruption of the
material world. *Memoirs of a Dinar* contained little in the way of an
explicit religious doctrine of its own; this was not a book that sought
to explain the message of Daheshism. Instead, Dahesh inveighed
against organized religion, tyranny, and loose sexual morals. It was,
in the words of his great disciple Dammous, "a book that destroyed,
not a book that built anything."[25]

The narrative, which sometimes moved slowly through its didactic
vignettes, was enlivened by cameos from some of the biggest figures
of the twentieth century, including Gandhi, Stalin, and Mussolini.
The dinar traveled through the trenches of the First World War, to
lavish parties hosted by the nizam of Hyderabad, to poetry readings
by Rabindranath Tagore, and to brawls in an Egyptian opium den.
Dr. Dahesh closed the book with his grand predictions for the coming
decades. He prophesied that Adolf Hitler's unknown son, Helmut,
would return to avenge his father's defeat. He would rise to power

in the 1990s, standing at the head of a nuclear-armed Germany, and usher in the end of the world.

As well as depicting great, world-changing events, Dr. Dahesh also used the book to settle some old personal scores and promote his movement. There is an appearance by a real-life Daheshist, the dermatologist George Khabsa, who was one of the only righteous and honorable people in the whole narrative. Likewise, Abd al-Rahim al-Sharif was given a brief role, sneakily picking up the coin as it fell out of a woman's handbag and then giving it to a Beiruti journalist, who agreed to plant false stories against Dr. Dahesh in the press. From the hands of this journalist, it reached Marie Hadad's sister, Laure, who was cast as scheming and sexually promiscuous and whose husband, Bishara al-Khouri, was painted as a fat, boorish fool. The attacks were not subtle.

Memoirs of a Dinar was Dr. Dahesh's most significant creation during his years in exile and is now considered his greatest literary work. It has since been translated into French, English, Spanish, and German and it is not hard to acquire a copy in the twenty-first century. Halim Dammous, who never missed an opportunity to extoll Dr. Dahesh's virtues, went as far as to describe it as a "literary miracle" on a par with the other physical miracles that he had performed.[26] He also spread the word about the book, asking people to review it and handing out copies, including one to the politician Ahmed Hilmi Pasha, who would go on to become prime minister of the all-Palestine government in 1948.

However, Dr. Dahesh did not have time to enjoy his accomplishment. In the summer of 1947, reports emerged that he had made it to the Iranian province of Azerbaijan, around one thousand miles from Beirut. However, the news about him was not happy. The holy man was dead, newspapers announced, executed either by rebels or by the Iranian government. At first, details of the story were vague. No one knew what had brought the exiled prophet to this area of Iran, which just a year previously had been a war zone, as Iran fought the Soviet Union for control of the area. Iran had emerged victorious, with the diplomatic help of the United States, but the province was still a dangerous place to be. Dr. Dahesh had apparently been traveling in the disputed land without any papers and his presence in a politically sensitive province was a recipe for disaster. People were not even sure whether his killers were Iranian authorities, who took him for a spy, or pro-Soviet rebels, who thought he had been sent by Iranian authorities. Either way, it was shocking news. Dr. Dahesh had finally met a force he could not evade, and the strange holy man who could communicate with the spirits of the dead had crossed over to the other side.

The execution came as a shock to everyone who had been following Dr. Dahesh's saga, and news appeared in Arabic newspapers from Beirut to Brooklyn to Buenos Aires. For his followers, the past few years had been very difficult, but they had never given up their faith. "The students did not abandon their teacher in his time of hardship but stayed with him until the final hours of his life," one sympathetic obituary noted with admiration.[27] Just days after his death was announced, Dr. Dahesh's will was made public in the Lebanese press. He had left tens of thousands of lira to help disadvantaged families and to support people wrongly imprisoned across the Arab world. He also left funds to support his own movement, enough money to begin a Daheshist publishing house, which would print his own work, and a modest prize of 500 lira to be awarded to the person who wrote the best book about Daheshism.[28] The Daheshists vowed to continue their guide's mission. The message was bigger than the man himself, his followers claimed. Some grandly quoted the words of Abu Bakr, the first caliph of Islam, after the death of the Prophet: "Whoever worshipped Mohammed, then Mohammed is dead," he said, "but whoever worshipped God, then God is alive and shall never die."[29]

Even then, Dr. Dahesh continued to be a living presence to many of his followers. In 1948, a year after his death, Marie Hadad and Halim Dammous brought a libel case against one newspaper that had called Dr. Dahesh a charlatan. The defendant was confused about the legal justification for this charge under the circumstances—"The case might be worth bringing if Dr. Dahesh was still alive but since he is dead it is pointless," he said. Dammous saw no reason to end their fight just because the claimant was dead; his soul was still with them, Dammous believed, and so could still claim damages for attacks in the press: "Dr. Dahesh has two natures, a mortal one that died with his body and another one which lives forever."[30]

Part III

RESURRECTION

Chapter 16

THEY ARE RISEN

IN THE SUMMER OF 1953, THE BRITISH ÉMIGRÉ ALDOUS Huxley was living in Los Angeles with his wife, Maria, exploring all the mystical and psychic experiences available on America's West Coast. The author of *Brave New World* had been in California since the late 1930s, when he had come as part of a small group of British writers, including the novelist Christopher Isherwood. Huxley and Isherwood had worked with varying degrees of success as screenwriters and simultaneously engaged in a parallel quest for personal spiritual enlightenment. Aldous and Maria Huxley spent much of their time in America experimenting with different philosophies, including Taoism, Buddhism, Spiritualism, and L. Ron Hubbard's new self-help movement of Dianetics. Aldous was fascinated by all the gurus and spiritual movements that found their homes in Los Angeles, from the high-minded to the bizarre. "He took as much pleasure in speculating about these cults as their devotees did in practicing them," his friend Anita Loos, author of *Gentlemen Prefer Blondes*, later wrote.[1]

In the early 1950s, Huxley was also beginning to investigate the effects of hallucinogenic drugs. In May of 1953, he took mescaline for the first time and it had a powerful effect on his psyche. When he wrote up his experiences in the book *Doors of Perception*, Huxley said that the drug had finally allowed him to comprehend the complex mystical writings and Hindu scriptures he had been studying for years. In his trip, he finally grasped the vedic philosophy of sat-chit-ananda, "being-awareness-bliss," and finally grasped Buddhist doctrines about

Dharma-Body that had previously seemed to him to be nonsense.[2] He was convinced that anyone who went through this door into the psychedelic world would come back a changed person. "He will be wiser but less cocksure, happier but less self-satisfied," Huxley claimed. He would also have a much deeper and more complex understanding of the world's secrets and "the relationship of words to things, of systematic reasoning to the unfathomable Mystery which it tries, forever vainly, to comprehend."[3]

While Aldous Huxley was in this heightened spiritual state, working on the manuscript of *The Doors of Perception*, which would be published in early 1954, he and his wife hosted an unusual visitor. Tahra Bey, the once-world-famous fakir, was a guest in their West Hollywood home for much of the summer. The Huxleys had witnessed his fakir performance in the French Riviera several decades earlier and they were excited to see him again. They seized the chance to dissect his skills as he came to America in one last attempt to revive his career.

Since the end of the Second World War and the liberation of Paris, Tahra Bey had been slowly trying to cast off the disgrace of the war years. In 1946, he began to perform again, putting on a demonstration of his skills on the beach at Cannes to a small but intrigued audience.[4] On February 29, 1948, he returned to Paris and took to the stage at the Palais de Chaillot, where later that year the UN would adopt the Universal Declaration of Human Rights. Sponsored by the newspaper *Le Parisien Libéré*, which was running a series on supernatural phenomena, he performed his old set—burial alive, inserting knives into himself, hypnotizing animals—to a new generation of Parisians. In the run-up to the performance he was visited by a correspondent from the magazine *Images du Monde*. The journalist, apparently oblivious to Tahra Bey's expulsion from France, his questionable wartime activities, and his recent attempts to revive his show, said that the fakir was "reappearing after 15 years of retirement."[5]

As he received this reporter in his luxurious ground-floor apartment on the boulevard Malesherbes, Tahra Bey quickly settled back into his role as the Egyptian fakir of the 1920s, dressed in the oriental robes that had become his signature. He recalled, as usual, his early years in Egypt, his initiation into the rites of the fakirs by his father, then his travels from Turkey, across Europe, to France. He explained his cataleptic trance to the readers and told old stories about a fakir he knew in Tanta who had stayed buried alive underground for over two decades. At his performance a few days later, some nostalgic observers were transported back to that period with him as they remembered "the wonderful evenings before the war when people literally fought each other at the ticket offices of theatres advertising the prestigious name of Tahra Bey."[6]

But his comeback suffered from many of the same problems as his earlier appearances. Before long, a challenger had arisen, the sexologist and psychologist Dr. Pierre Vachet, who had, in pleasingly cyclical fashion, been present as a younger man at Tahra Bey's first demonstration in Paris back in 1925. By 1948, Vachet was less tolerant of this fakir's experiments; he took to the stage to become the Paul Heuzé of postwar Paris.[7] This great comeback was starting to look like a repeat of his downfall. It was time for him to leave Paris and find somewhere else. In 1949, the fakir settled in Beirut, just a few years after the dramatic expulsion of Dr. Dahesh.

Tahra Bey would spend most of the rest of his life in Lebanon. However, he did not give up on his international ambitions. In 1953, he made one last attempt to break into the lucrative American market, hoping that a real-life holy man from the East might win a new generation of admirers in the postwar United States. "Lots of people have read about Masters, occult powers and occultism," he told one writer on paranormal subjects, "but hardly any one seems to have witnessed actual demonstrations of these powers or met even a single master of occultism."[8] His tour began in February at Boston's Symphony Hall, where he was joined onstage by "Professor Sanjean," who was also known as the manager of "Emir, the only dog in the whole world who can read your mind."[9] It was not a success. He made too many mistakes in the mind-reading section of the show and, during his burial alive, the impartial witnesses who had been brought onto the stage to certify the act accused him of cheating.[10] In April he put on a show at Carnegie Hall but it passed with little comment in the press.

By the time he reached California, Tahra Bey was jaded; he had argued with bookers about his pay and parted ways with his tour manager. But he had some reasons to be optimistic that he would receive a more enthusiastic welcome on the West Coast. He had managed to find two Armenian impresarios who, unlike his previous bookers, had no desire to cheat him: James T. Agajanian (who happens to be Kim Kardashian's great-great-uncle) and his son J. C. Agajanian. They managed to secure a series of Californian shows for Tahra Bey, including some at the over-one-thousand-seat Wilshire Ebell. Tahra Bey himself was already beginning to rewrite his war story for American audiences, giving himself a small but noble role in the Nazi defeat. When the Nazis took Paris, he claimed, he was summoned by Hitler himself to predict the future of the war but he refused. After several attempts to convince him to reveal his secrets, the Germans finally gave up and sent him to Paris's Cherche-Midi Prison, where he remained until liberated when Paris was retaken. He told a newspaper in Los Angeles that he had escaped death by Nazi firing squad thirteen times using his supernatural powers.[11]

Huxley, a thin, bookish Englishman whose eyesight was gradually failing him, made a strange companion for Tahra Bey, the extravagant mystical entertainer. However, Huxley's curiosity about the strange powers of the mind and Tahra Bey's willingness to explain his abilities gave the two enough to talk about. No manifestations connected to the human spirit were too unusual or far-fetched for Huxley to consider. Christopher Isherwood observed that a "fearless curiosity was one of Aldous' noblest characteristics, a function of his greatness as a human being." People might have mocked him for his credulity, but he never cared. "They laughed at him for consulting unlicensed healers and investigating psychic phenomena, and it was true that many of the healers proved to be wrong and many of the mediums frauds," Isherwood continued. "That was unimportant from Aldous' point of view. For his researches also brought into his hands some very odd and precious pieces of the jigsaw puzzle of Truth."[12]

Tahra Bey, for his part, was happy to play the part of a jigsaw piece and help uncover the mysteries of the mind alongside Huxley. He told him that the cataleptic trance he demonstrated during his set had several potential medical uses. In Lebanon, he claimed, he ran a mental hospital where he cured people of their psychological maladies by putting them in this trance "for two or three days at a time, leaving Nature to do the trick of making them well—which she often does." Huxley appears to have had complete faith in Tahra Bey's purported abilities. He also found him to be a pleasant house guest and, in letters to friends, described the fakir as a "charming man," if somewhat "child-like in spite of, or perhaps because of, the odd powers he possesses."[13]

Huxley did have to admit that Tahra Bey's stage shows themselves were somewhat hampered by his inability to speak any English and often descended into "a chaos of incomprehensibility."[14] However, as a loyal supporter of this strange man from Beirut, Huxley invited his friend the composer Igor Stravinsky to a July show at the Wilshire Ebell. Stravinsky, who had moved to Los Angeles in the 1940s, was unimpressed by the demonstration—a low point came as Tahra Bey's robes opened to give the legendary Russian composer an uncomfortably full view of his "jowlish genitalia."[15] Stravinsky could barely contain his embarrassment a few weeks later when he was forced to dine together with Tahra Bey and the Huxleys, who made no secret of the fact that they were believers in the fakir's powers.[16]

It is tempting to imagine an alternative version of Tahra Bey's life, one in which he moves to Los Angeles to lead his own Californian religious movement, wins some devoted followers, or, at the very least, makes a lot of money. Unfortunately for Tahra Bey, it was not to be. In America, he met one of the few enemies that he could not evade: U.S. Immigration. At the beginning of October, the government informed him that, since he had been working on a tourist visa, he would be deported. He did not put up a fight or argue as he had in 1930s France. Soon after his last show on October 9, 1953, he left Los Angeles for New York. Then, on October 22, he took a flight out of New York and returned to the safety of his Beirut home.

The Huxleys did not forget their visitor. The next year, they traveled to meet him in Beirut, partly in the hope that his powers might offer some kind of cure for Maria's aggressive cancer. Aldous wrote an article about his trip for *Esquire* magazine where he referred to Tahra Bey as a "professional thaumaturge" with a black beard and a silently expressive manner.[17] Sadly, Tahra Bey did not manage to cure Maria Huxley's disease and she died in 1955.[18]

If Tahra Bey's successful resurrection of his career, out of the ashes of shameful wartime spivery, was impressive, Dr. Dahesh accomplished an even more miraculous resurrection. As Tahra Bey was settling into his life in Beirut in the early 1950s, Dr. Dahesh literally returned from the dead.

The first signs appeared in 1950, as Lebanon was gripped by a new series of strange miracles. High up in the hills between Tripoli and Beirut, in a small Maronite monastery, a strange blood-like liquid started oozing from one of the coffins in the crypt. The source was quickly located as the tomb of Father Charbel, a popular Maronite holy man who had died in 1898 and whose body was buried in the monastery. The priests, worried that his earthly remains might be in danger, quickly opened up the zinc-lined casket to check his body. On removing the lid, they discovered, to their shock and confusion, that the corpse, which had been dead for over half a century, had no visible signs of decomposition at all and, in some accounts, even appeared to be gently perspiring.

Word soon got out about this portentous event and the monastery was flooded with visitors seeking blessings from this saintly grave. For the next few years, a steady stream of pilgrims came to visit Father Charbel. Many were healed of terrible diseases, and crowds of people from different religions—Christians, Muslims, and Jews—came from as far away as America to pray for the saint's intercession. It was one of the defining religious events of early 1950s Lebanon. A year after the pilgrims had started, the remote monastery was still receiving 10,000 visitors a day.[19] By 1953, 2,200 people had reported that they had experienced miracles when they visited the tomb—the majority were healed by Charbel's intercession.[20] One observer claimed: "There has never been anything like it in the history of the Church."[21]

At the same time, strange rumors began to filter through the Daheshist community. A hooded figure resembling their executed prophet, Dr. Dahesh, had been spotted in this very same Maronite monastery in the mountains of Lebanon. Among the pilgrims, a trembling woman was seen bowing before a figure who looked exactly like Dr. Dahesh; there were reports that Halim Dammous was also present amid the crowds. Back in Beirut, Daheshists began to whisper the news: Dr. Dahesh had returned from the dead and he was conducting miracles in a Maronite monastery. Father Charbel was taking the credit, they said, but the incredible events of the early 1950s could only be traced back to the incredible powers of the leader of Daheshism.[22] In September 1952, Bishara al-Khouri, the great enemy of the Daheshists, stepped down as president of Lebanon and ended his nine-year rule, which, toward the end, was increasingly dogged by accusations of corruption, mismanagement, and greed. Al-Khouri was succeeded as president by Camille Chamoun, who was much less hostile to the Daheshists, and Dr. Dahesh seized his opportunity to make a triumphant return to public life. In 1953, his followers revealed definitively to the world that he was alive.[23] The shadowy figure in the monastery was no longer a rumor. Dr. Dahesh was back in Lebanon—there could be no doubt. Once this news of his return had been announced, there were some obvious questions that needed answering. A few years earlier, he had been declared dead; newspapers had printed official announcements and run obituaries. He could not just come back to Beirut, claiming to be alive and well, without giving some kind of explanation.

The Daheshists had an answer ready, though it was probably not one that anybody could have predicted. This was no Christlike resurrection story, they said, but a uniquely Daheshist phenomenon. It could all be explained through the belief that six different "avatars" or incarnations of Dr. Dahesh walked the earth at the same time. These doppelgangers all looked identical to Dr. Dahesh but they existed apart from him, with no physical connection to him. His followers had known about these phantom materializations long before his execution. Dammous, the poet and so-called historian of Daheshism, recalled encountering these strange doubles during his earliest days in the Daheshist movement. Once, as he was watching Dr. Dahesh casually talk to one of his followers, an exact copy of Dr. Dahesh, wearing exactly the same clothes as him, walked into the room and strolled around as if nothing was happening. On another occasion, Dammous had walked in on Dr. Dahesh to find him in a fistfight with one of his avatars. Dr. Dahesh sometimes used these avatars to run errands for him when he was not able. Dammous recalled one time when two of these avatars went to meet followers many miles apart at the same time, all while Dr. Dahesh was taking a nap in the living room.[24] In Iran in 1947, one of these avatars had been executed and the original Dr. Dahesh was completely unharmed.

This far-fetched story proved unconvincing to Dr. Dahesh's more hostile critics, who offered some considerably less miraculous explanations of their own. They believed that the Daheshist inner circle had cooked up the story of his execution and planted it in the press in an attempt to ease the pressure that the Lebanese government was putting on their movement. Who, after all, is going to come after a dead prophet? There had been suspicions about the story of Dr. Dahesh's execution since it was first announced in 1947. Just weeks afterward, one newspaper ran a story under the simple headline "Dahesh Did Not Die," detailing what they believed to be the Daheshists' plan to "spread news everywhere about Dr. Dahesh's passing until people believed that he has crossed over into the world of the dead and then, when he returned to life, his followers could proclaim his divinity." The article said that "it would not be surprising if Dr. Dahesh was in Lebanon and that the news had been announced to deceive the authorities."[25] Another journal, which conducted some research of its own in Iran as early as 1948, concluded that the execution had never happened, and assumed, as the others had, that Dahesh must be "alive and well in some unknown place."[26]

This cynicism did little to dampen the spirits of the Daheshist faithful, who were ready to welcome their prophet back and start spreading his message again. Dr. Dahesh and Tahra Bey had returned to life in the 1950s, living in the same city on the Mediterranean and keen to revive their former glories. They each had one roll of the dice left.

Chapter 17

"I AM JUST A DOCTOR"

BY THE END OF 1953, TAHRA BEY AND DR. DAHESH WERE both living in Beirut, on the eve of the city's fabled golden age. In the decades after the Second World War, Lebanon was a melting pot of cultures, political beliefs, and creeds. It attracted many visitors, from political exiles seeking freedom to the international jet set drawn to the pleasures of Beirut's legendary nightlife. Lax censorship turned the city into the Arab world's hub of radical politics and seedy pornography alike. Lax banking regulations made it a place for the super-rich to put their money. Beirut was a magnet for poets, politicians, spies, and bohemians from across the world. Kim Philby spent long evenings in the bar of the Saint-Georges Hotel, Malcolm X addressed the Sudanese Cultural Center at the American University, Brigitte Bardot came for the beaches and the high fashion. Different populations lived in an uneasy but apparently functioning equilibrium: Sunni Muslims, Shia Muslims, Maronite Christians, Palestinian refugees, Islamists, Leftists. Lebanon was the only Arab country whose Jewish population increased after the establishment of the state of Israel in 1948—it more than doubled, mostly due to those fleeing from Iraq and Syria. There was also a large and thriving Armenian community, largely survivors of the Armenian genocide and their descendants. It was a city unburdened by the shackles of the past, moving into an uncertain but exhilarating future. When the Syrian poet Adonis arrived in the city from Damascus in 1956 he described this feeling of living in a place that looked forward, not backward: "It was not a city of 'endings' like Damascus, but a city of 'beginnings'; it was not a city of 'certainty' but a city of 'exploration.' . . . Beirut was embarking on a different kind of history, not one that was written for it but one that it could write for itself."[1]

The complex religious-sectarian balancing act that Bishara al-Khouri had helped create in the 1940s was holding firm, and for many, Beirut looked like a utopian experiment in religious diversity. Lebanese sociologist and historian Samir Khalaf, who was a student at the city's American University during the 1950s, remembered that time with a rose-tinted nostalgia. He has argued that the downtown area of Hamra, a short walk from where Dr. Dahesh lived, was "the only genuinely 'open' community in the entire Arab world." It had "room for everyone: the devout and the heathen, pious puritans and graceless hedonists, left-wing radicals and ardent conservatives."[2] People recalled this as a golden age of tolerance and coexistence—"No one cared who you prayed to or how you prayed, just that you were a good neighbor," one resident of Beirut later said.[3] As other countries in the postcolonial Arab world were controlled by increasingly authoritarian regimes, the state of Lebanon seemed to be building a culture of freedom and cosmopolitanism.

Tahra Bey, with his inexplicable abilities and supernatural skills, quickly settled into this liberal and vibrant city. By day, he ran in high society "dressed in a black suit and a brightly coloured bowtie" and was consulted by the police about their cases.[4] By night, he continued to put on his fakir shows just as he had before. These performances (and, as in Greece and France, the alleged power he held over female fans) prompted much gossip in the newspapers in Lebanon. "Never has the East seen a greater fakir, said some, never has it seen a greater swindler, claimed others."[5]

He was well known within Beirut's Armenian community and performed many of his old tricks in more private settings too. When his cousin Aida, Charles Aznavour's sister, visited Beirut with her husband, Georges Garvarentz, Tahra Bey could not resist demonstrating some of his powers. As they were having a coffee in the café of the Saint-Georges Hotel, Tahra Bey casually said that he could cast a spell on the waiter that would make him take out all the money he had on him and hand it over. The couple laughed, so Tahra Bey decided to prove that he still had powers of mind control. Staring the waiter directly in the eyes, Tahra Bey told Garvarentz to ask for the bill. As he did, the waiter absent-mindedly opened his own wallet and emptied it into Garvarentz's hands.[6]

By the 1960s, Tahra Bey was drifting out of Beirut's limelight, and the frenetic pace of his earlier career slowed to a crawl. By this point he was in his sixties, and he appeared more fragile than he ever had before. When asked, he claimed to be running a small hypnotic clinic, where he used his powers to help ease people's suffering. On a few occasions, he advertised performances of his old show, but many of them were canceled at the last minute. In 1965 he was supposed to perform at the Phoenicia theater but claimed that the owner had not got the correct license from the government. A few years later, his gig at the luxury al-Bustani Hotel in the hills above Beirut was canceled at the last minute because of an argument over the fee.[7] In 1965, he gave a short interview to the French-language newspaper *Le Jour*, where he talked about his canceled shows. "I know what you're thinking," he said, "Tahra Bey is afraid that he is too old to accomplish his former prodigies." Even as he raised this possibility, he immediately denied it, explaining that the fakir's skills did not work like that. Age had nothing to do with it; it was just that he had no need to appear onstage anymore. The mission to which he had devoted his life was almost complete. The Congress for Hypnosis and Psychosomatic Medicine in Paris, he claimed, had finally recognized the value in his experiments. His forty-year-long quest had borne fruit and now he could live a quieter life, his goals accomplished. He made light of the scandals that had surrounded him for his entire career. "For some I am a charlatan, for others I am a superman. I am neither one nor the other; I am just a doctor."[8]

Tahra Bey may have been drifting slowly toward retirement, but Dr. Dahesh was not yet ready to wrap up his spiritual mission. In

the open atmosphere of 1950s and 1960s Beirut, he and his movement lived in relative peace. There were no large-scale government
or press campaigns against Daheshism; if anything, he was treated
as an unusual curiosity and allowed to continue how he wanted. Surrounded by old, devoted followers, he continued to harness the power
of the spirits from the "Daheshist Message House" on one floor of the
opulent Heneine Palace in one of Beirut's most exclusive areas. It was
decorated much like his villa in Musaytbeh, with artworks, trinkets,
taxidermied animals, and books—some forty thousand volumes in
French, English, and Arabic. "The house is mysterious just like its
owner," wrote one journalist. "If you open the door and go up the long
staircase . . . your eyes move to all corners of the room rich in Middle
Eastern and Asian artefacts and your nose is filled with the scent of
incense, musk, and ambergris."[9]

In 1957, one of the most significant events since Dr. Dahesh's resurrection occurred. Halim Dammous, the "historian of Daheshism"
who had written so many detailed stories about the mystical leader
and his miracles, died. Dammous's influence on the rise of Daheshism cannot be overstated. He had done so much work spreading the
doctrine across the world, convincing his friends in the press to publish articles about Daheshism, and publicizing Dr. Dahesh's literary
works. Dammous had been the face of Daheshism in the late 1940s,
but to outsiders, he had always been hard to fathom. Even those who
were convinced that Dr. Dahesh was a fraud were divided on Dammous. Some saw him as an innocent victim of a scam—a true believer
who had been deceived by the charismatic holy man. Others saw him
as complicit—a scheming partner to Dr. Dahesh or perhaps even the
real power behind the entire operation. Even the circumstances of his
death were uncertain. One of his old friends had heard a story going
around that, in his final years, Dammous had argued with the other
Daheshists and left the mission house to live by himself. In this final
stage of his life, he was alone, isolated from everyone he had once
known, with barely enough money to afford food. According to the
story, Dammous was seen going into his small bedsit one day and

he never reemerged. Three days later his dead body was discovered.[10] Now that he was gone, the fate of Daheshism was uncertain.

One thing is clear. Without Dammous's meticulous documentation and controlling hand, the stories about Dr. Dahesh in the 1950s and 1960s grew increasingly far-fetched. One Beiruti resident wrote to an American magazine claiming to have seen Dr. Dahesh shrink himself to ten inches tall and then grow back to full size again before his eyes. On another occasion, Dr. Dahesh went to a party where the host had a large picture of Rembrandt on one wall and a picture of Beethoven on another. Dr. Dahesh ordered Rembrandt to get out of the picture and paint something for the guests; then he ordered Beethoven to step down and play the piano. These two great men from the past complied with Dahesh's request and the crowd were treated to the most amazing scene they had ever witnessed.[11] Another very popular tale that circulated about Dr. Dahesh at this time took place in a small local barbershop. He had come in for a haircut but there was a long queue and so the barber told Dahesh that he would have to wait. Unperturbed, the holy man simply removed his head from his body and placed it on a side counter; he told the barber that he would return to pick it up when the job was done, and his body jauntily strolled off into the street to kill time.[12]

However, Dr. Dahesh's popularity failed to keep up with the more outlandish stories that circulated about him. In the mid-1960s, Beirut's tolerant atmosphere meant that his movement suffered from less persecution but also received markedly less public airtime. Controversy was good publicity and during Dr. Dahesh's period of 1940s infamy, he was, at least, well known. Now, he was less feared but also less important. Still, a small group of dedicated Daheshists endeavored to keep his mission alive. In 1970, the message of Daheshism entered Lebanon's most esteemed educational institution as a recent convert, Ghazi Brax, delivered a lecture in the American University of Beirut titled "The Prodigies of Dr. Dahesh and the Unity of Religions." In the university's historic Assembly Hall, in front of an audience that included superstar Egyptian actor Youssef Wahby, Brax gave a long account of Dr. Dahesh's miracles. He recounted stories of the leader healing the sick, turning water into wine, and changing losing lottery tickets into winning lottery tickets. He wanted the crowd to know that Daheshism had an important message for people suffering from what he called "the tragic agony of this century." Thirty years after Dr. Dahesh had appeared in Beirut, Brax believed that this was the time for the world to adopt Daheshism's universalist message. "Since the dawn of history," he said, "humanity [has] not witness[ed] so much anxiety, growing despair, so much calamity, and a life so cruel and desperate, as the peoples of this twentieth century."[13]

The fact that these two influential holy men—Tahra Bey and Dr. Dahesh—were both living in Beirut at the same time, begs the question: Did they ever meet? Did Dr. Dahesh ever come face-to-face with the man who had pioneered the fakir act that he had used to launch his Palestinian career in 1929? The answer is complicated. I have found no evidence that both men were ever in the same room together. However, there are several accounts that show that they were, at the very least, aware of each other.

When Tahra Bey first arrived in Lebanon at the end of the 1940s, he almost immediately faced opposition from Dr. Dahesh's followers. For ardent Daheshists—at that point adrift without their leader—Tahra Bey's presence in Beirut was decidedly unwelcome. He was either competition or an unwanted reminder of their prophet's roots on the stages of the Middle East. In 1950, Dr. Farid Abu Sulayman, who had become a follower of Dr. Dahesh in 1942, encouraged by Youssef al-Hajj, and had been forced to leave his government employment because of his devotion to Daheshism, publicly confronted the fakir Tahra Bey.[14] Abu Sulayman poured cold water on Tahra Bey's supposedly miraculous abilities. "I challenge you," he said, as many before him had, "to accomplish your marvels in front of an audience, while I am present. I will explain how you do them all and if I can't . . . I will immediately pay you 200,000 Lebanese lira."[15]

Tahra Bey, a seasoned veteran with plenty of experience with challenges like this, used a strategy he had employed in Athens back in

1923. He was more than willing to submit to any kind of trial, he said, on just one condition. His challenger must deposit the money in a bank account for him first so that, in the inevitable event of his triumph, he would be able to collect it easily. Predictably, his Daheshist rival protested that he didn't have enough money to put down up front and the whole showdown fizzled out.[16] In its aftermath, Tahra Bey also revived a strategy that he had learned in Paris: he took his accuser to court. Early the next year he sued his Daheshist accuser for besmirching his reputation, and he won. His enemy was forced to pay a fine of 50 lira as well as legal costs.[17] Tahra Bey was proof that blind positivity can often make your problems disappear, if only for a while.

In 1965, Farid Abu Sulayman, who was by now regarded as Dr. Dahesh's right-hand man, reignited the challenge. In the 1960s, Dr. Dahesh was marketing himself as a campaigner against all types of charlatanry, especially hypnotism, which had done so much to launch his career in the 1930s. In interviews after his return from the dead, Dr. Dahesh declared that all hypnotism was a lie and a fraud—he maintained that any act involving a hypnotist and a medium was really based on elaborate systems of deception or code words, not on anything supernatural.[18] As part of this campaign, Farid Abu Sulayman arranged a showdown with Tahra Bey, in which he would demonstrate how all of his tricks were done. The event was rich with symbolism, as a movement that could trace its roots back to Tahra Bey's fakir performances in 1920s Paris tried to end his career in 1960s Beirut.[19] In many ways, the Daheshist campaign worked. Tahra Bey, now in his mid-sixties, made little attempt to fight back. In 1975, he died, with little fanfare to accompany his final interment. The end of Tahra Bey's journey was just as mysterious as the beginning.[20] Meanwhile, in the same year, his cousin Charles Aznavour, whose father had worked as Tahra Bey's secretary in Thessaloniki in the early 1920s, was at the peak of his international fame, playing sellout shows in London, Buenos Aires, and Rome, and appearing in an ill-fated film version of Agatha Christie's *And Then There Were None*, filmed in Iran. In April 1975, Aznavour recorded his melancholy anthem of the genocide, "Ils

Sont Tombés" ("They Fell"), cementing his place as one of the great Armenian voices of the twentieth century.

By the beginning of the 1970s, Dr. Dahesh himself was slowing down his pace of life. He spent most of the decade living the life of a wealthy retiree, traveling the world and visiting its most famous tourist spots. He went to India and Japan, to England and Hawaii, to France and Kenya. He toured wax museums, zoos, and art galleries. He also sampled the restaurants, theaters, parks, and palaces that caught his interest. As he neared death, Dahesh published a twenty-part series of lavishly illustrated books that he called his *Travels around the World*, documenting these pleasure trips, with all their humdrum details. Anyone hoping to find explanations of his message or philosophy in them will be disappointed. He comes across more like an eccentric uncle than the man who had once terrified Lebanon's political elite. His travels were largely touristic, his writing bland and diaristic, mentioning the names of hotels he stayed in and people he met but giving no detailed descriptions and, very often, no context at all. Dr. Dahesh, balding, often in a beige safari suit, posed for pictures in front of historic monuments or pointing at exotic animals in their cages.

A few of his trips stand out from the rest, as reminders that Dr. Dahesh had been a hugely important figure in the history of the modern Arabic occult. In 1971, he traveled to Egypt, forty years after his first appearance on the country's stages as a bright-eyed young stage fakir, hypnotist, and mystic. Politically and socially, much had changed since the 1930s, but Dr. Dahesh made the time to tour his old haunts, accompanied by his sister Antoinette, who had also been there four decades earlier as his hypnotic medium. He couldn't help but notice the differences. The Gloria Hotel, where they had stayed in the early 1930s, was sadly down at heel—so much so that he decided not to spend a night in its rooms. As he toured Cairo's Agricultural Museum, his eyes were caught by some distinctive taxidermied animals among the exhibits and he remembered that he had once seen them on display in the house of their original owner, the explorer Prince Youssef Kamal. Now he was looking at them like any other tourist. Dr. Dahesh was a ghost from a bygone era, returned after forty years to gaze upon the relics of a world that he had once known but which had now all but disappeared.

During his two months in Egypt, Dr. Dahesh also attempted to spread the word of his religious philosophy in a way that he had not done in Europe or Asia. He gave accounts in his diaries of how he won new admirers in Cairo by demonstrating his "Spiritual Phenomena." These demonstrations were a far cry from the amazing feats that he had accomplished in the 1940s—closer to magic tricks than miracles. He would, for instance, instruct someone to randomly pick a bank note out of their wallet, and then, without looking at it, he would tell them what denomination of note it was and, sometimes, its serial number. He would also magically reveal specific names that had been written on pieces of paper and sealed inside envelopes.[21] On his trip, Dr. Dahesh met several new people, including Cairo's top ballet dancer, Magda Saleh, and the committed Egyptian Spiritualist scholar Raouf Ubayd. He also reconnected with friends from his old life. He met up with the actress Mary Queeny, who had been a seventeen-year-old rising star when Dr. Dahesh first met her in 1931, and Bahiga Hafez, one of Egypt's earliest film stars, who barely recognized him after all these years. He reminisced with the former stars about the old days, and he took the time to explain the creed of Daheshism to them as best he could.

In 1975, six years after Dr. Dahesh first started these travels, Lebanon and the entire Middle East received a brutal shock. The sectarianism that Dr. Dahesh had preached against since the early 1940s erupted into violence. It started as long-running tensions between the Palestine Liberation Organization and the far-right, Christian nationalist Phalangist Party flared up, leaving several people dead. This, in turn, provided a spark for a wider explosion of interreligious fighting— what had started with Palestinians against Phalangists quickly ripped through Lebanon's fragile patchwork of religious groups. The political class had tried to restrain this with their array of convoluted constitutional solutions but they had not succeeded. Rapidly, Lebanon descended into a civil war, which would last fifteen years, as a dizzying array of rival militias and interest groups fought for control of the country. By 1976, the *New York Times* reported, dramatically, that Lebanon was "a society in [the] process of disintegration."[22]

As Dr. Dahesh watched these events unfold, he could not help but feel a little vindicated. The political elite of Lebanon had not heeded his radical message of religious unity and now they were paying the price. They had exiled him, destroyed his reputation, and persecuted his followers. The ordinary citizens of the country, who could have helped, did not come to his defense but just sat by and watched. Dahesh remembered that back in those dark days of persecution in the early 1940s, Halim Dammous had made an ominous prophecy. If Lebanon and its people did not stop sinning against Dr. Dahesh, they "would descend into terrible destruction and violent fear."[23] Two decades later, as the war raged, the Daheshists saw Dammous's prophetic words coming to pass—retribution had arrived late, but it had come drenched in blood.

Dr. Dahesh's reaction to the events unfolding in Lebanon sometimes came uncomfortably close to gloating. In the spring of 1976, he heard about the death of Kamal al-Hajj, the son of an enthusiastic Daheshist, and himself a well regarded, Sorbonne-educated philosopher and anti-sectarian thinker. Some years before, Kamal al-Hajj had mocked his father's belief in Daheshism and scorned the movement's message, calling it a naïve fantasy. In April, he was assassinated in his hometown, another victim of the sectarian violence. Rather than mourn, Dr. Dahesh thought back to another prophecy that Dammous had made. He had predicted that if Kamal al-Hajj did not embrace Daheshism, he would be killed. The prediction, like Dammous's other one, had come to pass and the Daheshists whom the young man had ridiculed many years before had the last laugh.[24]

As hostilities flared, Dr. Dahesh did not take up arms, nor did he take advantage of the chaos to spread his message. Instead, he turned his attention to something else—the precious art collection that adorned the walls and surfaces of the Daheshist Message House.

Over his life, he had amassed many paintings, prints, books, and objets d'art, which he did not want to become victims of the civil war. As the winter of 1975 approached, the gems of the collection—including 2,500 paintings and hundreds of statues—were entrusted to one of his followers, loaded into twenty large containers, each one containing dozens of individual boxes, sent through a war-torn city, and put on a plane to America.[25] Getting them out of the country was only half the battle. Shortly after the containers had been dispatched, Dr. Dahesh received the distressing news that his beloved artworks, which had dodged the bombs and bullets of Beirut, had been held up at customs in New York. American officials needed to determine their value and what taxes needed to be paid on them. At the beginning of 1976, Dr. Dahesh spent several months in America, wrangling with customs officials as the civil war raged in Beirut. To some, this might seem like a strange thing to do, but for Dahesh, this was a vital part of his life's last great mission. He wanted to create as part of his legacy a Dahesh Museum of Art in New York City, where his collection could be put on display for the world to see. After some complex back-and-forth, minutely detailed in the tenth volume of Dr. Dahesh's *Travels*, the crates of art eventually entered the United States. Sadly, Dr. Dahesh did not live to see his dream of a Dahesh museum take shape. He continued to travel the world in the late 1970s and early 1980s but became increasingly frail and ill. After many years of wandering, he passed away on April 9, 1984, in Greenwich, Connecticut, far from his Jerusalem birthplace. There was no great commotion when he died; the news passed largely unnoticed in both the Arabic press and the American press. His great enemies were gone—Bishara al-Khouri, the president who had exiled him, and Youssef Malik, who had written a long book denouncing him, had both died over twenty years earlier. Like Tahra Bey, Dr. Dahesh had outlasted his infamy.

His close followers, as many as were left, worked to keep the Daheshist message alive after his death. A Daheshist publishing house was set up in New York that churned out an enormous library of his works—from his old poetry to new editions of letters he exchanged with Arabic literary celebrities. A small group of people, mostly relatives of followers of Dr. Dahesh from the 1950s and 1960s, have struggled to continue Dr. Dahesh's teachings. Their work is largely informal, there is no central Daheshist organization, and precise numbers of Daheshists are very difficult to find—optimistic estimates say that the movement remains a few thousand strong.

The family to whom Dr. Dahesh had entrusted his artworks did not forget about his dream. The Dahesh Museum of Art finally opened in 1995, a decade after his death, in a narrow building in Manhattan's Diamond District that had previously housed a nail salon. Its collection was fittingly unusual. It largely consisted of the unfashionable genre known as "academic art," a style that peaked in late nineteenth-century Europe and is best remembered today as the stolid establishment style of painting, depicting historical, mythical, or allegorical scenes, which was so dramatically rejected by the radical innovations of impressionists like Monet and Renoir. Academic art, seen by its detractors as vapid and hackneyed, was so unpopular by the late twentieth century that the Dahesh Museum of Art was, almost by default, the premier museum of its kind in the entire world—and the only one in the United States. Many New Yorkers treated this new addition to their gallery world with raised eyebrows. The critic who reviewed the Dahesh's opening show for the *New York Times* said that the paintings had "the very special awfulness of expensive kitsch."[26] For some, the Dahesh Museum was something of a guilty pleasure—"too bad to be true," with "exuberantly insipid" paintings.[27] Eventually, through well-considered additions to the collection and a series of successful exhibitions, the museum managed to win a few converts to this forgotten style of art. By 2000, five years after its opening, one writer argued that the museum ought to be considered a "true gem of New York" and said that it had contributed to a revival of interest in academic art.[28]

Any burgeoning interest in academic art in the early twenty-first century was not enough to keep the museum running. At the time of writing, Dr. Dahesh's collection has lain mostly dormant since 2007, occasionally loaned out to other galleries or featured in traveling exhibitions. In 2017, I visited the only physical outpost of the Dahesh Museum of Art: the gift shop on Sixth Avenue, which mostly stocks museum catalogues and small tchotchkes decorated with reproductions of paintings in the collection. After a little searching, I did manage to find a copy of Dr. Dahesh's magnum opus, *Memoirs of a Dinar*.

For a man who accomplished so many miraculous and inexplicable wonders, it is ironic that his most enduring legacy is the Dahesh Museum of Art in New York. Still, its success has been hampered by Dr. Dahesh's controversial history and his spiritual mission, which loomed uncomfortably over the museum since its inauguration. In 1996 *ARTnews* magazine conducted a ten-month investigation into the museum and its links to Dr. Dahesh's movement. A journalist interviewed several members of the board and curators at the museum as well as other experts and some surviving Daheshists. In the end, he concluded that the Dahesh was a "legitimate museum operated by respected professionals who are not affiliated with Daheshism." Still, many members of the staff were unsure how to deal with the legacy of the man whose collection started the museum. The art historian Flora Kaplan, who later became the museum's director, insisted that Dr. Dahesh was simply a philosopher and a humanist, as she downplayed the wonders that had set Beirut ablaze in the 1940s. "He never proclaimed himself anything," Kaplan said. "Not a prophet, not a reincarnation. He never claimed anything that people are claiming for him." In a final sentence, which was undeniably true but not quite the whole truth, she declared simply, "He was born a Christian, and he must have been very charismatic."[29]

Epilogue

MODERN MYTHS

TAHRA BEY, DR. DAHESH, HAMID BEY, AND RAHMAN Bey—the holy men who made up this world of the occult, the irrational, and the miraculous—are almost mythical beings. The "real" people behind them—Krikor Kalfayan, Salim al-Ashi, Naldino Bombacci, and Antinesco Gemmi—are almost entirely obscured by the long shadows of their supernatural personae. With a careful eye, it is sometimes possible to catch glimpses of the human being. Krikor Kalfayan and Salim al-Ashi, for instance, were both from persecuted minority groups and both suffered hardship and displacement. From positions of powerlessness, they harnessed the wonders of the world beyond to become miracle-working celebrities. These are all crucial pieces of information. Yet their inner thoughts, their inner lives, and their true aspirations remain frustratingly out of reach. A conventional biography of people like Kalfayan and al-Ashi is not possible. Instead, this book tells the story of their mystical doppelgangers, Tahra Bey and Dr. Dahesh.

But how can you write the history of a myth—is that not a contradiction in terms? In the early twentieth century, at the same time that these holy men were winning acclaim, psychoanalysts like Sigmund Freud and Carl Jung came up with a radical new way to think about myths. They rejected ideas that fables and stories were remnants of long-forgotten religious practices or ways for people in a pre-scientific age to explain the marvels of the natural world. Instead, they asserted, myths were the embodiment of repressed desires and anxieties. For

Freud, this mostly meant sexual desires—he famously explained the Oedipus myth as a dramatization of men's repressed urge to sleep with their mother and kill their father. For Jung, myths had even broader and deeper roots in the psyche not just of a single person but of a whole society; they were outpourings from a larger "collective unconscious." In myths, it was possible to see all the aspirations and fears of humanity at large.

Tahra Bey and Dr. Dahesh created a new kind of folklore for the twentieth century. They were born from the chaos of the 1920s, as the world order collapsed, Europe stood in ruins, and the Ottoman Empire had been torn apart from the inside, and they held up a mirror to the desires and neuroses of that extraordinary century. They came into a broken world as mysterious prophets, promising that a bright future lay beyond the horizon, which anyone could attain with the help of unexplainable occult sciences. Their stories touch on many of the big issues of the early twentieth century: trauma, the fluidity of identity, internationalism, the remaking of the old world, the limits of modern science, and the complicated relationship between so-called East and West. Tahra Bey and Dr. Dahesh offered something that people around the world needed. Within a few years of Tahra Bey's appearance in Paris in 1925, his fakir character had spread from New York to Jerusalem, carried by different people who eagerly stepped into the role. These mystical characters could not have spread so fast and so far if they did not capture a feeling in the air.

These men were the heralds of a grander modern mythical cycle that continued to develop as the twentieth century continued. In the 1950s, Carl Jung conducted lengthy studies of UFO sightings in America. As a psychologist, he was not interested in saying whether they were *real* or not. Rather, he was interested in why so many people in this period believed they had seen them and what that said about their states of mind in an age of Cold War anxieties. For Jung, these UFOs were manifestations of a desire to see a superior, powerful (perhaps divine) intelligence come from outside the earth to restore the psychic equilibrium that had been thrown off-kilter over the previous decades. In the mid-twentieth century, this urge was not embodied in God or traditional religion. It manifested, instead, in the superadvanced technology of extraterrestrials.

In the twenty-first century, we are in a new age of anxiety. Our world is not too different from that of the 1920s. We have survived a pandemic, are in the middle of a huge refugee crisis, and are likely on the verge of much greater disasters, whether climatic, geopolitical, or something else entirely. I started writing this book as the COVID pandemic began and I am finishing it as both Gaza and Sudan have been devasted by war. What will be the defining myths of the 2020s? QAnon? Trumpism? Perhaps they have not yet arrived.

Since Tahra Bey and Dr. Dahesh first appeared, these holy men have been dogged by a persistent set of questions. Were they frauds or were they sincere? Were they cult leaders or philosophers? Did they believe in their own powers or was their act just a cynical ploy? Their opponents accused them of charlatanry and exploitation. Many readers will, no doubt, come to the same conclusion. And if they were simply international con men their stories would still be strangely compelling, but they were more than just that. Intoxicating followers and admirers with their messianic promises, they were manifestations of the zeitgeist, archetypes of the electromagnetic age. These men lived lives full of contradictions and fabrications, each one appearing entirely different depending on who was looking at him. They were mystics, apostles of science, holy men, charlatans, frauds, and tricksters all at the same time. To ask if they were genuine is like asking if myths are genuine; it is the wrong question.

There is another question, though, that could be answered through their stories; it is the one posed at the start of this book: Is another world possible? The stories of these holy men of the early twentieth century told in this book suggest that the answer is no. All of their movements ended without fulfilling any of their great promises. Most ended in outright ignominy. They channeled desires for rebirth into vessels that were ultimately empty and could never be filled, harnessing the power of miracles to produce nothing. All messiahs are false;

all their promises are broken. But these myths can have real power and people will never stop seeking new prophets. Harry Houdini, Paul Heuzé, and Youssef Malik could appeal to rationality all they wanted but they could not disprove the dreams that these men were selling. If the twenty-first century has proved anything, it is that logical argument and technocracy cannot defeat the appeal of wonder. Proving that a myth is false does not kill it. In difficult times, miraculous holy men increase their power as the anxious keep their eyes fixed on a new future. Another world is coming; but whose world will it be?

ACKNOWLEDGMENTS

THIS BOOK HAD A long and somewhat painful gestational period, much of it over the COVID-19 pandemic. There are more people to thank than I can fit on a few pages. I am particularly indebted to the libraries and archives, who were so generous over a difficult time, including but not limited to the American University in Cairo, the American University of Beirut, the New York Public Library, Columbia University Library, Durham University Library, the French National Archives, the Archives of the Police Prefecture of Paris, the National Library of New Zealand, and the British Library.

So many people helped me in so many ways (reading extracts, accessing difficult-to-access primary sources, translating passages, providing much-needed moral support, etc.) that I cannot name them all. Here are just a few: Alex Grammatikos, Alex Jovanovic, Carol Kino, Elif Su Isik, Elsa Mitsoglou, Humphrey Davies, Ifdal Elsaket, Jennifer Manoukian, Joseph Leidy, Joy Garnett, Kevin Dean, Kevin Eisenstadt, Kieran Hodgson, Konstantinos Gkotsinas, Marilyn Booth, Mary Beard, Nareg Seferian, Nektaria Baxevanaki, Nikhil Krishnan, Olga Taxidou, Peter Cherry, Peter Stothard, Rana Haddad, Tom Hardwick, Yair Wallach, Victor Kattan, and William Kattan. Thanks to Alane Mason, Mo Crist, and YJ Wang at W. W. Norton, George Lucas at Inkwell, and Sarah Johnson for extremely insightful copyediting (which much improved the text!). All faults are my own.

Finally, to my two partners in life, Pamela Takefman and Elijah: I finished.

FURTHER READING

The Occult and Spiritualism

The literature on the occult, in general, is enormous and I will not attempt to give a comprehensive survey. James Webb's two books *The Occult Underground* and *The Occult Establishment* are very good (and very detailed) overviews. Gary Lachman has written several books on the nineteenth- and twentieth-century occult, including *A Dark Muse: A History of the Occult*. There are also too many histories of Spiritualism to list. I found Ann Braude's book *Radical Spirits* particularly interesting—on the role of women in the early Spiritualist movement. Another excellent and accessible book is Kate Summerscale's *The Haunting of Alma Fielding*. "The Global Occult: An Introduction," a special issue of the journal *History of Religions* (vol. 54, no. 4 [2015]), guest edited by Nile Green, opens up the study of the occult to a wider geographical range.

The history of the modern occult in the Middle East is a relatively recent area of study. Alireza Doostdar's book *The Iranian Metaphysicals: Explorations in Science, Islam, and the Uncanny* gives a good introduction to the history of modern Spiritualism in Iran. Özgür Türesay's article "Between Science and Religion: Spiritism in the Ottoman Empire (1850s–1910s)" in *Studia Islamica*, vol. 113, no. 2 (2018) gives a rundown of the history of Ottoman spiritualism; and Edhem Eldem's "Magic at the Imperial Palace, 1876–78" in volume 3 of *Aca'ib: Occasional Papers on the Ottoman Perceptions of the Supernatural* gives a view from inside the sultan's palace. There are sections on

Spiritualism in Majid Daneshgar's *Tantawi Jawhari and the Qur'an*, Marwa Elshakry's *Reading Darwin in Arabic, 1860–1950*, and On Barak's *On Time*. Sam Glauber Zimra has published widely on Jewish occultism in the twentieth century. Many of his works are available at https://www.samglauberzimra.com/publications.

The history of older forms of esotericism and the occult in the Islamic world is more comprehensively researched. One good place to look, if resolutely academic (with a price tag to match), is *Islamicate Occult Sciences in Theory and Practice*, edited by Liana Saif, Francesca Leoni, Matthew Melvin-Koushki and Farouk Yahya, or *Islamicate Occultism: New Perspectives*, edited by Matthew Melvin-Koushki and Noah Gardiner. *Aca'ib: Occasional Papers on the Ottoman Perceptions of the Supernatural* is also a good read and is open access. Marinos Sariyannis's "Of Ottoman Ghosts, Vampires and Sorcerers: An Old Discussion Disinterred" is also enlightening, and can be accessed through his academia.edu site (along with several other of his articles on the occult). Hager El Hadidi's book *Zar: Spirit Possession, Music and Healing Rituals in Egypt* is a good introduction to the practice of *zar*, which is not much discussed in this book but touches on many of the same questions. Taylor M. Moore's paper about *zar*, "Occult Epidemics" in *History of the Present*, vol. 13, no. 1 (2023), is also well worth the read.

Tahra Bey

There is a limited bibliography on Tahra Bey. Fleur Hopkins-Loféron wrote a short blog for the Gallica website in 2022 called "Tahra-Bey, Célébrité et Charlatan." She is working on a book on Tahra Bey but it is not yet published at the time of writing. There is a book in Turkish by Mustafa B. Bozkurt, published in 2023, that gathers several sources about Tahra Bey; its title is *Tahra Bey'in Akıllara Durgunluk Veren Maceraları*. Ronald Grigor Suny's *"They Can Live in the Desert but Nowhere Else"* is an accessible recent history of the Armenian genocide.

The literature on other fakirs is more comprehensive. Bertrand

Tillier's *Ni Fakir, Ni Birman* tells the story of another French fakir of the interwar years, Birman. Sofie Lachapelle's *Conjuring Science: A History Of Scientific Entertainment And Stage Magic In Modern France* features some fakirs too.

When it comes to the American fakirs, John Benedict Buescher's *Radio Psychics: Mind Reading and Fortune Telling in American Broadcasting, 1920–1940* tells some of the story of Rahman Bey, as does David Jaher's *The Witch of Lime Street*, particularly in relation to Houdini and Carrington. Many of Hamid Bey's writings are for sale online.

For more on the world of Russian clubs in 1920s Paris see Dimitri Galitzine's article "Le Monde des Musiciens Tsiganes Russes à Paris" in Ilsen About and Marc Bordigoni (eds.), *Présences Tsiganes: Enquêtes et Expériences dans les Archives*.

Dr. Dahesh

The primary source of written material on Dr. Dahesh in both Arabic and English is the Daheshist Publishing Company. This press (and previous official publishing houses of the Daheshist movement) put out huge numbers of books, which offer an extremely positive account of Dr. Dahesh and frequently repeat the same material but have a lot of minute details. This is no longer an active publisher, as far as I know, and while the books are becoming harder to find as time passes many are available on secondhand book sites. Youssef Malik's *Khalifat Iblis* (The devil's deputy) from 1945 is still the most comprehensive attack on Dr. Dahesh.

The Egyptian writer Sameh El-Gabbas recently published a novelization of his quest to research Dr. Dahesh's life, *Rabitat Karihi Salim al-Ashi* (The Salim al-Ashi haters' union). Dahesh also briefly appears in Osama al-Issa's novel *Majanin Bayt Lahm* (The madmen of Bethlehem) and in Elias Khoury's *Broken Mirrors: Sinalcol*. Alia Nour-Elsayed's "The Making of the Dahesh Museum of Art: An Account of Its Founding, Ten-Year History, Its Academic Art Collection, and Exhibitions" (master's thesis, Seton Hall University, 2006) is a detailed account of the Dahesh Museum.

NOTES

For the transliteration of Arabic in the notes, I am using a simplified version of the IJMES system.

Epigraphs

1. Taha Hussein, *The Future of Culture in Egypt*, trans. Sidney Glazer (1st Arabic ed. 1938; Washington, DC: American Council of Learned Societies, 1954), 22.
2. Aldous Huxley, "Miracle in Lebanon," *Esquire*, August 1955.

Prologue: The World Beyond

1. *Home Journal*, June 15, 1850, 2.
2. For more on the eventful career of John Murray Spear, see John Benedict Buescher, *The Remarkable Life of John Murray Spear: Agitator for the Spirit Land* (Notre Dame, IN: University of Notre Dame Press, 2006).
3. John Patrick Deveney, *Paschal Beverly Randolph: A Nineteenth-Century Black American Spiritualist, Rosicrucian, and Sex Magician* (Albany: State University of New York Press, 1996).
4. *Fortune Telling: Hearings before the United States House Committee on the District of Columbia, Subcommittee on Judiciary*, 69th Cong., 1st sess., February 26, May 18, 20, 21, 1926 (Washington, DC: U.S. Government Printing Office, 1926), 33. The White House denied these allegations.
5. James Webb, *The Occult Establishment* (La Salle, IL: Open Court, 1976), 7.

Part I: Strange and Wondrous

1. Albert Schweitzer, *The Decay and the Restoration of Civilization*, trans. C. T. Campion (London: A & C Black, 1923), 1:44.
2. Ella K. Maillart, *The Cruel Way: Switzerland to Afghanistan in a Ford* (1947; London: John Murray, 2021), 33.

Chapter 1: The Anti-Christ of Athens

1. Henry Morgenthau, *I Was Sent to Athens* (Garden City, NY: Doubleday, Doran, 1929), 48.
2. A. A. Pallis, "The Greek Census of 1928," *Geographical Journal* 73, no. 6 (1929): 547.
3. *Scotsman*, December 11, 1922, 8; Dimitra Giannuli, "American Philanthropy in the Near East: Relief to the Ottoman Greek Refugees, 1922–1923" (PhD diss., Kent State University, 1992), 173–74; *Times of London*, January 11, 1923, 12.
4. *Times of London*, February 2, 1923, 11, referenced in Bruce Clark, *Twice a Stranger* (Cambridge, MA: Harvard University Press, 2009), 142–43.
5. *He Charauge tou Anthropismou* [The dawn of humanity], August 10, 1923, 7–8.
6. *He Charauge tou Anthropismou*, April 18, 1923, 5.
7. *He Charauge tou Anthropismou*, January 3, 1921, 1.
8. *Sphaira*, June 16, 1923, 3.
9. *Sphaira*, June 16, 1923, 3.
10. *Sphaira*, June 16, 1923, 3.
11. Harry Boddington, *The University of Spiritualism* (London: Psychic Book Club, 1946), 263.
12. *He Charauge tou Anthropismou*, April 30, 1923, 4–5.
13. Edward William Lane, *An Account of the Manners and Customs of the Modern Egyptians* (London: Charles Knight, 1836), 310.
14. There are many accounts of the event, e.g., *Reynolds's Miscellany*, December 21, 1850, 341; W. G. Osborne, *The Court and Camp of Runjeet Singh* (London: Henry Colburn, 1840), 129–38.
15. *Popular Science Monthly*, June 1893, 192–96; *Current Literature: A Magazine of Record and Review*, April 1892, 548.
16. Even these simple facts of his life are disputed; his birth date appears in different places as 1887, 1897, 1900, 1901, or 1903, but 1900 is the most common and the one that Tahra Bey himself used on official travel documents.
17. Zabel Yessayan, *The Gardens of Silihdar*, trans. Jennifer Manoukian (Boston: Aiwa Press, 2014), 28.
18. Özgür Türesay, "Between Science and Religion: Spiritism in the Ottoman Empire (1850s–1910s)," *Studia Islamica* 113, no. 2 (2018), 166–200; Hasan Merzuk, *Cinlerle Muhabere Yahud Ispiritizm, Fakirizm, Manyatizm: Tarifi, Tarihi, Malumât-i Umumiye* (Istanbul: Necm-i İstikbal Matbaası, 1912).
19. For more of this early life story see the Armenian journal *Jamanak*, June 6, 1926, 1.
20. Arnold Toynbee and Great Britain Foreign Office, *The Treatment of Armenians in the Ottoman Empire: Documents Presented to Viscount Grey of Fallodon* (London: Hodder and Stoughton, 1916), 165.
21. Deniz Dölek-Sever, "Policing the 'Suspects': Ottoman Greeks and Armenians in Istanbul, 1914–18," *Middle Eastern Studies* 53, no. 4 (2017): 533–50.
22. The story of Tahra Bey's Smyrna years was serialized in the Armenian journal *Jamanak*, in June and July 1926, and later (slightly altered) in the Turkish journal *Halkın Sesi*, in July and August of 1936.
23. Marjorie Housepian Dobkin, *Smyrna 1922: The Destruction of a City* (1966; Kent, OH: Kent State University Press, 1988), 103.
24. Sona Seferian, "Translators-Enlighteners of Smyrna," in *Armenian Smyrna/Izmir*, ed. Richard G. Hovannisian (Costa Mesa, CA: Mazda Publishers, 2012), 158–65.
25. *Halkın Sesi*, August 3, 1936, 2 (trans. Elif Su Isik).

26. Dobkin, *Smyrna 1922*, 132.

27. Dobkin, 150.

28. *Irish Times*, September 18, 1922, 5.

29. *Los Angeles Times*, September 18, 1922, 1.

30. *Times of London*, October 5, 1922, 7, originally from the *Canterbury Diocesan Gazette*.

31. The interview is in *Hairenik*, June 20, 1930, 1; it does not mention Sheikh al-Falaki by name but others do (e.g., *al-Lataʾif al-Musawwara*, October 31, 1927, 1). Oddly, the story of his trip to Egypt also appears, in a way that doesn't make chronological sense, at a later stage in the previous narrative that took him to Smyrna in 1920. Compare *Ruz al-Yusuf*, no. 105 (1927), 13, for a less supernatural account of his trip to Egypt.

32. The family arrived in Marseilles in October 1923, so this period in Thessaloniki must have come before Tahra Bey's Athens period: see Laurent Wirth, *Le Madeleine et le Papillon* (Paris: Armand Colin, 2022), 246.

33. Charles Aznavour, *Le Temps des Avants* (Paris: Flammarion, 2003), 32 ff.; Charles Aznavour, *Yesterday When I Was Young* (London: W. H. Allen, 1979), 3.

34. Teotig, *Amēnun Taretsʿoytsʿē: Zbōsali u Pitani 1926*, trans. Jennifer Manoukian (Venice: Tp. Mkhitʿarean, 1926), 683. The quote is from an article by Yervant Odian in the Beiruti newspaper *Armenian Life* from 1926.

Chapter 2: "Tahranitis"

1. *Empros*, May 22, 1923, 1–2.

2. Giannis Kairophylas, *He Athena tou Mesopolemou* [Athens between the wars] (Athens: Ekdoseis Phillipote, 1984), 25–26. This book is a very useful source for the story of Tahra Bey in Athens.

3. *Empros*, July 11, 1923, 2.

4. Kairophylas, *He Athena tou Mesopolemou*, 26–27.

5. *Sphairos*, September 29, 1923, 5 (trans. Nektaria Baxevanaki).

6. *Sphairos*, September 29, 1923, 5 (trans. Nektaria Baxevanaki [with minor edits]); *Empros*, October 10, 1923, 1.

7. *Empros*, June 24, 1923, 7.

8. Dr. Tahra Bey, *Mes Secrets* (Paris: Editions Fulgor, 1926), 107.

9. *Sphairos*, October 6, 1923, 5 (trans. Nektaria Baxevanaki [with minor edits]).

10. *Empros*, November 4, 1923, 1.

11. League of Nations, *Supplementary Report to the Fifth Assembly of the League on the Work of the Council, on the Work of the Secretariat and on the Measures Taken to Execute the Decisions of the Assembly* (Geneva: August 30, 1924), 36–37.

12. For a detailed discussion on Arturo Reghini, his life, and his beliefs, see Christian Giudice, *Occult Imperium: Arturo Reghini, Roman Traditionalism, and the Anti-Modern Reaction in Fascist Italy* (Oxford: Oxford University Press, 2022). There is a discussion of pagan imperialism, 91–110.

13. *Ignis: Rivista Mensile di Studii Iniziatici*, January–February 1925, 45–46.

14. "Il Fachiro Tahra Bey," *Luce e Ombra*, April 1925, 177. *Chavk* means "light" in Ottoman Turkish.

15. "Il Fachiro Tahra Bey," 177.

16. See *Ignis*, January–February 1925, 31–46, and "Il Fachiro Tahra Bey," 176–84.

17. *Le Petit Parisien*, July 14, 1925, quoted in Sabine Brazier, *Le Fakir Tahra Bey à Paris* (n.p.: n.d. [Paris: 1925]), 5–6.

18. "Il Fachiro Tahra Bey," 181. (Passage is a quotation from *Sicilia Nuova* without specific reference.)

19. *Le Quotidien*, July 20, 1925, 2.

20. *Baltimore Sun*, November 15, 1925, pt. 2, sec. 3, p. 2.

21. *L'Homme Libre*, August 7, 1925, 2.

22. Brazier, *Fakir Tahra Bey à Paris*, 7. It is unclear what the "Arab revolution" of 1905 was.

23. "Le Fakir Tahra Bey Contre Heuzé et Editions de France," *Revue des Grands Procès Contemporains* 37 (1931), 563–636 (quote from 593).

24. Paul Valéry, "The Spiritual Crisis," *Athenaeum*, April 11, 1919, 182–84; pt. 2: May 2, 1919, 279–80. It was published in English, and published in the original French in *La Nouvelle Revue Francaise*, August 1, 1919, 321–37.

25. Dominique Kalifa, *The Belle Époque: A Cultural History, Paris and Beyond*, trans. Susan Emanuel (2017 [French ed.]; New York: Columbia University Press, 2021), 32–33.

26. Richard Overy, *The Twilight Years: The Paradox of Britain between the Wars* (New York: Penguin, 2009), introduction, Kindle.

27. André Breton, *Manifestes du Surréalisme* (Paris: Gallimard, 1969), 64.

28. Edwin E. Slosson, "Weeping and Bleeding Images," *Independent* (New York), October 9, 1920, 47–49.

29. Peter Fisher, *Weimar Controversies* (Bielefeld: Transcript, 2020), 25–26, quoting "Sling und Der Okkultismus," *Vossische Zeitung*, November 6, 1925 (Fisher's translation).

30. *Phoenix* (Cairo), December 7, 1925, 28, 31.

31. *Phoenix* (Cairo), December 7, 1925, 33–34.

32. Katherine Mansfield, "To J. M. Murry" [ca. November 27, 1922], in *The Collected Letters of Katherine Mansfield*, vol. 5, *1923*, ed. Vincent O'Sullivan and Margaret Scott (Edinburgh: Edinburgh University Press, 2022), 328, 319.

33. *Le Figaro*, July 24, 1925, 1.

34. *Chicago Tribune and the Daily News New York* (European Edition), August 13, 1925, 6; August 14, 1925.

35. Georges-G. Toudouze, "Maroc et Logique," *Le Phare de la Loire, de Bretagne, et de Vendée*, May 30, 1925, 1.

36. *L'Avenir*, July 24, 1925, 1.

Chapter 3: A Fakir in Montmartre

1. *Civil and Military Gazette* (Lahore), October 17, 1925, 11.

2. *Comeodeia*, September 25, 1925, 3.

3. *Le Gaulois*, September 20, 1925, 1.

4. *New Yorker*, October 24, 1925, 28.

5. *South China Morning Post*, September 25, 1925, 1.

6. *Le Siècle*, September 21, 1925, 2. The same article mentioned the eight faintings.

7. *Le Petit Parisien*, April 14, 1926, 1–2.

8. Program of the Théâtre des Champs-Élysées, September 18, 1925.

9. Paul Heuzé, *Dernières Histoires de Fakirs* (Paris: Montaigne, 1932), 160n1. Large parts of *Mes Secrets* are based on articles that Tahra Bey published in *Le Petit Journal* in the summer of 1925.

10. Tahra Bey, *Mes Secrets* (Paris: Editions Fulgor, 1926), 24.

11. Tahra Bey, *Mes Secrets*, 12.

12. Tahra Bey, 22.

13. Tahra Bey, 12–13.
14. Tahra Bey, 13.
15. Tahra Bey, 135–37.
16. Maud S. Mandel, *In the Aftermath of Genocide: Armenians and Jews in Twentieth-Century France* (Durham, NC: Duke University Press, 2003), 11.
17. *Paris-Midi*, July 17, 1929, 2, cited in Anouche Kunth, *Exils Arméniens: Du Caucase à Paris* (Paris: Belin, 2016), 158.
18. Aznavour, *Le Temps des Avants*, 30.
19. Claude Farrère, *Fin de Turquie* (Paris: Dorbon-Aîné, 1913), 21, cited in Anouche Kunth, "Dans les Rets de la Xénophobie et de l'Antisémitisme: Les Réfugiés Arméniens en France, des Années 1920 à 1945," *Archives Juives* 48, no. 1 (2015): 72–95.
20. For more see Stefan Ihrig, *Justifying Genocide: Germany and the Armenians from Bismarck to Hitler* (Cambridge, MA: Harvard University Press, 2016), 301–19.
21. George Orwell, *Down and Out in Paris and London* (1933; London: Penguin, 2009), 75.
22. Tahra Bey, *Mes Secrets*, 24.
23. "Fakir Tahra Bey Contre Heuzé et Editions de France," 563–639. For wages, see Alain Bayet in *Le Travail en France, 1800–2000*, ed. Olivier Marchand and Claude Thélot (Paris: Nathan, 1997); *Monthly Labor Review* 25, no. 1 (July 1927): 112–13.
24. *Observer*, September 27, 1925, 8.
25. *New Yorker*, October 24, 1925, 28.
26. *Boston Globe*, May 18, 1926, 2.
27. Albert de Courville, *I Tell You* (London: Chapman and Hall, 1928), 234.
28. *Chicago Tribune and the Daily News New York* (European Edition), September 28, 1925, 1.
29. Dimitri Galitzine, "Le Monde des Musiciens Tsiganes Russes à Paris. Transformation des Cadres Artistiques et Réseaux Familiaux dans l'Entre-Deux-Guerres," in *Présence Tsiganes: Enquêtes et Expériences dans les Archives*, ed. Ilsen About and Marc Bordigoni (Paris: Le Cavalier Bleu, 2018), 309–39; *New York Herald* (Paris Edition), October 12, 1924, 2.
30. *New York Herald*, March 29, 1919, 7.
31. *New York Herald* (Paris Edition), October 12, 1924, 2.
32. *Le Courrier de Saône-et-Loire*, February 14, 1926, 1.
33. *Le Figaro*, February 13, 1926, 1.
34. *Le Quotidien*, June 8, 1926, 2.
35. *Le Figaro*, June 18, 1926, 2.

Chapter 4: Rahman Bey (Almost) Conquers America

1. *Empros*, October 15, 1923, 1.
2. Ioannis Metaxas, *To Prosopiko tou Hemerologio* (Athens: Govosti, 1963), 5:404–5.
3. *Corriera della Sera*, May 16, 1925, 5.
4. *Corriera della Sera*, October 26, 1925, 3.
5. Sisley Huddleston, *Paris Salons, Cafés, Studios* (Philadelphia: J. B. Lippincot & Co., 1928), 96.
6. Edward Portnoy, "Freaks, Geeks, and Strongmen: Warsaw Jews and Popular Performance 1912–1930," *Drama Review* 50, no. 2 (Summer 2006): 129–30.
7. *Daily News* (London), April 28, 1925, 5.
8. *Daily News* (London), April 28, 1925, 5.

9.   *Evening Standard*, April 28, 1926, 6.

10. *Variety* (London), May 12, 1925, 2; *Evening Standard*, April 29, 1926, 9.

11. *Variety* (London), May 12, 1926, 2.

12. F. Yeats-Brown, "A Path to Peace," *Spectator*, May 29, 1926, 902.

13. *Evening Standard*, April 30, 1926, 4.

14. *New York Times*, March 3, 1923, 4.

15. *Address of President Coolidge at the Celebration of the 150th Anniversary of the Declaration of Independence* (Washington, DC: Government Printing Office, 1926), 10.

16. *Orient* 1, no. 1 (February 1923): 3.

17. *Herald of Gospel Liberty*, August 16, 1923, 20, quoting an article by George C. Henderson in *Christian Herald* [n.d.].

18. Charles W. Ferguson, *The New Books of Revelations: The Inside Story of America's Astounding Religious Cults* (New York: Doubleday, 1929), 1.

19. Joseph Fort Newton, "Preaching in New York. II," *Atlantic*, October 1922, 456–64.

20. *The Oriental Fakir Rahman Bey* (Program, 1926) in Princeton University Archive, Hereward Carrington Papers, Box 3, Folder 2, Rahman Bey.

21. *Daily News*, May 30, 1926, 33.

22. *Brooklyn Daily Eagle*, May 26, 1926, 34; *Brooklyn Citizen*, May 26, 1926, 5.

23. *Billboard*, June 5, 1926, 25.

24. *Daily News*, May 30, 1926, 33; *Variety* (Los Angeles), June 9, 1926, 36. If there were around 900–950 seats in the theater and the tickets ranged from fifty cents to two dollars and fifty cents, this means that most nights were mostly full.

25. *Daily News*, May 30, 1926, 33.

26. *Sunday News*, May 30, 1926, 33.

27. *Daily News*, May 30, 1926, 33.

28. Nandor Fodor, "A Personal Note on Hereward Carrington," *Tomorrow* 7, no. 1 (1959): 110–13.

29. See short biography at the back of his Haldeman-Julius editions, e.g., Hereward Carrington, *A Book of Rogues and Impostors* (Girard, KS: E. Haldeman-Julius, 1948), 29.

30. *New York Times*, April 18, 1920, *Book Review*, 5: 189.

31. Hereward Carrington, *Hindu Magic* (London: The Annals of Psychical Science, 1909), 44–45.

32. Harry Houdini, *A Magician among the Spirits* (New York: Harper and Brothers, 1924), xix.

33. *Strand Magazine*, August 1927, 135.

34. *Billboard*, January 24, 1925, 17.

35. *New York Times*, December 21, 1924, sec. 9, p. 8.

36. *New York Times*, December 20, 1924, 18.

37. *Chicago Tribune*, February 12, 1925, 9. For more details about this whole affair, including those rumors, see David Jaher, *The Witch of Lime Street: Séance, Seduction, and Houdini in the Spirit World* (New York: Crown, 2015).

38. *Fortune Telling: Hearings*, 114.

39. Joseph Rinn, *Sixty Years of Psychical Research* (New York: Truth Seeker Company, 1950), 509–12.

40. *New York Herald Tribune*, July 8, 1926, 4.

41. *New York Herald Tribune*, July 8, 1926, 4; *New York Times*, July 8, 1926, 12.

42. *Boston Daily Globe*, August 6, 1926, 3; *New York Times*, August 6, 1926, 32.

43. *Wilkes-Barre Record*, August 7, 1926, 3.

44. *Brooklyn Eagle*, August 10, 1926, 3.

45. *Sunday Times* (Sydney), October 21, 1928, 24; *Bathurst National Advocate*, December 18, 1928, 2.
46. See Mandy Sayer, *Those Dashing McDonagh Sisters* (Sydney: NewSouth Publishing, 2022), 143, 172.
47. Gianfranco Cresciani, "Refractory Migrants: Fascist Surveillance on Italians in Australia, 1922–1943," *Italian Historical Society Journal* 15 (2007): 9–58. Citing, Archivio Centrale dello Stato, Rome, Ministero dell'Interno Direzione Generale di Pubblica Sicurezza, Casellario Politico Centrale, Italians in Australia Screened by the Fascist Government—1922–1940, Gemmi, Federico, b. 2328, f. 27598.
48. See, e.g., *Brooklyn Daily Eagle*, November 5, 1926, 12; *American Magazine*, July 1928, 123.
49. Hereward Carrington, *The Story of Psychic Science* (London: Rider and Co., 1930), 187.

Chapter 5: The Man from Juan-les-Pins

1.   Willie Cobb, *L'Amoureuse du Fakir* (Montrouge, France: J. Ferenczi, 1929), 63, 91. See also Sofie Lachapelle, *Conjuring Science* (New York: Palgrave Macmillan, 2015).
2.   Cobb, *L'Amoureuse du Fakir*, 71.
3.   Paul Heuzé, *Do the Dead Live?*, trans. from the French (London: John Murray, 1923), 37.
4.   *La Victoire*, October 30, 1925. Quoted in Paul Heuzé, *Fakirs, Fumistes & Cie* (Paris: Les Éditions de France, 1926), 109.
5.   Heuzé, *Fakirs, Fumistes & Cie*, 88n1.
6.   Heuzé, 128–29.
7.   Heuzé, *Dernières Histoires de Fakirs*, 111.
8.   *Manchester Guardian*, December 13, 1928, 6.
9.   Heuzé, *Dernières Histoires de Fakirs*, 120.
10. Heuzé, 121n1.
11. *Psychic Research*, February 1929, 113.
12. *La Presse*, December 13, 1928, 1.
13. "Fakir Tahra Bey Contre Heuzé et Editions de France," 606.
14. Paul Heuzé, *Dernières Histoires de Fakirs*, 131.
15. *L'Ami du Peuple*, December 12, 1928, 4; *La Presse*, December 13, 1928, 1; *Psychic Research*, February 1929, 114.
16. Heuzé, *Dernières Histoires de Fakirs*, 126.
17. *Le Petit Parisien*, December 12, 1928, 1.
18. *Paris-Soir*, December 14, 1928, 5.
19. *Observer*, December 16, 1928, 12.
20. Heuzé, *Dernières Histoires de Fakirs*, 240–41.

Chapter 6: Hamid Bey: Self-Help Guru

1.   The main details of the story come from the local New Jersey newspaper *Bergen Evening Record*, January 21, 1927, 1–2; other details are in *New York Herald Tribune*, January 21, 1927, 8; *New York Times*, January 21, 1927, 36.
2.   John Benedict Buescher, *Radio Psychics: Mind Reading and Fortune Telling in American Broadcastings 1920–1940* (Jefferson, NC: McFarland & Co., 2021), 90.
3.   *Variety*, January 5, 1972, 14.

4. *North Adams Evening Transcript*, April 15, 1929, 8.
5. *Billboard*, September 6, 1930, 124.
6. *St. Louis Daily Globe*, November 22, 1930, 7.
7. *New York Tribune*, November 25, 1923, 3.
8. *Los Angeles Times*, January 28, 1925, pt. 2, p. 4.
9. *Washington Post*, January 15, 1927, 8; *New York Times*, January 15, 1927, 9.
10. *New York Times*, February 4, 1927, 1.
11. *Buffalo News*, May 25, 1927, 24; May 27, 1927, 28.
12. *East-West*, September–October 1927, 23–24.
13. See, e.g., *Los Angeles Record*, April 11, 1931, 3.
14. *Oakland Tribune*, February 29, 1932, 17.
15. *Santa Cruz Sentinel*, August 3, 1932, 7.
16. Ferguson, *New Books of Revelations*, 315.
17. *Santa Cruz Evening News*, January 19, 1933, 8; January 21, 1933, 4.
18. For more on the life of the McCollum family, see Elmer Verner McCollum, *From Kansas Farm Boy to Scientist* (Lawrence: University of Kansas Press, 1964).
19. John Greenwood, "Psychology in America: The Early Years," in *A Conceptual History of Psychology: Exploring the Tangled Web* (Cambridge: Cambridge University Press, 2015).
20. Lee R. Steiner, *Where Do People Take Their Troubles* (Boston: Houghton Mifflin, 1945), 2.
21. *Evening World* (New York), March 3, 1922, 3; *Salt Lake Herald*, May 3, 1919, 6; *New York Tribune*, February 26, 1922, 17.
22. *Brooklyn Daily Eagle*, June 18, 1922, 5.
23. *Brooklyn Daily Times*, March 11, 1922, 3.
24. *Illustrated Daily News* (Los Angeles), November 28, 1931, 6; *Buffalo Evening Times*, October 7, 1921, 6; Harriet Luella McCollum, *Analytical Outline of Applied Psychology* ([n.p.], 2018), 60.
25. Hamid Bey, *My Experiences Preceding 5,000 Burials* (Buffalo, NY: Ellicot Press, 1933), 134.
26. *Aegyptus*, January 1941, 6.
27. *Evening News* (Harrisburg, PA), October 3, 1933, 15.
28. *Richmond Times-Dispatch*, March 30, 1936, 9; *Memphis Commercial Appeal*, March 26, 1935, 8; *Richmond Times-Dispatch*, May 8, 1926, 2.
29. Hamid Bey, *The Sacred Teachings of the Coptic Fellowship of America* (n.d. [ca. 1938]), Lesson 19–20, 3.
30. Hamid Bey, *Sacred Teachings*, Lesson 47–48, 8.
31. *Aegyptus*, November 1941, 25.
32. *Aegyptus*, May 1942, 5.
33. *Arizona Republic*, November 23, 1952, sec. 5, p. 2; *Detroit Free Press*, January 11, 1953, sec. B, p. 6; Food, Drug and Cosmetic Act, Notices of Judgment, "Drugs and Devices Actionable Because of Failure to Bear Adequate Directions or Warning Statements," Case Number 6587, July 1962, https://fdanj.nlm.nih.gov/catalog/ddnj06587.

Chapter 7: Funeral Oration for a Fakir

1. Dr. Tahra Bey, Carnegie Hall program, May 28, 1930, 3.
2. *Evening Standard*, September 17, 1929, 11.

3.   *Les Temps*, January 8, 1926, 3.

4.   "Fakir Tahra Bey Contre Heuzé et Editions de France," quotes from 599.

5.   "Fakir Tahra Bey Contre Heuzé et Editions de France," 593.

6.   Henry Torrès, *Accusés Hors Série* (Paris: Gallimard, 1957), 91.

7.   Henry Torrès, *Accusés Hors Série*, 92; "J'ai tué un assassin"; *Le Rappel*, October 19, 1927, 1.

8.   Geo London, *L'Humour au Tribunal* (Paris: Librarie Generale de Droit et de Jurisprudence, 1931), 191–92.

9.   *Le Canard Enchaîné*, April 22, 1932, reproduced in Heuzé, *Dernières Histoires de Fakirs*, 162–65.

10. *Tao: Revista Psychica*, available online at http://obscurofichario.com.br/fichario/krikor -tahara-kalfayan/ (accessed 9 April 2024). This online collection of documents also contains a police file on Tahra Bey, which mentions his Spanish passport.

11. *Diario da Noite*, March 12, 1932, 3.

12. *La Volonté*, December 19, 1933, 2.

13. *La Volonté*, Decmber 27, 1933, 2.

14. *Al-Dunya al-Musawwara*, November 6, 1929, 4.

15. Paul Brunton, *A Search in Secret Egypt* (London: Rider and Co., n.d. [1936]), 105.

16. *Detective*, April 4, 1935, 15; Archives of the Préfecture de Police, Paris: "Krikor Kalfayan dit Fakir Dr. Tarha [*sic*] Bey," 77W567, 208.332.

17. The following account is largely based on Tahra Bey's file in the French National Archives: "Intérieur. Fichier central de la Sûreté nationale : dossiers individuels de KA à KJ (fin XIXe siècle-1940): Kalfayan, Krikor: Dossier 2098.

18. *L'Eclaireur du Soir* (Nice), September 16, 1938.

19. *Le Journal*, June 2, 1938, 3; *L'Oeuvre*, June 16, 1938, 6.

20. *La Gazette de Bayonne, du Pays Basque, et des Landes*, November 3, 1938, 1; Police files.

21. Aldous Huxley, "Letter to Humphry Osmond, September 25, 1953," in *Psychedelic Prophets: The Letters of Aldous Huxley and Humphry Osmond*, ed. Cynthia Bisbee et al. (Montreal: McGill-Queens University Press, 2018), 37–38.

Chapter 8: "A Fakir in Jackboots"

1.   *La Republique*, July 31, 1938, 3.

2.   Konrad Heiner, *Der Fuehrer: Hitler's Rise to Power* (Boston: Houghton Mifflin, 1944), 17.

3.   See Eric Kurlander, *Hitler's Monsters: A Supernatural History of the Third Reich* (New Haven: Yale University Press, 2017).

4.   Kurlander, *Hitler's Monsters*, 99–130.

5.   Giudice, *Occult Imperium*.

6.   Leonard Woolf, *Quack, Quack!* (London: Hogarth Press, 1936), 28.

7.   R. G. Collingwood, *An Autobiography and Other Writings* (Oxford: Oxford University Press, 2017), 167. See also Nikhil Krishnan, *A Terribly Serious Adventure* (New York: Random House, 2023).

8.   Adorno's "Theses against Occultism" was written in 1946–1947. It has been reproduced in many places. I quote from the E. F. N. Jephcott translation, which is available in, e.g., Theodor Adorno, *The Stars Down to Earth and Other Essays on the Irrational in Culture*, ed. Stephen Crook (London: Routledge, 2001), 172–80.

9.   Piers Brendon, *The Dark Valley: A Panorama of the 1930s* (New York: Knopf Double-

day, 2002), 616. NB: Brendon is not giving his own opinion of Hitler but speculating about the opinion of Lord Halifax.

10. For more details on the Aznavour family and their sheltering of Jews during the war, see Yair Auron, *Saviors and Warriors: Compassion and Heroism* (Tel Aviv: Contento-Now, 2016).

11. The details of this story are largely told through Archives of the Préfecture de Police, Paris: file 253 W 55.

12. See Bundesarchiv der Bundesrepulik Deutschland, "Memorial Book: Victims of the Persecution of Jews under the National Socialist Tyranny in Germany 1933–1945," Chronology of Deportations from France, https://www.bundesarchiv.de/gedenkbuch/chronology/viewFrance.xhtml.

13. *Boston Globe*, September 4, 1966, 43.

14. Werner Lange, *Artists in Nazi-Occupied France: A German Officer's Memoirs*, trans. Leonard Rosmarin (Oakville, ON: Mosaic Press, 2018), chap. 3, Kindle.

15. See, e.g., *L'Aurore*, November 29, 1945, 1; *Paris-Presse*, November 30, 1945, 1; the letter was reproduced in many French newspapers.

16. *France Soir*, November 28, 1945, 1.

17. See Alan Riding, *And the Show Went On: Cultural Life in Nazi-Occupied Paris* (New York: Knopf, 2010).

18. *Le Figaro*, September 8, 1942, 2; Fred Adison, *Dans Ma Vie y a d'la Musique* (Paris: Clancier-Guénaud, 1983), 112.

19. Archives of the Préfecture de Police, Paris 253 W 55/Audition de Kalfayan, Krikor, 18 September 1942.

20. "New York, New York Passenger and Crew Lists, 1909, 1925–1957," 7834, vol. 17012–17013, May 20, 1950; accessed at familysearch.org, citing NARA microfilm publication T715 (Washington, DC: National Archives and Records Administration); U.S. National Archives and Records Administration, Departing Passenger and Crew Lists, New York, A4169—New York 1948–1956, 079, accessed August 25, 2023, at ancestry.com.

Part II: Ghara'ib wa-'Aja'ib

1. Munir Wuhayba, *Asrar al-'Ulum al-Ghamida* [Secrets of the occult sciences] ([Beirut], 1948), i.

2. *La Revue du Liban*, April 1929, 23–24.

Chapter 9: Dr. Dahesh Takes the Stage

1. *Al-Samir*, June 19, 1946, 2. This is from a 1946 novelization of Dr. Dahesh's movement, first published in the Beiruti journal *Alf Layla wa-Layla*.

2. *Al-Samir*, June 19, 1946, 2.

3. *Lisan al-Hal*, May 15, 1928, 4.

4. *Al-Massara*, June 1928, 372–73.

5. *Al-'Irfan*, August–September 1929, 71; *Al-Dunya al-Musawwara*, June 26, 1929, 8; *Israel* (Cairo), August 9, 1929, 3.

6. *Al-Iqdam*, June 1, 1930, 2.

7. *Al-Dunya al-Musawwara*, August 21, 1930, 4–5.

8.   *Miraat al-Sharq*, June 25, 1929, 3; *Sawt al-Shab*, July 3, 1929, 4.

9.   The core story of Dr. Dahesh's early life comes from a series of articles by Halim Dammous that ran monthly in the Cairene journal *'Alam al-Ruh* from January 1952 to November 1952.

10. Most official documents give the date 1912, but most of his followers use 1909.

11. *'Alam al-Ruh*, January 1952, 19.

12. *'Alam al-Ruh*, February 1952, 8–9.

13. *'Alam al-Ruh*, February 1952, 8–12; Lutfi Radwan, *Mu'jizat wa-Khawariq al-Duktur Dahish* (New York: Daheshist Publishing House, 1997), 65–69.

14. One source (*al-Mukhtasar*) dates Dr. Dahesh's father's death to 1918 but most put it in 1920.

15. Yusuf Malik, *Khalifat Iblis: Dahish* (n.p. [Beirut], 1945), 187–88.

16. *'Alam al-Ruh*, September 1950, 22.

17. *'Alam al-Ruh*, March 1952, 20–23; Jabra Ibrahim Jabra, *The First Well: A Bethlehem Boyhood*, trans. Issa J. Boullata (Fayetteville: University of Arkansas Press, 1995), 66.

18. Malik, *Khalifat Iblis*, 75–78.

19. League of Nations, *Mandate for Palestine* (Geneva: League of Nations, 1922), 2.

20. *A Survey of Palestine: Prepared in December 1945 and January 1946 for the information of the Anglo-American Committee of Inquiry* (Jerusalem: Government Printer, 1946), 140–64.

21. Hillel Cohen, *Year Zero of the Arab-Israeli Conflict 1929*, trans. Haim Watzman (Waltham, MA: Brandeis University Press, 2015).

22. See Rena Barakat, "Thawrat al-Buraq in British Mandate Palestine: Jerusalem, Mass Mobilization and Colonial Politics, 1928–1930" (PhD diss., University of Chicago, 2007), esp. 167–98. Figures of the dead come from *Report of the Commission on the Palestine Disturbances of August, 1929* (London: H. M. Stationery Office, 1930), 65–66.

Chapter 10: The Mysteries of Magnetic Sleep

1.   *Al-Lata'if al-Musawwara*, October 31, 1927, 1.

2.   *Filastin*, December 30, 1932, 6. (This article mistakenly calls his medium Henriette.)

3.   Mayy Ziyada, *Warda al-Yaziji* (1922; Cairo: Hindawi, 2017), 36.

4.   *Al-Muqtataf*, May 1, 1889, 543–44 has a short biography of Dimitri Nahhas, an early proponent of hypnosis in the Arab World.

5.   *Al-Mu'ayyad*, November 12, 1902, 3.

6.   Muhammad Rushdi, *al-Tanwim al-Maghnatisi wa-Ghara'ibuhu* [Hypnotism and its marvels] (Cairo: al-Muqtataf, 1913), 7.

7.   Muhammad Shawqi, *'Ilm al-Tanwim al-Maghnatisi wa-'Aja'ibuhu* [The science of hypnotism and its wonders] (Cairo: Muhammad Muhammad Matar, 1915), 34–39.

8.   Details of the trial reprinted in Rushdi, *al-Tanwim al-Maghnatisi*, 95–141. The doctor's name comes from *al-Ahram*, September 4, 1913.

9.   At first the court report censors the name of the disease (out of taste) but later in the published trial documents they use the term *silan*, which often means gonorrhea.

10. Muhammad Lutfi Jum'a, *Shahid 'Ala al-'Asr: Mudhakkirat* [Witness to an era: Memoirs] (Cairo: GEBO, 2000), 333.

11. Under Egyptian law it was legal for a Muslim man to take multiple wives.

12. *Al-Ahram*, September 4, 1913.

13. Rushdi, *al-Tanwim al-Maghnatisi*, 129.

14. *Do'ar ha-yom*, August 5, 1931, 2.
15. *Mirat al-Sharq*, April 4, 1931, 4. In Dr. Salomon's defense, he never denied that his father was Syrian but he did claim to have grown up in Naples. The author of the article clearly believed that he was hyping up his credentials as a "European." In one of the earliest articles about Dr. Salomon, in 1926, he is identified as French, not Italian, which reveals either his duplicity or the fluid boundaries between different European identities: *al-Musawwar*, May 21, 1926, 9.
16. Tawfiq al-Hakim, *'Usfur min al-Sharq* [Sparrow from the East] (1938; Cairo: Hindawi, 2017), 119.
17. *Al-'Alam*, June 7, 1926, 9; *al-Musawwar*, August 30, 1929, 19.
18. *Al-Ahram*, July 30, 1926, 7.
19. *Al-Musawwar*, July 23, 1926, 4; *al-Ahram*, September 9, 1926, 6.
20. *Do'ar ha-Yom*, May 20, 1931, 4.
21. *Palestine Bulletin*, April 9, 1931, 3.
22. Wasif Jawhariyya, *al-Quds al-'Uthmaniyya fi-l-mudhakkirat al-Jawhariyya* [Ottoman Jerusalem in Jawhariyya's memoirs] (Jerusalem: Mu'assasat al-Dirasat al-Maqdisiyya, 2005), pt. 2, 471–72.
23. *Al-Ahram*, March 15, 1931, 11.
24. *Al-Shura* [Ashoura] (Cairo), March 18, 1931, 2; *al-Ahram*, February 24, 1931, 8.
25. *Al-Shura* [Ashoura] (Cairo), March 18, 1931, 2.
26. *Al-Shura* [Ashoura] (Cairo), April 1, 1931, 2.
27. *Al-Sarkha*, May 3, 1931, 22.
28. *Al-Jami'a al-Islamiyya*, September 11, 1933, 7; *Kull Shai' wa-l-'Alam*, May 23, 1931, 33.
29. *Sawt al-Sha'b*, January 31, 1931, 4; December 20, 1930, 4; *al-Jami'a al-'Arabiyya*, October 8, 1930, 1.
30. *Al-Sirat al-Mustaqim*, August 28, 1940, 2. The article does not specifically name Dr. Dahesh but it is written by an N. Q. from Bethlehem, almost certainly Nasri [Q]attan, who was a close associate of Dahesh in the 1930s.
31. *Misr al-Haditha al-Musawwara*, October 10, 1930, 6–7.

Chapter 11: The Spiritual Sciences

1. Muhammad Farid Wajdi, *Da'irat Ma'arif al-Qarn al-'Ishrin* [Encyclopedia of the twentieth century] (Cairo: Da'irat al-Ma'arif, 1925), 10:410–20 (quote from 420).
2. *Al-Musawwar*, January 22, 1930, 17.
3. 'Abd al-Hamid Najib Qinawi, *Mu'allim al-Tanwim al-Maghnatisi* [Guide to hypnotism] (Cairo: Matba'a 'ataya, 1923), 19–31 (quote from front cover).
4. *Al-Mufid*, April 16, 1916. Cited from On Barak, *On Time: Technology and Temporality in Modern Egypt* (Berkeley: University of California Press, 2013), 106. His translation.
5. Wajdi, *Da'irat Ma'arif al-Qarn al-'Ishrin*, 4:365.
6. Tantawi Jawhari, *Nahdat al-Umma wa-Hayatuha* [The life and renaissance of the nation] (Cairo: Matba'at al-Liwa', 1908), 28.
7. British Library Archives: Tantawi Gauhari, of Cairo, author: Letter to Lord Avebury: 1906.
8. Tantawi Jawhari, *Nahdat al-Umma*, 2nd ed. (Cairo: Mustafa al-Babi al-Halabi, 1934), 17.
9. Tantawi Jawhari, *al-Arwah* [The spirits] (Cairo: al-Matb'a al-Misriyya, 1919), 5.

10. Tantawi Jawhari, *Bara'at al-'Abbasa Ukht al-Rashid* [The innocence of Abbasa sister of al-Rashid] (Cairo: Mustafa al-Babi al-Halabi, 1936).
11. *Al-Ma'rifa*, February 1933, 1193–95, 1200.
12. Al-Hakim, *Usfur min al-Sharq*, 65.
13. *Miraat al-Sharq*, November 30, 1932, 2, 4; *Filastin*, November 29, 1932, 7.
14. See, e.g., *Miraat al-Sharq*, December 3, 1932, 5.
15. *Filastin*, November 18, 1932, 11.
16. *Al-Karmil*, October 8, 1932, 5.
17. *Filastin*, May 27, 1933, 4.
18. *Miraat al-Sharq*, December 3, 1932, 5.
19. *Filastin*, May 28, 1933, 9.

Chapter 12: Jinn, Charlatans, and Miracles

1. *Al-Ahram*, August 16, 1934.
2. *Al-Kawakib*, June 8, 1954.
3. Muhammad Rushdi, *Al-Tanwim al-Maghnatisi wa-Ghara'ibuhu* (Cairo: al-Muqtataf, 1913), 107–8.
4. D. B. Macdonald et al., "Djinn," in *Encyclopaedia of Islam*, 2nd ed., ed. P. J. Bearman (Leiden: Brill, 2005).
5. *Al-Hilal*, January 1, 1926, 392–95.
6. Munir Wuhayba, *Asrar al-'Ulum al-Ghamida* (n.p., n.d. [Beirut, 1948]), 48–51.
7. Abraham Frumkin, "The Ghettoes of Cairo," *Reform Advocate*, June 11, 1910, 907–9.
8. Accounts of the trial were published in *al-Ahram* between June 10, and July 7, 1935.
9. *Al-Ahram*, June 11, 1935, 15.
10. *Al-Ahram*, June 10, 1935, 10.
11. *Al-Ahram*, March 3, 1934, 1.
12. *Al-Ahram*, June 17, 1935, 10.
13. *Al-Ahram*, January 17, 1936, 10.
14. See *al-Ahram*, March 10, 1935, 11; June 5, 1935, 10.
15. *Al-Ahram*, August 20, 1935, 10.
16. *Al-Ahram*, February 12, 1934, 2.
17. *Filastin*, July 3, 1931, 2.
18. See, e.g., the novel by Mahmud Taymur, *Rajab Afandi* (Cairo: Salafiyya, 1928); Badia Khayri's play *'Ala 'Aynak ya Tajir* (available in AUB Jafet Library, Muhammad Yusuf Najm Collection, Box 6, File 5, esp. 60–65).
19. *Al-Ahram*, January 22, 1934, 2.

Chapter 13: "The Dandy of the Spirit World"

1. Malik, *Khalifat Iblis*, 194. Some say that al-Asrawi was a Lebanese poet, but all the details known about him suggest he was a tour guide in Petra (of course, both may be true). See, e.g., Nasir al-Din Asad, *Muhammad Ahmad al-Asad: Sira watha'iqiyya* (Dar al-Fath, 2008), 124; Yusuf Ibish, ed., *Mudhakkirat al-Amir 'Adil Arslan: Al-mustadrak, 1948* (Beirut: Dar al-Taqaddamiyya, 1994), 264.
2. Malik, *Khalifat Iblis*, 169.
3. *Al-Difa'*, July 8, 1935, 8; August 12, 1935, 4.

4. *Al-Jami'a al-'Arabiyya*, September 19, 1933, 1, 8.

5. *Filastin*, July 8, 1934, 10.

6. Al-Duktur Dahish Bey, *Daj'at al-Mawt aw Bayna Ahdan al-Abadiyya* [The sleep of death, or in the embrace of eternity] (Jerusalem: Dar al-Aytam al-Suriyya, 1936), 204.

7. *Guardian*, January 31, 2018.

8. *Al-Jamia*, March 19, 1936, 41.

9. *Akhir Sa'a*, March 1, 1936, 51.

10. *Al-Liwa'* (Jerusalem), January 29, 1936, 2.

11. *Al-Difa'*, March 4, 1936, 13.

12. *Al-Jami'a*, March 19, 1936, 30.

13. Hisham Sharabi, *Suwar al-Madi* [Images of the past] (Beirut: Dar Nilsun, 1993), 60–61.

14. Matthew Hughes, "The Banality of Brutality: British Armed Forces and the Repression of the Arab Revolt in Palestine, 1936–39," *English Historical Review* 124, no. 507 (April 2009): 313–54, citing *From Haven to Conquest*, ed. Walid Khalidi (Beirut: Institute for Palestine Studies, 1971), 846–49.

15. Ghassan Kanafani, *The 1936–39 Revolt in Palestine*, unknown translator (1972; London: Design Atelier, 2020), 29.

16. W. F. Boustany, *The Palestine Mandate: Invalid and Impracticable* (Beirut: American Press, 1936); see also Esmat Elhalaby, "Empire and Arab Indology," *Modern Intellectual History* 19, no. 4 (2022): 1081–105.

17. Mutlaq 'Abd al-Khaliq, *al-Rahil* (Nazareth: Mutlaq Abd al-Khaliq Cultural Foundation, 2011), 224–28.

18. Several sources state that he died January 10, 1937, including Dr. Dahish, *Daj'at al-Mawt* (Nazareth: Mutlaq Abd al-Khaliq Cultural Foundation, 2011), 15. I have not been able to verify this.

19. Malik, *Khalifat Iblis*, 196–97.

20. Akhir Sa'a, May 29, 1938, 36; Malik, *Khalifat Iblis*, 198, 245–48.

21. *Al-Sirat al-Mustaqim*, May 24, 1938, 7.

22. Malik, *Khalifat Iblis*, 150.

23. *Al-Difa'*, June 12, 1938, 6.

24. *Akhir Sa'a*, no. 212, 51.

25. Although no one had made the connection between Abd al-Rahim al-Sharif, the Palestinian political figure, and Abd al-Rahim al-Sharif, the companion of Dr. Dahesh, their biographies (and their physical appearances) are so similar that they must be the same person.

26. *Al-Sirat al-Mustaqim*, May 31, 1938, 7.

Chapter 14: The Rise and Fall of Daheshism

1. *Los Angeles Times*, June 10, 1938, pt. 3, 9.

2. See, e.g., *al-Akhbar*, May 23, 1950, 3.

3. For a brief biography see Carl Brockelmann, *History of the Arabic Written Tradition*, supple. vol. 3-i, trans. Joep Lameer (Leiden: Brill, 2016), 275.

4. *Al-Akhbar*, May 18, 1950, 3.

5. *'Alam al-Ruh*, February 1948, 18–20; *al-Dabbur*, February 16, 1948, 2, 35; *al-Jumhur*, March 10, 1945.

6. *'Alam al-Ruh*, February 1948, 19; *Al-Akhbar*, May 18, 1950, 3.

7. *'Alam al-Ruh*, September 1948, 17.

8.   *Dirasat wa-Maqalat al-Udaba' wa-al-Kuttab wa-al-Suhufiyyin fi Kitab Mudhakkirat Dinar li-Mu'allifihi al-Duktur Dahish* [Studies and articles by writers, litterateurs, and journalists about Dr. Dahesh's book *Memoirs of a Dinar*] (Beirut: Dar al-nisr al-muhalliq, 1980), 68–69.

9.   *Al-Jazira* (Amman), November 2, 1945, 3, 8.

10. Salim Onbargi, *Born Again with Doctor Dahesh* (New York: Daheshist Publishing Company, 1993), 19. For more on these beliefs see *al-Dabbur*, June 20, 1949, 28–29.

11. Robert Darnton, *Mesmerism and the End of the Enlightenment in France* (Boston: Harvard University Press, 2009), 8–18.

12. *Miraat al-Sharq*, June 25, 1929, 3.

13. Malik, *Khalifat Iblis*, 82.

14. *Al-Jumhur*, April 21, 1945, 8.

15. See, e.g., *al-Samir*, June 4, 1946, 2 (reprinted from an original article in *al-Nahar*).

16. *Al-Jazira* (Amman), 2 November 1945, 3, 8.

17. Michael Hudson, *The Precarious Republic: Political Modernization in Lebanon* (New York: Random House, 1968), 264.

18. *Beaux-Arts*, May 7, 1937, 2.

19. Mari Haddad, *Mu' jizat al-Duktur Dahish wa-Zahiratuhu al-Ruhiyya* [The miracles of Dr. Dahesh and his spiritual phenomena] (Beirut: Dar al-Nar wa-l-Nur, 1983), 13–14.

20. *Al-Akhbar*, May 22, 1950, 3; *Al-Dabbur*, April 26, 1948, 22, 26.

21. *Al-Diyar*, March 20, 1944, 2.

22. *Al-Bashir*, September 29, 1942, 1.

23. *Al-Bashir*, September 20, 1942, 1.

24. Lebanese Penal Code, article 768: *Supplément au Journal Officiel No 1404*, October 27, 1943, 66.

25. See, e.g., *'Alam al-Ruh*, July 1950, 23–25; August 1950, 18–19.

26. The events of the next few paragraphs largely come from Mari Haddad, *Al-Kitab al-Aswad: Ana Attahim* [J'Accuse] (n.p., n.d. [Baghdad, 1945]), 11–33, 124–26.

27. From "Decree K/1842." This decree is reproduced in several Daheshist publications: e.g., Haddad, *Ana Attahim*, 27, 29. The decree was not published in the official gazette but its numbering is consistent with the date given.

28. *Al-Muqattam*, February 12, 1945, 6; *Sawt al-Ahrar*, January 31, 1945, 2.

29. *Al-Usbu' al-'Arabi*, June 22, 1954. Reprinted in Iskandar Shahin, *al-Duktur Dahish Rajul al-Asrar* [Dr. Dahesh: Man of secrets] (New York: Daheshist Publishing House, 2001), 136–56.

30. *Al-Mukhtasar*, October 1946, 2.

31. *Al-Mukhtasar*, October 1946, 1–2.

32. *Al-Mihmaz*, May 19, 1946, 11, 22.

Chapter 15: Black Books and the Arab Rasputin

1.   Al-Duktur Dahish Bey, *Jahim* (Beirut: Rihani-Sadir, 1944), 38.

2.   Malik, *Khalifat Iblis*, 118.

3.   Malik, 2.

4.   Dr. Dahesh Bey, *Daj'at al-Mawt* (Nazareth: Muntada Mutlaq 'Abd al-Khaliq al-Thaqafi, 2011), 16.

5.   Malik, *Khalifat Iblis*, 31.

6.   Malik, 108.

7.   *Al-Samir*, May 27, 1946, 2, citing the Lebanese magazine *Marqad al-'Anza*.

8.   *Al-Mihmaz*, May 19, 1946, 11.

9.   *Time*, April 21, 1947, 34.

10. Al-Duktur Dahish, *Mudhakkirat Yasu' al-Nasiri* [Memoirs of Jesus of Nazareth] (Beirut: Dar al-Nisr al-Muhalliq, 1980), 27. An English translation of this text is available in Fawzi A. Burgess, "Dr. Dahesh's Arabic Work: Memoirs of Jesus, the Nazareth: An Edited Translation and an Introduction" (PhD diss., Middle Tennessee State University, 1982).

11. Haddad, *Ana Attahim*, 96.

12. Haddad, 98–100.

13. *Alif Ba*, May 20, 1945, 3; *'Alam al-Ruh*, January 1953, 10–19; American University of Beirut, Jafet Library, Archives and Special Collections: LHMND: List of Patients April 2, 1914–March 21, 1960: July 1945.

14. *Al-Muqtataf*, June 1946, 52–53.

15. *Al-Wahda*, April 13, 1946, 4.

16. Ja'far al-Khalili, *Hakadha 'Ariftuhum* [This is how I knew them] (Baghdad: Dar al-Ta'aruf, 1968), 5:69.

17. *Al-Ahram*, April 20, 1946, 4.

18. "Cairo Panorama," *Sphinx*, May 4, 1946.

19. *Al-Muqattam*, May 17, 1946, 3.

20. *Alif Ba*, December 16, 1947, April 15, 1947.

21. *Al-Mukhtasar*, October 1946, 15.

22. Abo Adel (@_AboAdel), "Hadhihi al-risala muwajjaha min (Jubran Massuh) ila (Riyad Bak al-Sulh)" [This letter was sent from Jubran Massuh to Riyad Bey al-Sulh], Twitter, January 18, 2018, 8:54 a.m., https://x.com/_AboAdel/status/954019116431659014.

23. *Al-Mukhtasar*, June 1947, 2.

24. Al-Khalili, *Hakadha 'Ariftuhum*, 5:53–70, esp. 64–68.

25. *O Oriente*, January 1, 1949, 8.

26. Dr. Dahish, *Mudhakkirat Dinar* (n.p. [Beirut], 1946), 5.

27. *Al-Mukhtasar*, August 1946, 14.

28. *Al-'Irfan*, August 1948, 1242; *al-Wahda*, July 27, 1947, 3.

29. *Marathi al-Udaba' wa-al-Shu'ara' wa-al-Suhufiyyin wa-al-Atibba' wa-al-Muhamin wa-Rijal al-Din wa-al-Hukkam wa-al-Quda bi-Mu'assis al-'Aqida al-Dahishiyya* [Eulogies by writers, poets, journalist, doctors, lawyers, men of religion, rulers, and judges on the founder of the Daheshist creed] (Beirut: Dār al-Nisr al-Muḥalliq, 1979), 16. Quote is from Sahih Bukhari 3667.

30. *Alif Ba*, January 15, 1948, 4.

Chapter 16: They Are Risen

1.   *Harper's Magazine*, May 1, 1964, 52.

2.   Aldous Huxley, *The Doors of Perception* (1954; London: Vintage, 2004), 7–8.

3.   Huxley, *Doors of Perception*, 50.

4.   *V: Magazine Illustré de MLN*, March 17, 1946, 2–3.

5.   *Images du Monde*, February 25, 1948.

6.   *Le Petit Journal*, March 6, 1949, 39.

7.   *La Domenica del Corriere*, February 19, 1950.

8.   Paul Brunton Archives at Cornell University, Talks in the Occident, Box 32, W087, 13.

9.   *Harvard Crimson*, February 19, 1953.
10. *Harvard Crimson*, February 19, 1953.
11. *Mirror* (Los Angeles), July 15, 1953, 15; *Le Petit Journal*, March 6, 1949, 39.
12. Christopher Isherwood, "Aldous Huxley in California," *Atlantic*, September 1964.
13. Huxley, "Letter to Humphry," 37–38; Aldous Huxley, "Letter to Frieda Law-rence," August 30, 1953, Murry Family Papers, National Library of New Zealand, MS Papers-11327-061.
14. Huxley, "Letter to Humphry," 37–38.
15. Robert Craft, *Chronicle of a Friendship* (Nashville: Vanderbilt University Press, 1994), 102.
16. Craft, *Chronicle of a Friendship*, 386.
17. *Esquire*, August 1955.
18. Craft, *Chronicle of a Friendship*, 386.
19. *À la Page*, April 19, 1951, 6–7.
20. P. Daher, *Vie Survie, et Prodigies de L'Ermite Charbel Makhlouf* (Paris: Editions Spes, 1953), 115.
21. "Sharbal Makhlouf (1828–1898)" in *La Vie Spirituelle*, April 1951, 404–14, cited in J. G. McGarry, "Charbel Makhlouf," *Furrow* 5, no. 1 (1954): 28–35.
22. *Al-Jabal*, May 29, 1950, 3; *Al-Samir* 25 September 1950, 4–5.
23. *Al-'Irfan*, May 1953, 800–2.
24. *'Alam al-Ruh*, July 1949, 25–26; *'Alam al-Ruh*, January 1951, 21–22.
25. *Al-Dabbur*, 4 August 1947, 9.
26. *Al-'Irfan* 35, no. 6 (May 1948): 930.

Chapter 17: "I Am Just a Doctor"

1.   Adunis, *Ha Anta Ayyuha al-Waqt: Sira Shi'riyya Thaqafiyya* (Beirut: Dar al Adab, 1993), 31–33. For more on the Beiruti literary scene of the 1960s see Robyn Creswell, *City of Beginnings* (Princeton: Princeton University Press, 2009), incl. 21–22, which cites this passage (and takes its name from it).
2.   Samir Khalaf, *Lebanon's Predicament* (New York: Columbia University Press, 1987), 263–65, quoted in Creswell, *City of Beginnings*, 22.
3.   Maria B. Abunnasr, "The Making of Ras Beirut: A Landscape of Memory for Nar-ratives of Exceptionalism" (PhD diss., University of Massachusetts–Amherst, 2013), 213 (Ibrahim Takkoush interview, September 17, 2012).
4.   Salah al-Lababidi, *Mudhakkirat Mudir al-Bulis* [The memoirs of a police chief] (Bei-rut: Dar al-Hadara, 1970), 81–82.
5.   See, e.g., *Al-Akhbar*, November 28, 1949, 1; *Oberoesterreichische Nachrichten*, March 25, 1950, 5.
6.   Aida Aznavour-Garvarentz, *Petit Frère* (Paris: R. Laffont, n.d. [1986]), 32–33.
7.   *Le Jour*, June 2, 1965, 8; *Al-Anwar*, October 5, 1969, 2.
8.   *Le Jour*, June 2, 1965, 8. The congress was held in Paris 1965. The proceedings make no mention of Tahra Bey.
9.   *Al-Liwa'*, June 26, 1964. Reprinted in Shahin, *al-Duktur Dahish Rajul al-Asrar*, 157–63.
10. Ja'far al-Khalili, *Hakadha 'Ariftuhum* (Baghdad: Dar al-Ta'aruf, 1968), 5:70. Jaafar notes that he could not verify this story.
11. *Billboard*, April 24, 1954, 1; also repeated in Yvon Yva, *Les Fakirs et Leur Secrets* (Paris: Gallimard, 1963), 59; *Hugard's Magic Monthly*, June 1955, 292, 297.

12. This story is repeated in Maurice N. Khoury, *It All Started in Nazareth* (Bloomington, IN: Archway Publishing, 2023) and in many other places. It is also sometimes told about Tahra Bey.

13. Ghazi Brax, *Prodigies of Dr. Dahesh and the Unity of Religions*, trans. A. Z. Touma (Beirut: Al-Nisr Al-Mohallek, 1971), 5, 37.

14. *Al-Usbu' al-'Arabi*, June 22, 1954. Reprinted in Shahin, *al-Duktur Dahish Rajul al-Asrar*, 136–56.

15. *Al-Akhbar*, November 28, 1949, 1.

16. *Al-Akhbar*, December 5, 1949, 2, 4.

17. *Al-Samir*, January 25, 1950, 3.

18. *Al-Usbu' al-'Arabi*, June 22, 1954. Reprinted in Shahin, *al-Duktur Dahish Rajul al-Asrar*, esp. 155–56.

19. *Al-Nahar*, March 14, 1965, suppl., 4–6.

20. The only book that I have found that references Tahra Bey's death date is Harut'yun Minasyan, *100 Hay Hogebuyzhner* (Yerevan: Zangak-97, 2002), 1:70–71. It does not give his place of death but Beirut seems by far the most likely.

21. Al-Duktur Dahish, *al-Rihalat al-Dahishiyya Hawla al-Kura al-Ardiyya* [Dahishist trips around the globe] (1971; Beirut: Dar al-Nar wa-l-Nur, 1983), 4:78, 209–11, 338–39, 115–16.

22. *New York Times*, March 19, 1976, 1, 6.

23. Al-Duktur Dahish, *al-Rihalat al-Dahishiyya Hawla al-Kura al-Ardiyya* (1976; New York: Dahishist Publishing Company, 1991), 10:136–38.

24. Dahish, *al-Rihalat al-Dahishiyya*, 10:205–6.

25. *ARTnews*, December 1996, 108.

26. *New York Times*, January 20, 1995, C:27.

27. *New York Times*, July 4, 2014, The City, 14:3.

28. Carol Kino, "The Baddest of Bad Art," *Atlantic*, April 2000.

29. *ARTnews*, December 1996, 109.

IMAGE CREDITS

INDEX

Page numbers in *italics* refer to illustrations.